T0277528

The
Longest
Winter

The
Longest
Winter

A Season with England's
Worst Ever Football Team

MARK HODKINSON

First published by Pitch Publishing, 2022

Pitch Publishing
9 Donnington Park,
85 Birdham Road,
Chichester,
West Sussex,
PO20 7AJ
www.pitchpublishing.co.uk
info@pitchpublishing.co.uk

© 2022, Mark Hodkinson
www.markhodkinson.com

A CIP catalogue record is available for this book
from the British Library.

ISBN 978 1 80150 157 6

Typesetting and origination by Pitch Publishing
Printed and bound in Great Britain by TJ Books Ltd, Padstow

Contents

Acknowledgements 7

Preface 9

1. A Beautiful Quiet 13

2. Tough Start for Dale 29

3. The Baiting and Biting of Fred Ratcliffe 53

4. Soft as Silk, Solid as Granite 73

5. A Sash of Blue and Yellow 96

6. Moto-Psycho Nightmare 113

7. A Socially Divided Society 146

8. A Poor Urban Environment 172

9. A Dire Capitulation and Complete Collapse 203

10. New Year, Old Rochdale 229

11. They're Like Bloody Ghouls 253

12. April Fool's Day, 1974 270

Epilogue 286

Afterwards 291

Bibliography 303

Also by the Author

No One Round Here Reads Tolstoy (Canongate)

The Overcoat Men (Pitch Publishing)

That Summer Feeling (Pomona)

The Last Mad Surge of Youth (Pomona)

Blue Moon: Down Among the Dead Men with Manchester City (Penguin/Random House)

Life at the Top (Queen Anne Press)

Acknowledgements

I WOULD like to thank, most of all, Kellie While for her understanding, kindness and invaluable help in the writing of this book. Jane Camillin at Pitch Publishing was wholly supportive, from a quick decision to commission, to seeing it home. Ivan Butler did a thorough but sensitive editing job. Richard Whitehead offered sound advice throughout. Wayne Skeffington kindly supplied some wonderful pictures and souvenirs that have never been seen before, or for a long time, at least. Mark Wilbraham, the Voice of Spotland, provided great photographs too. Fred Eyre passed on excellent contacts and checked through an early draft. Richard Lysons and Jim Stringer were my superlative proofreaders (or is it proof-readers?) once more: true friends.

James Heward, James Wallace and my agent, Kevin Pocklington, took care of other business on my behalf while I was absent. Chris Hewitt gave great insight into Rochdale's counter-culture scene of the early 1970s. Dale Hibbert supplied essential technical support. My two sons, George and Alec, gave constructive advice. Lisa Edgar and Emily Wood generously provided a writing bolthole in a Cornish paradise.

Thank you to the following for either their friendship or giving up their time to help make this a better book: John Abraham, David Bartlett, Dave Bell, Ashleigh Bland, Colin Bland, Pauline Bland, Mike Brennan, Mark Brierley, Dennis

Butler, Gary Canning, John Clarke, Francis Collins, David Cross, John Dennis, Bobby Downes, Terry Eves, Chris Fitzgerald, David Gartside, John Gilder, Ian Goodwin, David Hammond, Keith Hanvey, Andrew Harrison, Keith Hicks, Andrew Hilton, Judith Hilton, Harold Holburt, Stan Horne, Trevor Hoyle, Darran Hurst, John Keith, Karen Kerr, Tony Kerr, John Matthews, Julie Matthews, Graham Morris, Miles Moss, Steve Murray, Richard Partington, Guy Patrick, Mike Pavasovic, Dave Reed, Dave Seddon, Andy Sharrocks, Graham Smith, Nige Tassell, Don Tobin, Stan Townsend, Chris While and Bernie Wilcox.

Preface

THE WALK along the main street at Beer in east Devon is a joy. Shops, houses, cafés and pubs are painted either white or pink with dashes of nautical blue on the window sills and drainpipes. Sunlight slants around the buildings and the sky above is big and bright and open. Leading the way to the shingly beach is a brook set in a stone channel on the pavement, which flows from the chalk hills all around. It was here – at a point equidistant to the café with a boar's head attached to the wall and the Church of St Michael – that I had the idea for this book.

It was mid-summer. I was a long way from home and, finally, I had reached that point when you become detached from the routine and the mundane and start to *reflect*. Most people, finding themselves at this peaceful berth, ponder on their job, marriage, health or family. I was thinking about Rochdale AFC. I do this a lot. Ordinarily at that time of year, I appraise the season just gone and contemplate the season to come. Instead of this appraising and contemplating, a very particular thought entered my head and stayed there all day, all holiday and then revisited me frequently over many years – Rochdale AFC's nadir, its *annus horribilis*. Namely, the unprecedented, disastrous, catastrophic season of 1973/74.

Rochdale's squad of 1973/74 is statistically the worst ever assembled in the Football League. The club finished bottom of the Third Division, winning twice in 46 league matches – the fewest ever victories in a 46-match season. They were 21 points adrift of safety from relegation and closed the season with a 22-match winless run. One home match was played in front of the lowest ever post-war 'crowd' for a Football League fixture – *about* 450 (the club was too embarrassed to release a genuine figure).

The season of our grave discontent predates my family moving to Rochdale and my becoming a diehard supporter. The same as most fans, I was conceited enough to presuppose that my club only came into existence when I discovered it, so I seldom speculated on teams and seasons gone by. Until that day in Beer. I am not sure why I thought of the club's darkest time on such a cheery, sunny afternoon. Maybe it felt sufficiently long ago to lend it a soft sepia nostalgia – a painful past now viewed from a place of safety and comfort. I tried to imagine what it must have been like to play in such a poor team, one that had fallen out of the win-lose-draw pattern of most clubs and did not 'turn a corner' or 'see light at the end of the tunnel'. All they had was a Saturday ritual of defeat upon defeat.

Who were these players? What went wrong? How had they ended up at Rochdale? Where did they go to next? What effect did it have on them, as sportsmen and people? To find answers, I tracked down and interviewed as many people as possible who were in and around the club during this period. Occasionally I have had to use a little poetic licence to relate the story but these incidents and episodes are as true to life as possible, their tone and content corroborated by first-hand or nearby witnesses.

Meanwhile, at the same time, the country had been in meltdown. The Arab–Israeli War had sent energy prices soaring, causing a near-economic collapse. Edward Heath, the prime minister, declared a state of emergency. Bombs were being detonated across England by the IRA. Power cuts were frequent and the BBC and ITV were instructed to end broadcasting each night at 10.30pm. As inflation took hold, a three-day working week was inaugurated. Mineworkers and others went on strike. Rochdale suffered more than most. The cotton industry was in the midst of a slow but inevitable close-down. Thousands working at TBA (Turner Brothers Asbestos), the town's main employer, were becoming aware of the threat their job had on their health and lifespan. *A Clockwork Orange* devotees were on the prowl. Racists were attacking Asians. Violence and vandalism seemed to be everywhere. The football club was a mirror image of the town and country – tired, dark, clinging to life.

There is, then, a landslide of woe in this tale but it should be viewed as a bewitching melancholy, similar to, say, a song by Joy Division or The Cure, or a painting by Edvard Munch or Walter Sickert, or a film by Ingmar Bergman or Roberto Rossellini. Everything turns out fine in the end. Rochdale AFC survived and thrives to this day; the world still turns. So, hope can gold-splash the murk as it evolves from chaos to order, bleak to better, monochrome to colour. Horace Walpole (1717–1797), the art historian, man of letters and celebrated dandy – surely this is the first time he has been referenced in a football book – tendered the word *gloomth* to the world, a harmonious marriage of gloom and warmth. Enjoy the gloomth herein.

Mark Hodkinson
August 2022

1

A Beautiful Quiet

BEFORE THE winter comes the summer. And, in and around a football club, even a lower-league one such as Rochdale, it is a place to be when the sun shines and the days are long and languid. Ask the groundsman about the pitch and he'll tell you it is *immaculate* or *perfect*. He'll crouch on his knees to show you. Look, he says, pulling at a handful of deep-green strands and then forming an arc with his pointing arm: not a single divot in sight. The sit-on lawnmower is still, parked at the side of the pitch, but the smell of petrol is in the air, mixed with the tang of cut grass. Towards the stands, there is another smell: fresh paint, blue and white, has been daubed across wooden panels. It is the last week of June.

Last season, 1972/73, Rochdale finished mid-table. They won 14 times and lost 15, a typical and acceptable mix of a season that brought forth cheers and moans, chants and groans in equal measure as players battled through the mud and cold, driving rain and occasional sunshine. It has all gone now – over there, blown up and over the moors and far away; out of sight, out of memory. The ground, forlorn in November fog, feels today to be a snapshot of heaven fallen to earth. Terraces are brushed clean. Stands are neat and symmetrical, framed by foliage, the sycamores strong and verdant behind the Sandy Lane End. 'The Hill' is at the corner of the Pearl Street End and the Main

Stand. Here, in November 1948, soil and debris heaved from the pitch in an attempt to reduce the five-foot slope from one end to the other was piled high. A handful of crush barriers are driven down hard into the mound but it is too steep and uneven to terrace. Buddleia, dandelions and, at the highest point, rosebay willow herb flourish, almost as if placed there to garland a Pennine hill caught and set among the people at play.

From the halfway line on the pitch, it is possible to see the steeple of St Clement's Church peeking above the top of the stand at the Pearl Street End. Curiously, as if prearranged by a higher force, the spire pierces the sky at the exact centre of the crossbar down below. Rays of sunlight criss-cross the four metal structures that hold aloft the floodlights at each corner of the pitch. What are those for? Surely the light never fades around these parts. All around, there is newness and hope and promise and giddiness for a season soon to begin.

A football ground is a village, an encampment of disparate souls. The villagers here at Rochdale, those who work on the grass and others who set down in the dugout, offices or boardroom, are few in number, at least until the players return in a week or so. This morning, today, Fred Ratcliffe, club chairman, has invited a few pressmen and radio lads to meet the new manager. In years to come, such events will be branded 'press days' and the terminology – lads? press*men*? – recast to fit a wider social agenda.

For now, this small band is doing what they did last season and many more before that. Ratcliffe leads the way on to the pitch. He is chatting to Walter Joyce, the man he appointed as manager a few weeks earlier – Tuesday, 5 June 1973, to be precise. They are a mismatch of men. Ratcliffe is small, slightly bowed and walks in short steps. Joyce is 35 years old, sure-footed and lithe, still with the resplendent aura of a sportsman, as if living within a halo. The *Rochdale Observer* will later describe him as a 'fitness fanatic'. He is wearing a short-sleeved polyester shirt and check trousers. Before leaving the family home in Sutton, St Helens, he'd asked his wife, Doreen, whether the shirt was 'a bit feminine'; it was bright and seemed to wear him as much as he wore *it*. She'd reassured him that it was fine and he looked smart, very smart. 'Lemon is all the rage this summer,' she said, smiling. 'It's not lemon, it's yellow,' he protested.

Looking on at pitchside, respectful of the pre-eminence of the chairman and manager, is the back-up team: Peter Madden, assistant manager; Angus McLean, secretary/assistant manager (a position that would clearly need reviewing: no club had *two* assistant managers); Fred O'Donoghue, chief scout; Beryl Earnshaw, office assistant; Albert Sanderson, groundsman; and Tom Nichol, a man without a formal position but the avuncular figure found at most football clubs, with too many roles to audit.

The press corps that had made its way to Spotland to meet Walter Joyce was only three-strong – Mike Smith of BBC Radio Manchester, Stan Townsend of the *Rochdale Observer* and local freelance journalist, Jack Hammill. Was Joyce surprised to get the job? 'I suppose I was, really. Most football directors prefer someone with managerial experience but I'm pleased they chose me.' Would he be bringing in the players early for pre-season training? 'Footballers, like everyone else, need a break and most of them will have already made plans for their holidays. So I think I'll let them have their rest, but once they come in for training, I expect 100 per cent effort.'

Fred Ratcliffe was listening in, taking it in; ever thus. He knew the buggers (Rochdale supporters) would accuse him of going for the cheapest option; an established manager would invariably have commanded a higher wage. He knew also that if Joyce succeeded, the thinking would be reversed and he'd receive acclaim for having the vision to detect and foster untried talent. Ratcliffe had been on the board for more than 25 years, 20 as chairman. He knew more than enough about football fans, how they were both loyal and fickle, that they complained and congratulated, and, of course, they each felt they could run a football club better than him. On this particular deal, what they didn't know was that Joyce had been enticed from his job in the youth set-up at Oldham Athletic on the promise that he could bring a couple of coaches with him – and they wouldn't be paid in brass washers.

The microphone was also placed in front of Ratcliffe; he was known to be good for a quote. He said a principal reason behind Joyce's appointment was his promise to assemble a squad of young players. As Ratcliffe said this, he imagined the mutterings, Brimrod to Castleton, Norden to Littleborough: Fred's cutting the wage bill again. Salaries were seldom revealed in football but everyone knew that a kid drawn from amateur football, brought to Spotland after running his guts out for Torchbearers (a local amateur club) on Lenny Barn (a nearby playing field), would earn about a fifth as much as a well-fed, well-trained stopper or striker who had played 200 matches for Scunthorpe United or similar.

And what if he *was* trying to save a few bob? The latest accounts, up to 31 May 1972, showed that the club was £108,289 in debt (more than £1.5m in today's terms) and had a bank overdraft of £40,819. Ratcliffe had these figures seared into his brain, as he did the constituent costs: salaries and pensions £91,166; travelling and refreshments £11,443; bank interest and charges £7,795; social club administration £7,552; and ground maintenance £4,723. Over a two-year period, Ratcliffe, along with fellow directors, had introduced £74,327 to the club's finances as 'unsecured loans'. When asked what these were, Ratcliffe was unequivocal: 'It's a posh way of saying we've tipped the money out of our pockets and thrown it down a bloody big hole.'

The board at Rochdale AFC was typical of most lower-league football clubs. Fred Ratcliffe, the wealthiest and most charismatic, aged 59 in 1973, was essentially the club's owner, courtesy of holding the most shares. He had 12,263 of a total of almost 50,000 issued, while no other individual had more than 500. If the other directors combined all their shares, they would still have less than half the number of Ratcliffe. Many described him as a 'natural chairman' – an autocrat who, true to the cliché, didn't suffer fools but was prudent enough to listen to those whom he respected. Under his stewardship, the board had fallen together naturally, each of them local, middle-aged and moderately wealthy. Much the same as Ratcliffe, they viewed running the club largely as a call of duty – propping it up or bailing it out was how they most often described it. The drip-drip of money from their own accounts into the club's and out again was constant but, by way of recompense, they enjoyed their soirées and Saturday match routines; all pals together.

Football was easy in June, when even the most experienced pros succumbed to hope and optimism. They looked at the pitch and it was, as Albert the groundsman had said, 'immaculate'. They imagined dancing across it, this way, that way, pass, move, dribble, another pass, shoot – goal. All that space to run into and time enough to chip the ball from one wing to the other, to even pose for the photographer, snap, while the ball was in arc-flight. There was no mud slowing them down, no opponents shifting their weight to block a run or raking studs against their shins, ankles or calves. Quiet was on all sides, a beautiful quiet, no grumbles or groans from the crowd, no fat bloke leaning on the perimeter fence imploring you to lump it forward or screaming that you were a mardarse or shithouse for not making a tackle that was always two yards out of reach.

Players were sparkly-healthy in June and relaxed after a summer break, even if it had only been a week or two. That dip in the sea at Scarborough or Majorca had 'worked wonders' on their old war wounds – the achy knee, tight hamstring or an ankle injury that sent a sharp stabbing pain into their shin when they pushed off in a particular direction. For now, today, mid-summer, they were without pain or fear of pain. In their imagination, they were running as if they were children again or in a dream, floating across the grass, quick as sprites. They tried, but couldn't fathom, what had made it all seem so difficult last season and all the seasons before that. Football really was a beautiful game.

The cheer was shared by everyone gathered upon the Spotland turf. Stan Townsend joked with Ratcliffe about the press box chiselled into the Main Stand, so small that journalists were squashed up against a narrow ledge barely wide enough to take a notebook. The light bulb hanging above the box was invariably missing and reporters often worked in the dark, especially at evening matches. 'Are you going to sort it, Fred?' asked Townsend. 'If it's toss-up between signing a decent full-back from Rotherham and having a joiner in for a couple of weeks building you lot a new press box, I think you know what I'm going to do, don't you? And, come on, you're not having to climb up a 14ft ladder to get to the press box like you do at Port Vale. And none of that's for printing,' said Ratcliffe.

Stan Townsend had reported faithfully and often bluntly on the club's many disappointments but he was upbeat in his preview of the forthcoming season: 'With eight goals coming in the final three games of last season, it only proved that if The Dale can relax in all the games, then they could well be challenging for promotion this season.' Walter Joyce was new to the balancing act between anticipation and realism, but volunteered: 'I can't promise promotion this season, but if the players give me their all in the games and we get off to a good start, who knows, we may well get there.'

* * *

On the other side of the stands and walls, the offices and car parks that form Spotland the football ground, is Spotland, the district of Rochdale. The name sounds comical when mispronounced as Spot-*land* rather than with the soft hybrid of 'u' and 'e' in place of 'a' in the second syllable. Rochdale people do this often with place names, as if to purposely catch out incomers and outsiders. In the local tongue, for example, Kirkholt becomes Ki'Kolt, Turf Hill is T'Fill, Whitworth is Whit'th and Milnrow is Milnrer.

'Spotland' means 'area around the Spodden', which refers to the River Spodden, a tributary of the River Roch that emanates high on the Pennine moors encircling most of the town. At different times, the water tumbles or surges down from these hillsides, through the peat and millstone grit and is responsible for all that is Rochdale. At first, it was used to power mills where wool was woven and, later, during the Industrial Revolution, it was converted to steam as Rochdale became one of the world's most productive cotton-spinning towns of the 19th century. The incessant rainfall – it rains on average 161 days per year – provided both the energy and an attendant damp climate, so that cotton fibres, when spun, were less likely to snap.

By 1900, the population of Rochdale had increased from a few thousand before industrialisation to 120,000. The town had more than 125 mills, Acre Works to Yew Vale, with tall, belching chimneys jabbing the skyline. Dunlop Mill was believed to be the biggest in the world, built over six years using 14 million Accrington bricks. Inside this cavernous structure, the Dunlop Rubber Co. spun cord on a round-the-clock basis for use in car tyres. More than 3,000 people worked there and, over a year, it was said to consume the equivalent of one-third of Egypt's cotton crop.

Almost 90 per cent of workers in the town were employed in the manufacture or trading of textiles. They moved into cheap terraced houses, many of them back to back, hewed into narrow streets abutting the mills, several storeys high. Demand for living accommodation was so high that 'cellar communities' were established beneath houses, mainly close to St Chad's Church above the town centre; in 1870 almost 600 people lived in these dark, dank hovels.

Mills were infernal places. They were cramped. The air was clogged with cotton dust that snagged in lungs, making breathing difficult and often leading to a condition called byssinosis or brown lung disease. Machines were thunderously noisy. The temperature, which had to be maintained at between 65 and 80°C to save thread from breaking, was stifling. Operatives, a good number of them children, spent between 12 and 16 hours a day, Monday to Saturday, at their machines. They were fined for misdemeanours such as staring out of a window. Accidents were rife, many occurring in the last few hours of a shift when workers were exhausted; it wasn't uncommon for people to lose fingers and limbs or suffer gruesome deaths trapped in machinery.

Debris from mills, along with oils and toxins from the associated dyeing industry, was pumped into streams and rivers; in 1915 Rochdale was the most polluted area in England. Life expectancy in the town during the Industrial Revolution was 21 – it was 38 in rural Westmorland. One in every three babies born in England didn't reach the age of five and the ratio was often one in two in industrial areas such as Rochdale. In growth terms, Rochdale boys, at the age of 13, were a full year behind those from elsewhere. This was the town and these were the people from which Rochdale AFC was formed.

* * *

It was his first day. Moral dilemmas and potential life-changing episodes shouldn't occur on your first day in a new job. He was still telling Beryl, the secretary, how he preferred his tea, when the phone rang. 'Is that Walter?' It took a few seconds before Walter Joyce could determine the words through the syrupy Glaswegian accent. 'Speaking,' he replied. 'Tommy Docherty, Manchester United.' As if Tommy Docherty needed to identify himself. Most days, he was on the sports pages of the national newspapers or on television, answering questions about the release of Denis Law and retirement of Bobby Charlton, or pondering on the whereabouts of George Best. 'Walter, I've heard good things about you. I'd like you to come and sort out the youth set-up here at Old Trafford,' he said.

Fred O'Donoghue, Rochdale's chief scout, was sitting across from Joyce. 'It's Tommy Docherty,' mouthed Joyce, his hand held over the mouthpiece. O'Donoghue had already heard and recognised the voice. 'But I've just taken over at Rochdale,' said Joyce, returning to the telephone conversation. 'It's my first day.' Docherty was persistent. He asked if Joyce had signed a contract. 'Not yet,' he replied. 'Aye, that's what Frizz told me,' said Docherty. Jimmy Frizzell was manager of Oldham Athletic, from where Joyce had joined Rochdale. Joyce immediately recognised the link. Frizzell had been born in Greenock, 25 miles west of Glasgow. Everyone knew that Scots looked out for one another. 'They're sorting out the contract for me to sign,' said Joyce. He promised Docherty that he'd 'think about it' and get back to him in a day or two. Turning to O'Donoghue, Joyce asked: 'Who have you got for me?' It was their first proper meeting. O'Donoghue began running through a list of players who were still not fixed up with clubs and might be interested in joining Rochdale. Joyce interrupted: 'I'm sorry, Fred, I can't concentrate. I've got the United offer on my mind. What do you think I should do?'

O'Donoghue had seen this conundrum played out before. The role of youth coach was without the do-or-die pressure to secure wins at all costs. The only measurement of efficacy was on how many young players were successfully readied for the first team. They tended to stay longer in their jobs, many even withstanding managerial changes. A manager, however, was much better paid and – board of directors willing – granted a fiefdom to govern as he saw fit: *his* players, *his* coaching, *his* tactics, *his* philosophy and, always, *his* responsibility. Within the game, those who embedded themselves at a club as youth coaches were sometimes viewed as patsies – lacking ambition, playing it safe – while, alternatively, those seeking manager status were heroes or egotists, savants or fools, setting themselves up for a fall, often so great that finding a job in football thereafter might be denied them. Two or three years on from their pay-off by a football club, many ex-managers, especially from the lower leagues, were spotted doing 'normal' jobs, maybe working in garden centres, pubs or driving a taxi to get by. Few returned to coaching or less prestigious roles at football clubs, either because their ego couldn't endure the diminution or, more likely, fans and directors alike considered them 'tainted' by failure.

'Tell me, most of all – what do you want to be?' asked O'Donoghue. 'A manager,' replied Joyce. 'Well, you've answered your own question.'

Later, Joyce informed Fred Ratcliffe of the approach from Manchester United. 'I know all about it,' said Ratcliffe. 'Docherty phoned me a couple of weeks ago and asked if he could speak to you. I told him I'd rather he didn't, that we had an agreement you'd manage Rochdale.' Joyce was impressed. Most lower-league chairmen would have kowtowed to Docherty, reduced in the shadow of Manchester United. To Ratcliffe, it clearly didn't matter; hands had been shaken, a deal was a deal. Joyce was concerned that he'd offended Ratcliffe by broaching the subject. 'It's Oldham that have jiggered me off,' said Ratcliffe. 'The stirring buggers. They know full well that you're our man and yet they've been on the phone to Docherty telling him we've not sorted out the contract.' Joyce said he was 'in shock' and needed time to consider. 'Fine,' said Ratcliffe. 'Take as much time as you want – let me know by the morning!'

* * *

Sport in a codified form was played initially by upper-class men who had more time available than manual workers and were healthier and generally less tired. They were also educated enough to set down rules and record results; 40 per cent of men and 60 per cent of women were illiterate in England in 1800. Earlier, 'games' such as mob football, involving an unlimited number on opposing teams, took place in the streets. The heaving mass would struggle to carry, kick or throw an inflated pig's bladder to markers at each end of town.

The first team to formally represent the town was Rochdalians, who travelled to Liverpool in 1812 to take part in a cricket match. Twelve years later, Rochdale Cricket Club was formed, thought to be the oldest organisation in the town aside from religious institutions. Rochdale Athletic Club was inaugurated in 1866 and, in the same year, a magistrate and a handful of businessmen formed a rugby team, Rochdale Football Club. In Rochdale, the sport of choice for the working man was predominantly rugby. Alongside Rochdale Football Club (despite its name, a wholly rugby-playing entity), others formed to provide competition – St Clement's, Rochdale Juniors, Rakebank, Rochdale United and Rochdale Wasps. At a meeting held in the Roebuck Hotel, Rochdale, in April 1871, three of these clubs merged (Wasps, United and Rochdale Football Club) to form a team strong enough to represent Rochdale against other town teams. Officials considered Grasshoppers and Butterflies before settling upon the suffix of Hornets.

The growth of sport, as either a participant or spectator, was stymied because most people worked on Saturdays. The Early Closing Association, formed in 1842, lobbied employers to allow workers to have Saturday afternoons off and 'foster a sober and industrious workforce'. The burgeoning leisure industry backed the campaign. Train operators charged reduced Saturday fares for day-trippers to the countryside. Theatres and music halls put on star turns on Saturday afternoons. Ultimately, employers (mill owners especially) were most persuaded by the increased productivity and reduced absenteeism from workers refreshed by an extra day or half day away from their machines. Sport benefited greatly from this incremental shortening of the working week, which by the 1890s saw most mills fall quiet and still on Saturday afternoons, if not the whole day.

An 'association football' club bearing the town's name had been established in 1896 but foundered after five years. Another, Rochdale Town, lasted two seasons, before a third attempt was undertaken. The *Rochdale Observer* of Wednesday, 15 May 1907 reported: 'At a meeting convened by Mr Harvey Rigg in the Central Council School, Fleece Street, last evening, with Mr Herbert Hopkinson in the chair, it was decided to form a club to be called Rochdale Association Football Club.'

* * *

On the drive back home from Spotland, Walter Joyce pulled in to the car park at Birch Services on the M62; it had opened a few months earlier and workmen were still banging in fence posts and marking out parking spaces. He was anxious to return home and discuss the matter with Doreen and to have his usual back garden kick around with his son, Warren, aged nine. Before then, he needed some quiet time, alone time. He had a lot on his mind. The same as all ex-footballers, if asked about his playing career, he'd say how wonderful it had been to be paid for carrying out an activity he loved and to have the crowd cheering him on. He'd mention how much he'd enjoyed keeping fit and feeling fit and the kudos of being a *footballer*, a prince among the hoi polloi. In more wistful moments, in his car on an overcast afternoon parked up by a hawthorn hedge at a service station, for example, he'd think back, dissect his career and ponder on the incidents, episodes and decisions that comprised the whole.

Walter Joyce was born in Oldham in September 1937. At school, he excelled at sport – cricket, running, athletics, but most of all, football. Scouts from several Football League clubs had knocked at the family door and, at 16, he became a groundstaff boy – a precursor to the formal apprenticeship scheme – at Burnley, an established top-tier club with a progressive reputation. At the time Joyce signed, the club was investing in splendid training facilities. Bob Lord, their chairman, had bought 80 acres of land on the estate of the nearby Gawthorpe Hall, an Elizabethan country house, and was overseeing the installation of three full-size pitches, an all-weather pitch, a medical room and gymnasium. The club was going to 'rear' players and avoid spending excessively on transfer fees.

Joyce signed as a professional in November 1954 but waited six years before making his first-team debut, in a 2-1 away defeat at Manchester City. He was three weeks short of his 23rd birthday but the period had embraced two years of National Service, when he trained at RAF Catterick and served in Cyprus. He acknowledged that he 'wasn't the quickest' but he was athletic, strong in the tackle and able to play in several defensive and midfield positions. He played 71 matches in ten seasons at Burnley, suggesting his versatility had marked him down as a 'covering' player rather than being fixed to a single position and a regular place in the team. He'd also been competing with some of the finest players in English football. Burnley had won the league championship in 1959/60 with a team comprising footballers of the calibre of Jimmy Adamson and Jimmy McIlroy.

In February 1964, Joyce moved to Blackburn Rovers and played much more often (120 times) before signing for Oldham Athletic in September 1967, where he was a regular first-team player (71 appearances). He ended his playing career after breaking his right foot, then left and right foot again in quick succession.

Jimmy Frizzell, Joyce's team-mate at Oldham, had been appointed manager at Boundary Park in March 1970. He recognised that Joyce's enthusiasm and experience made him an ideal choice as youth coach. One of Joyce's mantras to young players was: get over it. If your last shot on goal was wide, you forgot about it, pretended it hadn't happened and demanded the ball, to try again. Similarly, if you'd had a 'mare', you put it out of mind as soon as the final whistle was blown; you moved on. These fundamental elements of performance were easily resolved, assuaged with a little cod philosophy.

On the more substantial issues across a footballer's career, regrets (although they preferred the kinder phrasing of doubts, qualms or misgivings) were inevitable. So, Joyce pondered occasionally whether he'd chosen the right club when he'd signed for Burnley. Might he have had more opportunities with a less successful team? Had he waited too long for his professional debut, been too patient? Should he have insisted on being played in his preferred position (wing-half) instead of filling in here and there? Had he overestimated his talent, thinking he could dislodge the finest players in the country from their place in the team?

Alone in his car a few miles from Spotland, he recognised that he was at a pivotal moment of his new career, the one that came after being a professional footballer. He didn't want to make a decision he'd regret or later have doubts, qualms or misgivings about – dress it up any way you wanted. Rain began to fall heavily and washed away the view through the windscreen and on all sides of the car. He liked this feeling of being cocooned; it concentrated the mind. What to do? Youth coach at Manchester United? Manager at Rochdale? What to do? What was best – working with some of the most talented young players in the country or being king of a small-town club? What to do? He'd given his word to Fred Ratcliffe but surely he'd forgive him an about-turn. It was Manchester United, after all. *Manchester United*. What to do?

In the meantime, the press had become aware of the contest for Joyce's services. Tommy Docherty was typically bullish, using the media to do his bidding. 'We feel Walter is the ideal man for

United. He has done a good job with little resources at Oldham and we are trying to develop our youth side this year. It's now up to him to decide. I want him here, but so do Rochdale,' he told the press. Docherty was about to begin his first full season at Old Trafford and had been granted the support of the chairman, Louis Edwards, and board of directors, as he set about a restructure of the club that he insisted was necessary after the 18-month tenure of Frank O'Farrell.

Stan Townsend, with his excellent network of contacts – players, directors and other journalists – had heard that United were constantly improving their offers to Joyce. Townsend felt it was his duty to prepare Rochdale fans for the loss of a manager who hadn't overseen a single match, not even a pre-season friendly. 'I feel the latest offer by Manchester United is too good for him to turn down,' he wrote in the *Rochdale Observer*.

* * *

At a meeting convened by Mr Harvey Rigg. Indeed, Harvey Rigg was a supreme convenor – 'a person whose job it is to call people together for meetings of a committee'. Unlike most people who were reluctant to take on titles and responsibility, Rigg relished both. Aside from his involvement with sport, he cheerfully amassed civic positions, among them honorary secretary of the Rochdale Agricultural Society and the presidency of both the Rochdale Head Teachers Association and the Rochdale branch of the National Union of Teachers.

Before he petitioned to set up a football club, Rigg had devoted much of his time to rugby. He was blessed with great eloquence and energy. He was the eldest of five sons born to Isaac and Elizabeth Rigg, long-time publicans at the Church Inn, Willbutts Lane, Spotland. The pub bordered a large field and in the 1870s the family marked it out as a rugby pitch; it had previously hosted cricket matches and a small pavilion was on the site. A rugby club was formed, St Clement's, named after the nearby church, where the nucleus of the team were members of the Young Men's Class. The Rigg brothers – Harvey, Wilford, Louis, Edgar and Arnold – all played for the club, for whom Harvey volunteered himself as treasurer and, later, secretary. By 1881, they had three teams and played matches as far away as the Midlands and South Wales.

Rugby grew in popularity but a schism formed. The rules stated that participants had to hold full-time jobs but players asked for 'broken time payment', effectively compensation for wages they had to forego to either train or play matches. In 1895, the Northern Rugby Football Union broke away from the Rugby Football Union to enable its clubs to pay players on a lawful basis; it was previously done clandestinely or on a quid pro quo basis – players granted positions at club owners' businesses, for example. Clubs leaving the Rugby Football Union – all based in the north – reduced teams from 15 to 13 players, introduced the 'play-the-ball' and did away with rucks and mauls. Hence, two codes of the same sport were fashioned, rugby union and rugby league – although the latter version wasn't named as such until 1923.

Harvey Rigg backed the wrong code. He chose to maintain St Clement's on an amateur footing and follow the Rugby Football Union's diktat of 'if men can't afford to play, then they shouldn't play at all'. As their rivals joined the new code, St Clement's were left without key opponents. The next season, 1896/97, the club converted to the 13-a-side game but the better local players were settled at other clubs and, due to dwindling attendances, finance wasn't available to tempt them to St Clement's. The club went bankrupt in March 1897 while, on the other side of town, Rochdale Hornets prospered. Undeterred, Rigg was determined to make best use of the field next to his parents' pub for both the health and wellbeing of the townspeople and his family's finances. Soon afterwards, he convened that famous meeting.

2

Tough Start for Dale

'I'M STAYING,' sang Walter Joyce to everyone he passed in the village of Rochdale AFC. 'I knew you would,' said Angus McLean. 'How?' asked Joyce. 'Just knew.' Joyce had promised Stan Townsend he'd give him a call, whatever his decision, so that he could run the story in the midweek edition of the *Rochdale Observer*. 'Two things swayed me to stay at Rochdale,' he told the reporter. 'The main one being it has always been my ambition to manage a club. Also, having been announced that I was to take charge here, I felt I couldn't go back on my word by taking the job at Manchester United. My mind is settled now. I have put the offer from Tommy Docherty out of my mind but, I must admit, the terms were difficult to turn down.'

Over the weekend, Joyce had barely slept and had paced the floor so much that Doreen had joked that he'd wear out a patch of carpet. Late on Sunday afternoon, she'd noticed a change in his mood. He was smiling, light on his feet. He tried to explain but struggled to shape thoughts into words. He'd realised, he said, that it wasn't a choice between Rochdale or Manchester United, Fred Ratcliffe or Tommy Docherty, or the now and the future. In fact, there hadn't been a choice at all. And if there were no choice, there was no need to fret. Put simply, it wasn't possible for him to give back-word to Fred Ratcliffe; it was an affront to Joyce's integrity. In football, he'd learned to keep his counsel at times and hide his true feelings but he stood by an absolute: he didn't renege on a deal – the handshake between him and Ratcliffe was binding.

Fred Ratcliffe, back at Spotland after a business trip, reacted in typically paternalistic fashion: 'As you can see, the lad has made up his mind to stay with us and I am pleased he has honoured his word.'

* * *

Harvey Rigg had learned bar-room oratory while listening to regulars pontificating on all manner of subjects in the Church Inn. He'd also had a sturdy traditional education. At first, he went to St Clement's Church School, before making his way across town each morning to Henry Street in Deeplish, where he attended classes given by a private tutor, Mr Wrigley. At the age of 22, Rigg enrolled at Trinity College, a teacher-training establishment in Carmarthen, South Wales, known for its 'monastic' regime. Students started the day at 6.30am with a cold bath and often washed with rainwater collected from the roof.

He returned to Rochdale and, at 30, became headmaster at Newbold Free School. His teaching career was interrupted when he answered the call from the British government to serve in the Second Boer War in southern Africa. During 'Black Week' in December 1899, almost 3,000 soldiers had been killed or wounded in three separate battles, prompting a plea for reinforcements. Rigg served as a trooper in the Duke of Lancaster's Own Yeomanry for 16 months; cavalry troopers were considered a cut above regular soldiers because they had to be reasonably wealthy to supply their own equipment and, sometimes, their own horse.

Back in Rochdale, Rigg, as the eldest son, was charged by the family to ensure the sports field provided income to augment the pub takings. Rochdale Town FC had played there for a few months before their demise in December 1903 and it had hosted a few rugby tournaments. Rigg noted that football was now being played widely throughout the town. Two leagues had been established for amateurs – the Rochdale and District and the Rochdale Sunday Schools League. He surmised that, with Hornets newly settled at their Athletic Grounds, a new football club based at St Clement's might succeed.

Rigg had an evangelical belief in the value of sport, revealed in a speech given at Brickcroft Workmen's Club. A party had gathered for the unveiling of a photograph of William Waugh, a former captain and president of St Clement's, who had died a year earlier. 'If anything in the world elevates a man, it is sport,' announced Rigg. 'It shows whether he is an honourable man, or a cad.' The assembly at the Brickcroft was typical of the social bonding engendered by sport. William Waugh had worked as a weaver at Mitchell Hey Mill but, through rugby, he and many others had earned the respect of 'gentlemen' such as Rigg. Similarly, artisans were realising that not everyone from the professional or employer class was 'stuck-up' or dismissive of those less well-off than themselves.

The Brickcroft was itself evidence of a growing cultural and social enlightenment. The club had been built in 1874 on a site (literally a brick croft) close to Rochdale town centre where a notorious pub had stood for many years. The new venture offered its 900 members a ladies coffee room, chess and card rooms and hosted a debating society. The Rev. William Nassau Molesworth of St Clement's Church approved of its ethos. He wrote in a letter that he was pleased to see 'good tea, coffee, soda water and ginger beer within the reach of members'. The reverend, a lifelong advocate of veganism, said he'd have preferred the club to have a policy of teetotalism but conceded: 'It is sure to me that at present we cannot get rid of the drink but I believe we may get rid of the drunkenness.'

* * *

Before Walter Joyce had arrived at the club, Fred Ratcliffe conducted a piece of business that many supporters considered unduly ruthless, if not foolhardy. Reg Jenkins was widely considered to be the club's best *ever* player. He'd spent nine seasons at Spotland, scoring 132 goals in 345 league and cup appearances – a remarkable goals-per-game ratio while playing in a team often of poor quality, although he'd been a regular in the promotion team of 1969/70.

Born in the Cornish village of Millbrook, Jenkins had made a tour of clubs in the south-west, turning out for Plymouth Argyle, Exeter City and Torquay United before joining Rochdale, aged 25, in the summer of 1964, for £2,500. At first, neither he nor his wife, Norma, knew of Rochdale's whereabouts and had to buy a map to trace a route along 'A' roads and newly built motorways. Their first trip north, made in Jenkins's Morris Tourer, took 13 hours. He received a signing-on fee of £300, which was spent on a washing machine. His fair hair and broad, muscular stature made him easily distinguishable on a football pitch. He had a robust and direct style of play and a powerful shot. Fans referred to him as a 'giant' (he was actually 5ft 10in) and stories, whether apocryphal or not, were told of his shots ripping through goal nets and breaking goalkeepers' fingers. He was courteous with fans, signing autographs and driving ball boys home if it was raining. He was the club's longest-serving player but had suffered a series of niggling injuries during the previous season. 'He's always in the treatment room these days, having a bloody rubdown,' complained Ratcliffe.

Over many years, Fred Ratcliffe had learned that sentiment could play no part in football. Players always wanted higher wages, extra bonuses and longer contracts, while all the time having an eye out for their next move up the divisions (or down, if it was more lucrative). He knew of Jenkins's status among supporters and his talismanic value to the team but, as he often told fellow directors, no player was any use if he wasn't on the pitch. And how big was that bloody hole, the debt, the club was in?: £108,289. And rising. During the interviews with prospective managers, they had each been told that the budget was limited and it made best sense to focus on youth with a few 'old heads' helping them out – those who could still get up and down that heavy, sapping Spotland pitch.

Jenkins had played 24 matches during the 1972/73 season and scored ten goals. He was, though, about to turn 35, an age when footballers invariably slowed down and were less effectual, even those as committed to fitness as Jenkins. After training, he often ran on the moors above Norden with Peter Madden, competing with one another on sprints to the next tree, stile or mound of rocks. On weekday afternoons, Jenkins helped local freelance journalist, Jack Hammill, who kept hundreds of chickens on farmland in Bamford. This workaday bearing all added to Jenkins's lustre and he was known to fans as either 'Our Reg' or 'Big Reg'.

The *Rochdale Observer* asked Fred Ratcliffe about Jenkins and he responded (in noticeably impersonal terms): 'The player has told me that he thinks he can give Rochdale another season and in view of the fact that he has been such a good servant, we feel we do not want to get rid of him at the moment. But the final decision on Reg's future will rest entirely with the new manager when he is appointed.' A week later, Jenkins was told he wouldn't be offered a new contract regardless of the incoming manager's feelings on the matter. Ratcliffe might have been influenced by initial conversations with Walter Joyce who, to the chairman's delight, supported the emphasis on building a team of mainly young professionals; this made it easier for Ratcliffe to release the club's highest-paid player. He knew he'd get stick from the fans, a few letters maybe, people collaring him in the club car park, but he liked to think that whatever he said or did, they knew it was because he thought it was best for the club. They owed him that, all the hours and all the money he'd put in over the years.

Jenkins had settled in Rochdale with Norma and their children, Andrew and Helen, and he quickly made it known that he'd prefer to stay in the north-west. This alerted Oldham Athletic and they began a comical pursuit of the striker who had returned to Cornwall for a summer holiday. His mother-in-law, based in Plymouth, began to receive phone calls from journalists and Oldham's staff. 'All I could tell them was that Reg was somewhere on the other side of the county and that I would get him to ring Boundary Park when he returned here,' she said.

Jimmy Frizzell wanted Jenkins as his assistant. They had met a few times and he saw Jenkins's reserved but flinty demeanour as an ideal foil for his own more combustible nature. When Jenkins was eventually found, he turned down the offer, mainly because he'd bought a plot of land in Millbrook and a family friend had committed to building him a house. Afterwards, Jenkins played on a part-time basis for Falmouth Town and Bodmin Town until his mid-40s. He then worked as a lorry driver and helped run his local club, Millbrook FC; its ground is named Jenkins Park in his memory (he died in January 2013, aged 74).

Many years later, it emerged that a rumour had reached Ratcliffe that Jenkins had been feigning injuries. At the start of the 1973/74 season, Ratcliffe had asked him to sign a three-month contract during which he could prove his fitness. To Ratcliffe, this was common sense, safeguarding the club from a wasted wage but Jenkins viewed it as a slight on his honour. Either way, it meant the team went into the new campaign without one of the lower-league's most prolific goalscorers, a man who many felt embodied the very spirit of the club.

* * *

Harvey Rigg had a new impetus to find a tenant for the sports field. His father, Isaac, who had run the Church Inn for 45 years, died in August 1906. He'd left £1,077, a substantial sum at the time, but it spread thinly between a wife, five sons and two daughters. Harvey immediately made what he later referred to as 'strenuous efforts' to bring a professional football club to Rochdale. He assembled a ten-man committee of friends from teaching and sport to guide Rochdale Association Football Club to formation and the team was duly elected to the Manchester League.

Rigg's good friend, Herbert Hopkinson, although only 25, volunteered himself as secretary. Hopkinson was similar to Rigg – zestful and willing to undertake admin duties. He was a sportsman himself, taking part in 'pedestrianism' fairs throughout the north-west. These were competitive walking races that attracted a great deal of gambling money. His prowess was such that, to generate better odds, an opponent was often given a yard or two start over the routine 50-yard race. Later, Hopkinson spent 12 years as a Football League referee and officiated at an international match between Ireland and Wales.

The initial Rochdale team comprised young men who had impressed at trials or who had already played for established clubs. They had to live relatively close by because trams and trains were the only form of transport; only the very wealthy owned cars in the early 1900s. Rochdale's first match was a friendly: the First XI vs The Rest, on Saturday, 24 August 1907. The pitch was roped off and about 350 fans were charged a penny to watch. Next, a friendly was played at St Clement's against Oldham Athletic, newly elected to the Second Division of the Football League. Rochdale lost 4-1 in front of approximately 2,000 supporters.

Four days later, on Saturday, 7 September 1907, Rochdale made their competitive debut, at home against Tonge FC, a club based in Middleton, north Manchester. Rochdale wore black-and-white-striped shirts in homage to Newcastle United, who dominated English football in the 1900s, winning the league on three occasions. Again, about 2,000 spectators made their way to Spotland and the 2-2 draw augured well as Tonge had been Manchester League champions on four occasions.

The team had performed well in its first three matches but Rigg had expected greater numbers to attend. Staff at other clubs had emphasised the value of starting off with a substantial groundswell of support. 'The more that come straight off, the more will get hooked,' he was told. He'd imagined that a new team bearing the town's name would pique curiosity, even if they didn't become long-term fans. In the matches against Oldham Athletic and Tonge, at least half the crowd had supported the visiting teams.

Rigg recognised that there were mitigating circumstances. Rugby had established itself in the town and, already, most people tended to define themselves through their commitment to a single sport. The failure of the two earlier Rochdale football clubs had generated scepticism and mistrust – why should they lend their support to another club that might last only a few years? Another factor was the popularity of football in Heywood, a town less than four miles from Spotland. Heywood's population was a third the size of Rochdale but it boasted several successful football clubs – Heywood Central, Heywood FC and Heywood United. Heywood Central, until its demise in 1891, had played on a pitch with a grandstand to accommodate supporters, while Heywood United sometimes had up to 3,000 fans at their matches, many of them from Rochdale.

Handbills were printed, promoting Rochdale's matches. Regulars from the Church Inn passed them out in the town centre and outside mills at clocking-off time. Cheeky teenagers made paper planes from them and said they were busy on Saturdays, watching City or United or one of the other Football League clubs close to Rochdale – Burnley, Oldham Athletic, Blackburn Rovers, Stockport County, Preston North End or Glossop. Already, despite strong national interest in football, Rochdale's relatively late start meant they faced stiff competition for fans. This would become a familiar story over the years.

* * *

Walter Joyce informed Tommy Docherty of his decision and was now free to focus on his role at Rochdale. Within days, he assembled his back-up team. He brought Harold Holburt over with him from Oldham Athletic, to manage the reserves, and Frank Campbell to oversee, with Tom Nichol, the B team (a mixture of youth players and trialists). Both new coaches were employed on a part-time basis. Angus McLean was nettled. He was constantly being asked to make savings and felt these were unnecessary appointments; the club was running too many teams at various levels.

Most managers tended to bring their own assistant with them; very few 'inherited' an existing member of staff for this key position. Joyce had realised, however, from the first firm handshake, that Peter Madden was his kind of man: straight-talking, trustworthy and with enough nous to respect the hierarchy within a football club. Madden had served under the previous manager, Dick Conner, but Joyce could tell immediately that there was no pining for his former boss and, in football parlance, there would be no shit-stirring designed to undermine Joyce's authority.

Oddly, there was no mention of a role for Angus McLean within this new regime. Over the summer, McLean had been assigned to 'hold the fort' by Fred Ratcliffe and had done so diligently, sifting through more than 20 applications for the manager's job. Denis Law, aged 33, newly released by Manchester United, was reported to have made a tentative inquiry, possibly with a view to becoming a player-manager at the club. Fred Ratcliffe had responded with customary asperity: 'I have not seen Law around Spotland and I've certainly not interviewed him.' Angus McLean, perhaps worried about his future, was keen to relate his industriousness. He told the press: 'Everyone thinks we go to sleep here in the summer but it can be a very busy time for the staff and those players who help to renovate the ground during the close season.'

New crush barriers had been installed and a VIP room fitted into the space between the social club and manager's office. The pitch had been re-seeded and the stands repainted. Secretly, McLean had considered himself a candidate for the position as manager. To this end, sanctioned by Ratcliffe, he'd pursued and signed Steve Arnold, a midfield player released by Liverpool. 'I read in one of the papers that Liverpool had given Steve a free transfer, so I immediately contacted Bill Shankly for permission to see the lad,' McLean told the press.

* * *

The first Rochdale teams were fluid and makeshift but fans soon began to identify particular players and offer encouragement or criticism. They became familiar with players' traits – Matt Kingsley, the ex-Newcastle United goalkeeper, could punch the ball almost to the halfway line; winger J.T. 'Cracker' Manning would charge *through* defences rather than dribbling; and songs were sung in praise of the Page brothers, Tom and Jack, from Kirkdale, Liverpool, one of whom (Jack) was 'well-fed' and tall, the other (Tom) slender and 5ft 6in. As other clubs fell by the wayside (Heywood United included, unable to raise a team after the First World War), a spirit and partisanship was forged, season on season, at Rochdale. Fans began to invest in the players and the club, financially and emotionally, and believe it represented *them*, all they stood for and their environs: grit, hard graft, loyalty, decency and fraternity.

After a single season in the Manchester League, Rochdale joined the Lancashire Combination. Their new opponents were the reserve teams of established clubs such as Manchester City, Everton and Blackburn Rovers, with the first teams from towns of smaller population densities – Eccles Borough, South Liverpool, Haslingden, etc. They spent five seasons in the similarly structured Central League, before, along with 21 other clubs, joining the Football League when the Third Division (North) was created for the 1921/22 season.

St Clement's became better known as 'Spotland' and a low wooden stand replaced the cricket pavilion, from where the cries of 'Up the Dale' rang out. On the day of Rochdale's first match in the Football League – a 6-3 home win against Accrington Stanley in front of 7,000 fans on Saturday, 27 August 1921 – the club was in a reasonably healthy trading position with £726 in the bank. Both Harvey Rigg and Herbert Hopkinson had remained closely allied to the club. Rigg became vice-president and, in 1919, had assembled a new board, of which he was a member. He was to remain a loyal supporter until his death in February 1942, aged 77, in Southport, to where he'd retired. Hopkinson, meanwhile, undertook several roles at the club, including managing the team from April 1932 to January 1934.

Each season, only one club was promoted from the Third Division (North) and, as there was no relegation, several clubs, including Rochdale, found themselves in stasis for 30 seasons, despite twice finishing runners-up, and bottom three times. The North/South division segregation was abandoned in 1958 and Rochdale were placed in the Third Division. That season (1958/59), they finished at the foot of the table, 13 points adrift of safety and were relegated to the Fourth Division.

During a nine-year spell in the lowest division, an appearance in the League Cup Final of 1962 (losing 4-0 on aggregate to Norwich City) was a rare highlight. Then, in 1968/69, Rochdale were promoted. The previous three seasons, they had finished 21st, 21st and 19th (out of 24 clubs), giving no indication of an imminent upturn in form. In fact, in the summer of 1968, a miserly 98 season tickets had been sold, such was the lack of faith in the squad and the club.

Several Rochdale supporters, those given to reflection, perhaps on the walk to the ground or over a quiet pint in the Spotland Reform Club, would later wonder whether, amid the promotion jubilation and champagne-popping in the dressing room, this was where it all went wrong: was the abject failure of 1973/74 forged in the eye of this success? How, in five years, did it go from joy of joy to the club falling to its knees?

* * *

Steve Arnold's career trajectory was typical of many players, although perhaps condensed into a shorter period of time. As an outstanding schoolboy footballer, he came close to representing England Under-15s at a time when the team regularly played before sold-out crowds at Wembley Stadium; he took part in a final trial match but wasn't selected for the squad. He signed for Crewe Alexandra and, at 6ft 2in and weighing more than 13 stone, was considered robust enough to make his first-team debut at 18. After only 15 appearances with Crewe, Liverpool's canny scouting team reported to Bill Shankly that Arnold was 'solid and tough-tackling' and might complement his team's more lightweight and graceful players. Liverpool paid a transfer fee of £12,000, the equivalent today of approximately £300,000.

He appeared regularly for Liverpool reserves but struggled to bridge the chasm to the first team. He made a solitary full appearance in April 1971 in a controversial 2-2 draw at Manchester City. He was one of several reserves picked for the first team so that regular players could rest and stay free from injury. Two days later, Liverpool were due to play Leeds United in the semi-final, second leg of the Inter-Cities Fairs Cup (a precursor of the UEFA Cup). The Football League fined Liverpool £7,500 for fielding the weakened team at Maine Road.

While at Liverpool, Arnold had loan spells at Southport and Torquay United, and had accepted, at least for the time being, that he'd have to drop down a division or two for regular first-team football. He'd known Rochdale were without a manager at the time but this didn't matter; he was flattered by their interest and had enough confidence in his ability to impress whoever was appointed.

On the day of signing the contract, he drove from his home in Ellesmere Port to Spotland in his new Morris 1100. He posed for the obligatory press photograph alongside McLean; pen in hand, paper on the desk. He was much changed from the teenager with short back and sides who had joined Liverpool. The hair was longer. He had thick sideburns. He was wearing a leather jacket. He was 22 but could pass for several years older, already battle-hardened and ready for another season, another fight. Interestingly, it was Fred Ratcliffe and not McLean who supplied a quote to the press about the club's new addition: 'I am more than pleased with this signing,' he said. 'He is a good young prospect. I'm sure he will add bite to the midfield.'

Within a few days of pre-season training, Walter Joyce could see what others had seen in Arnold. He had the resolve that came with being among professional footballers from a young age. In short, and this was said of most players from Liverpool, he could 'look after himself' on a football pitch. In any team, you needed a few lads who stood strong, made themselves available for the pass, could gee up others and didn't mind taking a knock or two along the way. He wasn't *his* signing but Joyce could see that Arnold, on physique and enthusiasm alone, was worthy of a place in the team.

* * *

The people of Rochdale already had a tradition of banding together for the common good. A group of 28 men, most of them weavers, had formed the Rochdale Society of Equitable Pioneers in 1844. They had noted the profits made by wholesalers and shopkeepers, while ordinary workers were often impoverished, missing meals and going hungry. Over a period of four months, they each saved £1 and used the combined total to buy butter, sugar, flour, oatmeal and candles. A few days before Christmas 1844, they rented the ground floor of a warehouse at 31 Toad Lane (a derivation of The Old Lane, T'Owd Lane) in Rochdale town centre and sold these items over a counter fashioned from a plank of wood and two beer barrels. They had bought in relative bulk – one or two sacks of flour, for example – which meant they had paid wholesale prices and were able to pass this saving on to customers. Within three months, they also began to sell tea and tobacco, both considered life's necessities at the time. By the end of the first year of trading, the Pioneers had 80 members and held £182 of capital.

A dividend (share of the profits) was paid to everyone who bought from the store, commensurate to their individual spend over a period of time. On 'divi-day' they could receive this amount as cash or donate it to a cause of their choosing. Regular contributions were made to two orphanages planned for Rochdale, at Buckley Hall, opened in 1888, and the Moorland Home, 1894 (motto: 'Fresh air, fresh food and good fun'), burrowed in the hills between Wardle and Whitworth.

The Rochdale Pioneers had been influenced by socialism and Chartism, and a handful of members were of a religious persuasion, but they each subscribed to a make-do, pragmatic approach; they had acquired their knowledge and acumen through life experience. They bore surnames still common in Rochdale today: Tweedale, Kershaw, Ashworth, Holt and Garside, for example. Between them, they devised a philosophy, a set of seven 'rules', which became known as the 'Rochdale Principles' and formed a mandate and manifesto for a worldwide movement of co-operation. By 1900, the movement had grown to 1,439 co-operatives covering most of the UK. By 1916, in Rochdale alone, there were 47 branches of Pioneers stores

* * *

The fixtures for the 1973/74 season were announced. Rochdale were to play Brighton and Hove Albion at home, followed by away matches at Walsall and Plymouth Argyle. As much as Joyce knew what he was expected to relay to the press – we've got to play everyone at some time, we'll take each game as it comes, etc. – he recognised that it was a difficult start.

Brighton had been relegated from the Second Division but paid decent wages and always fielded experienced, strong teams. They would bring a few hundred fans with them and it would be noisy support, too – a reunion with hope after the relegation. Fellows Park, home of Walsall, was an austere environment, a ramshackle hotchpotch of timber, concrete and corrugated iron, while the pitch was heavy going, even in early autumn. And Plymouth away? No one won at Plymouth. All that bloody way. Stuck on a coach for hours. Lads moaning that they were hungry or wanted a piss stop, ten minutes after the last. If Ratcliffe tipped up enough for an overnight stay (which was unlikely), Joyce knew he'd have a job occupying them during the day, reminding them that they weren't on holiday and had a game of football to play, to win. Alternatively, if they had to travel down and play on the same day, they would be knackered, lethargic legs fastened to the turf, while the home team danced round them, a chuckle in their boots. No one won at Plymouth.

* * *

The British cotton industry peaked in 1912 – five years after Rochdale AFC had formed – when the UK led the world in production with eight billion yards of cloth per year. The outbreak of the First World War meant cotton could no longer be exported to foreign outlets, and many countries, particularly Japan, set up their own factories. The huge market of India, which accounted for 60 per cent of Britain's exported cotton, was decimated when Mahatma Gandhi, leader of the Indian National Congress, called for a boycott of British goods in 1929 as part of the campaign to free India from colonial rule. Between the wars, 800 mills closed and 345,000 workers left the industry in the UK.

The Second World War provided a short reprieve when textile companies were awarded contracts to make uniforms, bedding and parachutes. By 1958, for the first time, Britain imported more cotton goods than it exported. A year later, the Cotton Industry Act was passed, which encouraged new working practices and offered grants to replace equipment. Round-the-clock shifts, undertaken elsewhere in the world, were introduced. Extra employees were needed and there was mass immigration in the 1950s and 1960s, principally from the Indian sub-continent. The efforts to save the industry were in vain. Lower overheads in other countries – paltry wages and wretched conditions reminiscent of those during the Industrial Revolution – meant Britain couldn't compete. By the early 1970s, mills were closing across Lancashire at a rate of one per week.

* * *

Walter Joyce looked at the fixture list repeatedly and imagined various outcomes to the first few matches; all managers did this at the start of a new season. The back-page headline in the *Rochdale Observer* – 'Tough Start for Dale' – had peeved him. He complained to Stan Townsend. 'I don't write the headlines, Walter. That's the job of the sub-editors,' explained Townsend. 'I hope the players don't see it and it sets them off thinking negatively,' said Joyce. Townsend nodded. He knew full well that most of the players *would* see it; the *Observer* was practically the sole outlet for news about the club.

Joyce, after two decades in football, knew the value of a good opening to the season. Talent was essential for a footballer, of course, but it had to be bolstered by confidence. A couple of early wins could instil a self-belief and togetherness that might last for a run of matches – half a season, possibly, or a whole season.

Winning was, as everyone said, a habit. A couple of defeats, though, and confidence waned. Forward passes became square or backwards. Players declined to shoot or run with the ball and often 'hid', finding spaces on the pitch where they knew the ball wouldn't stray. Goalkeepers became jittery, the ball slipping from their grasp. Before too long, team-mates fell out, blaming one another, bawling at one another. Losing was a habit, too.

* * *

The job market in Rochdale was booming in 1973 despite the wind-down of the textile industry. Between 1,000 and 2,000 of the town's workforce was out of work at any given time but, in real terms, this was close to full employment because the fluidity of the market meant these figures corresponded roughly to the number of unfilled vacancies. As much as it was a mill town, Rochdale was also home to scores of engineering works, often built from the same red brick as houses, blending in on the same streets. Spring-making in particular had been carried out for more than 200 years and employed almost 1,000 people. Indeed, Fred Ratcliffe had started as an engineer at Milkstone Spring Works for Robert Riley Ltd, a spring-making company established for more than a century. At the age of 25, his astuteness noted, Ratcliffe was invited on to the board at Riley's. Four years later he formed his own company, F.S. Ratcliffe. He covered the staff's first week's wages by borrowing money from his aunt and uncle, who owned a fish and chips shop.

Jobs had been created by new businesses moving into vacated mills. Some were used as warehouses, for carpets and wallpaper, curtains and bedding, while, at others, engineering firms assembled machines for export to countries carrying out textile manufacture. Many were given over to the 'rag trade', where machinists, overlockers, cutters and pressers set to work on everything from eiderdowns to shirts and blouses, for premium clients such as Marks and Spencer or Woolworths.

Castleton Moor Mill housed Rochdale's first superstore, opened in May 1969. Asda Queens – known as such because the first Asda store was based in the former Queen's Theatre in Castleford – had 38,000 square feet of shopping space on the ground floor. Elsewhere, fitters used plywood and plasterboard to convert mills into bespoke sections and create offices for start-up companies; these later become known as 'business units' or 'enterprise centres'.

Workers were much in demand. Leesona, the 'recognised industry leader for quality, precision winding solutions', had moved into Unity Mill in Heywood and announced in June 1973 that it planned to increase its workforce to 1,000. The US-owned company offered a 40-hour week, canteen, pension scheme and a bus service to and from the site. F. Friedland & Co., housed in Fredo Mills, Littleborough, used its existing staff, photographed smiling in overalls, to ensnare new additions. 'Come and join us – we're a happy lot of Sew-&-Sews' read its advert. In another, the word 'SEX' was printed in huge letters across a full page with, beneath it, in much smaller print: 'Suitably ... Experienced ... Xperts'. The company was on the lookout for machinists able to make glass-fibre curtains and roller blinds. They were promised £35 a week, while trainees started at £15.

* * *

Fred Ratcliffe, in one of his first conversations with Joyce, had expressed concern about falling attendances. He told the same story to all Rochdale's managers, hoping to inspire them: 'Back in the day, you'd see folk making their way up to Spotland in their droves – all along Mellor Street, coming down Spotland Road and Sandy Lane. All cheering and shouting,' he said. 'Thousands of them, there were.' During the three seasons after the Second World War, the average attendance at Spotland had exceeded 8,000. If a particular manager looked at him incredulously, Ratcliffe felt obliged to qualify the figures. 'I think people were glad to be alive and that Hitler hadn't blown them up. So, football meant more to them because it felt like life was getting back to normal,' he said.

During the 1969/70 season, the first after Rochdale's promotion to the Third Division, crowds had averaged more than 6,000, but had since fallen markedly. The average attendance for the season before Joyce's arrival was 2,920, more than a quarter down on the season before when the average was 4,295. These figures were bolstered by virtue of playing several local derbies – against Blackburn Rovers, Oldham Athletic and Bolton Wanderers, for instance – who each brought support that outnumbered the home fans. As an exemplar of the true number of Rochdale's staunch, rain-or-shine, win-or-lose support, the attendance for a league match played against Rotherham United on Saturday, 7 April 1973 was pertinent: 1,588. 'The only way to induce them back to Spotland is to produce a winning side and that's what I intend to do,' said Joyce. He looked at the fixture list again: tough start for Dale.

* * *

A reasonable number of businesses were still able to eke a profit from cotton manufacture. A walk through Rochdale in 1973 would be interspersed with occasional rhythmic blasts of machine noise and the sweet, starchy smell of cotton emanating from an air duct set in a factory wall. Although a moribund industry, operatives were still required while there were at least *some* orders on the books. This meant the *Rochdale Observer* carried similar adverts for jobs as it had since its very first edition, in 1856, for, among others, beamers, loom overlockers, core winders, tenters, rocket winders, condenser ring spinners, draw frame tenters, beam crealers and ring doffers. Across town, a slaughterman and offal boy were needed at Wardlefold Abattoir, Wardle. A 'strong, intelligent girl to help in the cutting room' was required at Balderstone Mill. Burneys bakery in Dodgson Street was seeking a dough mixer, and the Highland Laddie pub wanted 'attractive lunchtime barmaids'.

The most unusual job on offer in Rochdale in 1973 was to become the town's Black Pea King. Arthur White, the previous incumbent, was retiring after 20 years of doing the rounds on his motor tricycle. He had arthritis and, at 54, felt it time to sell the family business. His wife, Irene, had cooked the peas at their home in Queen Victoria Street, Balderstone; the recipe had been in his family for generations. Arthur said children who could once hardly peep over the edge of his barrow would now wait for him every week and bring out their own children for a helping of black peas. He visited different parts of the town on particular days and his arrival was eagerly anticipated, with people peeking through their curtains, dishes at hand, waiting to be filled up. 'I never wanted to be Onassis [Aristotle Onassis, one of the world's richest men at the time]. I just wanted to make a living. And I've not done too badly. It's brought up two children, anyway,' he said. Trevor Jones, one of White's customers, of Derby Street, Deeplish, took over the business. He was taught the cry of 'Black peas – they're lovely' and took possession of the vintage motor tricycle and handbell.

* * *

Walter Joyce was loyal to the modus operandi of most football managers – he returned to his former club for players. Supporters imagine that talent is mined from a rich breadth of sources but this is a misnomer. In practice, managers mostly sign players they already know or who are known to someone within their trusted circle. Gary Cooper – *not* the American film star who often played cowboys (as the backroom staff joked when his name was mentioned) – was Joyce's first signing.

Cooper had recently turned 18 and had already experienced a fitful career. He'd been an outstanding schoolboy striker, selected to play for his county (Lancashire) and England but, after serving an apprenticeship at Burnden Park, was released by Bolton Wanderers. He'd played a handful of matches for his hometown club, Horwich RMI (now Leigh Genesis), in the Cheshire League, before Joyce had invited him for a three-month trial at Oldham Athletic. He hadn't been offered a contract by Oldham, but had now signed a two-year deal at Rochdale.

* * *

Bosses were easy to spot in blue-collar Rochdale. When almost everyone else was in overalls or a uniform of some kind, they wore suits and ties (they were almost always men). These directors carried themselves differently, shoulders back, and spoke with softer, rounder vowels and didn't drop the t's in butter or better. On rare sunny days, their cars glistened parked up outside mills and factories; sometimes young members of staff were asked to wash them and were flipped a few coins as a thank you.

Everyone knew that they earned more than those on the factory or shop floor; it was how the world worked. They were better educated and had usually been to university. Most were from out of town but those from Rochdale were from the landed or professional classes that had settled mainly on the new-build estates to the west of the town, in Bamford and Norden. They had gone to William Skurr private school or Bury Grammar, a selective school where fees were paid by either the local authority or parents. In contrast, the large majority of Rochdale people had received a humdrum comprehensive education. There had been little encouragement to reach university and professional status but, instead, an emphasis on physical or engineering work for boys and secretarial or retail for girls. Most understood that profit was made from their labour and this was a fundamental anatomy of capitalism. If asked (and they never were), they might have guessed that companies made a pro-rata profit equivalent of, say, two or three times the amount they received as a wage. They soon learned that they had significantly underestimated this differential.

A startling snapshot of the local economy was provided by *RAP* (Rochdale's Alternative Paper) in its round-up of the finances of companies operating in the town. TBA (Turner Brothers Asbestos but also known at different times as Turner and Newall or Turner's) was the largest employer and made £16.4m profit in 1972 – an extraordinary sum considering the danger of asbestos had been widely known for many years. That year, a dividend of £318,000 was shared between 12 directors, while chairman, Ralph Melton Bateman, also drew a salary of £800 per week; the average weekly wage for a TBA worker was £30. Bateman, later a president of the CBI (Confederation of British Industry), was granted a knighthood in 1975.

Meanwhile, about 800 people were employed at Thomas Robinson and Son Ltd of Railway Works, Rochdale, earning an average wage of £24 per week. The company's seven directors were paid between £76 and £290 per week. Alderglen Ltd, employing 600 people, declared a profit of £340,000. It paid staff £15.50 per week, while its five directors earned £140 per week and shared the 1972 annual dividend of £36,351.

Approximately 180 people worked at Vale Mill in John Street, on an average weekly wage of £16.23. The managing director, Miro Fuchs, received £172 a week. The John Bright Group, with seven mills in Rochdale, reported profits up by a third in 1973, to £880,000. Directors' annual salaries were £30,000. The Holroyd Group, an engineering company in Milnrow, Rochdale, made £591,976 profit, while 35 of its staff had been put on a four-day week to 'save money'. Fothergill & Harvey made £636,000 profit in 1973 – an increase of 45 per cent on the previous year. Its workforce, of approximately 1,000 staff, each received £30 per week. Directors drew £250 per week.

* * *

Walter Joyce had been impressed by Gary Cooper's exuberance, his willingness to 'put himself about'. He was lanky and, similar to most tall, thin players, it sometimes made him appear clumsy, as if he had to beat his own body before the opponent. Joyce was sure he could settle him down and teach him to have more poise on the ball. The biggest challenge with lads such as Cooper was making them believe they *belonged* on the pitch, especially after they had suffered a few knock-backs. There was a way of receiving the ball, settling it at your feet and moving on with it, which fellow professionals recognised instantly as 'someone who could play'.

One or two players and coaches at Oldham had been less convinced about Cooper. 'He was like a startled foal,' said one. 'You could see a mile off that, within a few minutes of playing in a proper match, a big, hard centre-half was going to smash him. He was a lick of paint, nothing to him.'

The day after Cooper joined Rochdale, another signing was announced. Keith Hanvey was his antithesis – three years older, three stones heavier and already fully initiated into the thorny and gnarled world of professional football. He'd even had a set-to with one of the toughest and most-feared figures in the game, Harry Gregg.

* * *

RAP had been set up by two men who had moved to the town during the 1960s. David Bartlett and John Walker had met at Rochdale Technical College, where they were lecturing in sociology and British government and politics, respectively. *RAP*'s manifesto was laid out on the front page of the first issue, published in November 1971: 'Questions asked, bubbles pricked, information open, workers heard, issues debated, rights explained, bosses challenged, the unspoken said and life explored'.

'We were interested in the working class and the disparity of income and set about trying to do something about it,' said Bartlett. 'We found our jobs weren't sufficiently challenging and had become routine so we decided to give *RAP* a shot.'

Similar radical magazines had been set up throughout Britain in the late 1960s and early 1970s, from the *The Snail* in Devon, *China-Cat Sunflower* (named after a song by Grateful Dead) in Birmingham, to *Spike* in Glasgow. They were influenced by national counter-culture titles such as *International Times*, *Oz* and *Frendz*, while *Private Eye*, founded in 1961, had set the template for lampooning public figures alongside in-depth investigative journalism. Closer to home, Bartlett and Walker had noted the popularity of *Mole Express*, which was first published in Manchester in May 1970 and had among its founders Mike Don, a self-defining, 'acid-head leftie'.

David Bartlett had arrived in Rochdale in 1962 as a Baptist minister with responsibility for four churches. 'I was straight out of a theology course when I took up the ministry. The first thing I remember of Rochdale was all the factory chimneys. I lasted five years as a minister. I'm not sure if I lost the faith or the faith lost me,' he said. He'd been raised in Copnor, a downmarket district of Portsmouth where his parents ran a grocery shop. 'It was there that I first saw poverty and met many struggling people and this became a driving force that led me into the ministry,' he said.

He left the church in 1967 to teach A level sociology at the college; the switch didn't feel especially unusual. 'Education in the late 1960s had a missionary element to it,' he said. Rochdale, with such disparity of income and wealth among its citizens, provided ample quarry for *RAP*. 'Our opponents were bosses, politicians, landlords, speculators, exploiters and all others who, by background or choice, had joined the respectable middle class,' said Bartlett.

Within a few issues, it had already identified a little man with a considerable wealth who lived in a palatial house in the posh part of town. He presided over both an industrial empire and the town's main sporting institution, Rochdale AFC. The word went out: get Fred.

3

The Baiting and Biting
of Fred Ratcliffe

THE LIST of all Rochdale's players, their home addresses and telephone numbers, were logged in a frayed red book that Beryl Earnshaw kept in the top drawer of her desk. Walter Joyce prided himself on being meticulous, doing a professional job. He asked for the book and phoned up every player. If they weren't in, he left a message with whoever answered, asking that the player contact him at the club 'as soon as convenient'. In each conversation, he introduced himself, hoped that the player had enjoyed a good summer and relayed the arrangements for pre-season training. He finished by asking whether there was anything they wanted to know or tell him. One or two gave updates on injuries outstanding from the previous season – still a bit sore, could do with some physio, etc. – but they each thanked him for the call and concurred that they, too, were looking forward to the new season.

Unlike many managers, Joyce eschewed the 'killing' opening sessions of pre-season, where players were run and run. He preferred to use the first few days for players to acclimatise to one another, the coaching staff and the surroundings. Rochdale trained at Sparth Bottoms, in the valley of the River Roch, close to the town centre where terraced houses merged with scrapyards and industrial units. Guard dogs barked on the other side of metal fences and the air was scented with the sweet-sharp tang of burning metal from foundries. Rochdale Gas Works was nearby, with a huge gasometer jammed tight to the streets, looking like an abandoned UFO. Ratcliffe Springs (company motto: 'They never lose their temper'), owned by Fred Ratcliffe, of course, was based at Crawford Spring Works in Norman Street. The company's site included a large swathe of grassland, which was given over to the football club for training. The early sessions were mainly limbering up, or 'getting the blood flowing', as Joyce called it; the hard work would begin soon enough.

At the end of one session, Peter Madden asked Joyce whether he could 'have a word'. 'What is it, Pete?' asked Joyce. 'Dick's been on the phone,' he answered. 'I thought he might call you,' said Joyce. Dick Conner, sacked a few weeks earlier by Rochdale, had been appointed manager at Darlington and wanted Madden as his assistant. 'I'm going, Walter,' said Madden. They shook hands.

Although Madden hadn't spoken to Joyce about it, others at the club had made him aware that he was disgruntled about the way Conner had been treated. 'They pissed him about something rotten,' was how it was described by a senior player. Conner had been summoned to the boardroom immediately after the home defeat to Rotherham United in April of the previous season, the match that had drawn the extremely low crowd of 1,588; directors often acted impulsively after such an occurrence. At that point, the team had won only once in ten matches. Conner was asked to resign but, the next day, the directors met at lunchtime and he was reappointed with a brief, delivered by Ratcliffe, to 'guide the team away from relegation'.

The team lost just once in the last six matches of the season, finishing four points above a relegation spot. Conner presumed his job was safe but began to hear rumours to the contrary. These were dismissed by Ratcliffe as 'press talk', even though two former Rochdale players had been linked with the role – Colin Whitaker, who had overseen Buxton becoming champions of the Cheshire County League, and Frank Lord, who was caretaker-manager of Preston North End until talks were completed to bring Bobby Charlton to Deepdale as player-manager. 'Dick Conner Stays – Mr Ratcliffe' was the headline in the *Rochdale Observer* of Saturday, 21 April. By Wednesday, 16 May, this had changed to: '1, 2 and Out Goes Dick Conner'.

Unknown to most at the club, Conner's contract had lapsed in March 1973. In football, it was unusual for staff to operate without a contract; most either 'rolled' on the same terms for a pre-agreed time period or were renegotiated immediately on expiring. Without a contract, Conner had yielded all power to the board. They could ask him to leave or stay or set a target (such as avoiding relegation) and, even if it were met, still release him without any financial obligation, as they duly did.

As a close friend of Conner, Madden had considered this an unfair and crafty way to treat someone who had given exemplary service to the club and had played a major role, as assistant manager and coach, in securing Rochdale's solitary promotion four years earlier. Conner had also moved to the town, placing his two young children at local schools. Madden viewed a 'contract' as a man coming in to work day after day, giving his all, and this should afford him absolute rights, irrespective of whether he'd scribbled his name on a piece of paper or not. 'Nothing personal,' Madden told Joyce. 'I know, Pete, I know.'

* * *

Fred Ratcliffe and *RAP* were near neighbours. A short walk down Edenfield Road, across Spotland Bridge and up the incline at Spotland Road, mapped out the distance from Ratcliffe's abode to 230 Spotland Road, the home of David Bartlett and *RAP*. Among a handful of others, Ratcliffe was everything *RAP* found objectionable: powerful, wealthy, avaricious, condescending, a Tory and a mason. He was a member of two masonic lodges, in Manchester and Rochdale, and, on two occasions, a worshipful master (effectively the chairman who presided over rituals and ceremonies). 'It would seem rude not to take a good look at Fred,' Bartlett had joshed to friends.

Fred Simpson Ratcliffe was born in January 1914 to a working-class family living in a two-bedroom terraced house in Clapgate Road, Norden, near the Brown Cow pub. He had a sister, Hilda, five years older. His mother, Mary, died when he was 14 and his father, Herbert, when he was 19; their early deaths were thought to have contributed to his independent nature. He registered F.S. Ratcliffe (Rochdale) Ltd in August 1942. The timing was perfect. Huge quantities of springs were needed in the production of aircraft engines for the war effort and his company quickly grew to more than 300 staff. He was a member of Hopwood Golf Club and the Central and Balderstone Conservative clubs; he'd stood unsuccessfully as a candidate for the Conservative party in the council elections of May 1949. He joined the board of Rochdale AFC, whom he'd supported from a boy, in September 1946, aged 32. He became, at 39, one of the youngest chairmen in the Football League.

Ratcliffe and his wife, Florence (nee Byron, and thought to descend from Lord Byron, whose family resided in Rochdale during the 1600s), lived with their children, Judith and John Frederick Stuart (known as Stuart), at Standrings in Bagslate Moor Road, Norden. The house, dating back to 1791, was a Grade II listed building with *six* bedrooms, valued at £30,000 in 1973. Many years before foreign holidays became within reach of most families, the Ratcliffes spent a few weeks each summer in Spain, usually Majorca, Torremolinos, Barcelona or Lloret de Mar.

Stuart Ratcliffe had a love of animals and his father financed a menagerie at the house, which included bush babies, monkeys, chipmunks, reptiles and snakes. Once, they were about to return from holiday in Spain, when Stuart saw a couple in a bar with a spider monkey. He was told it had been bought from a pet shop in Madrid. The flight back to England included a changeover in Madrid, during which time the Ratcliffes visited the pet shop and later had a monkey flown to England in a box placed on a seat in the cabin. 'Stuart had that monkey for years, long after all the other animals had died,' said Judith. 'They would have a cup of tea together when Stuart came home from school.'

Ratcliffe carried his wealth ostentatiously, driving through town in his Rolls-Royce with the registration number, FSR 880. Wiseacres at the spring works joked that he was so small and the car so big that he could barely see over the dashboard. His office at the factory was described as being 'like a posh living-room'.

RAP labelled its article on Ratcliffe as a 'personality profile' but its meticulousness and irreverence was a statement of intent, a 'we're-coming-to-get-you' warning to the elite and gentrified of Rochdale. Bartlett and his cohort, John Walker, weren't so much tapping on the shoulders of the privileged but poking them in the chest – take that. *RAP* presented a potted biography of Ratcliffe but was keen to colour in the outline, painting him for all to see. He was vulgar. The Rolls-Royce. The number plate. He kept rare cigarettes in a gold case. His watch cost £600. He wore mohair suits. He employed a chauffeur and handyman. He was mean and a traitor to his class – the flotation of his company in February 1956 had made him the astronomical sum of £500,000, while he drew £20,000 per year from directorships and dividends. He paid his staff £14 per week, the minimum permitted wage. Ratcliffe had warned that he'd 'shut the place' if staff insisted on joining a union. 'Fred has them all frightened to death,' said an unnamed union official. 'He could be very pointed if he wanted to be. He believed he should be respected. He spoke his mind. He was a very shrewd guy and didn't stand any nonsense,' said Stan Townsend.

On one occasion, Townsend sent a young reporter, David Rigby, to meet Ratcliffe at Spotland. 'He came back to the office looking very red-faced. I asked him what was wrong and he told me Fred had told him to leave. I rang Fred and asked him what had happened and Fred said, "He came walking in here and called me Fred, not Mr Ratcliffe." I told David to apologise next time he saw him. As much as Fred could be an awkward so-and-so, he could also be very generous at times, too.'

RAP claimed Ratcliffe was known as a 'Little Führer' by some of his workers. 'Fred remains living proof of what money and power do to a man,' the article closed. There was more to come.

* * *

The capacity to take a whack, smash, hiding, crunch – there were various euphemisms – was an integral feature of football in the 1970s. Pitches were heavy, tackles were hard and referees lenient. Fans winced at thunderous one-on-one, instep-to-instep tackles but these held little fear for professional footballers. The worst, the most painful, the career-enders, were the ones you didn't see coming, for which you hadn't 'set' yourself – a quick shift of weight or a leaning in of shoulder and knee to disperse the impact. The killing collisions were those you turned into inadvertently while your opponent had set his 13 stones rigid or where your legs caught around his legs but the knee buckled 'the wrong way' in that split second of entanglement. 'It looked so innocuous,' agreed fans on the way home.

By now, the footballer is in the ambulance. Soil and grass is being wiped from his legs. He is shivering but sweat pours from his forehead. He looks down at his knee, three times its normal size and flushed purple. 'Am I going to be alright?' he asks. 'Will I play again?' 'Sure you will, lad. Sure you will.'

Dennis Butler, although only 29, had spent enough time in ambulances and hospital beds. He'd been with Rochdale for five years. He played as a winger, a position that afforded more room to run, and into areas with usually more grass, unlike the middle of the pitch where, once the autumn rain arrived, it was often a heavy hack through sticky mud.

Butler had twice been seriously injured. He suffered a cartilage injury at the age of 20 while playing for Bolton Wanderers; it was done deliberately and kept him out of football for almost a year. He says he can't remember the name of his opponent but that it happened in a match against Everton. 'He went over the top and did me,' he said. 'I was never the same player afterwards. I couldn't properly put my weight on it and between games it was like having toothache in my knee. They operated on it but surgery wasn't like it is today. These days, they could probably have sorted it out so I was playing again in a few weeks. I was left with pain in my knee on and off for the rest of my life.'

His latest injury was a disc lesion – damage to the area around a disc in his spine. Backs, as various physios had told him, were 'funny things'. But no one was laughing. They were slow to heal. The soreness and pain recurred seemingly at random, sometimes weeks or months apart. There were secondary or tertiary symptoms – a 'buzzing' pain from thigh to ankle, spasms of nerve-jolts that felt as if you'd been peppered by a pellet gun or, most commonly, 'heaviness' around the middle of the body that made jogging a chore, and sprinting impossible. They didn't say it within earshot of the player but most physios agreed that once your back had 'gone', you were usually done for, finished.

'Can I help with the training?' asked Butler. Walter Joyce was happy to share the load and had expected the knock on his door from Butler once he'd learned of Madden's departure. Butler had played in the top flight with Bolton Wanderers and been an integral part of Rochdale's promotion of 1968/69; he appeared in every league match and scored 16 goals. Although Joyce wanted to build anew, he understood that links with the promotion squad were important (aside from Butler, the sole remaining player was Graham Smith); it showed that a marriage between Rochdale AFC and success was achievable.

Butler, originally from Atherton, had moved to Rochdale, living in Passmonds, and had forged strong links with the town. He was a talented cricketer and, earlier that summer, had turned out for Rochdale's 2nd XI. He notched an impressive 91 not out against Castleton Moor before recording a duck against Royton a few weeks later. In football terms, he'd scored goals at Highbury and had toughed out Tuesday night 1-1 draws at Southend United. He'd also completed an FA coaching course held at its centre at Lilleshall Hall, Shropshire. Joyce made him first-team coach. 'He is my sort of bloke,' Joyce told the press. 'He is completely dedicated and I am sure we will work extremely well together.'

* * *

'They're like a dog with a bone.' David Bartlett and John Walker were delighted when they heard this, or similar, in pubs, workplaces or at the college where they worked. They weren't trained journalists but prided themselves on having good 'news sense' and the determination to chase down a story. Readers and potential contributors were invited to meet them every Thursday in the Golden Ball pub on Spotland Road. Within a few weeks, they had about 40 contacts (better known as 'moles' or 'spies' by their employers) at local companies, willing to pass on information about their workplaces and bosses, whether substantial or tittle-tattle.

RAP felt it had an incentive to undertake thorough, hands-on journalism because it viewed the *Rochdale Observer* as a mouthpiece of the 'establishment', running to a listless formula. In an early edition of *RAP*, for example, all 53 places of worship in Rochdale were visited for an in-depth piece on faith (its main finding was that church attendance had fallen by 50 per cent over 60 years); such a feature was beyond the ingenuity and imagination of the *Rochdale Observer*.

RAP steadfastly adopted the workers' perspective, examining – as they saw it – the minutia of exploitation. To this end, Walker or Bartlett travelled each month to Companies House in London and examined the public records of local firms. They also bought single shares in most of them, which meant they received annual reports and invitations to meetings. 'I once had the distinction of being outvoted at one company by three million to one,' said Bartlett. 'We used to come back on the train and start pasting up the magazine. I can still smell the cow gum after all these years.'

In contrast, the 'industrial notes' in the *Rochdale Observer*, compiled by Harold Knott, reported on companies securing contracts or appointing new managing directors, revealing nothing of the working conditions or differentials of pay. Workers appeared on these pages only if they were being presented with a gold watch after decades of service or had been chosen as employee or apprentice of the year.

Fred Ratcliffe remained a fascination for *RAP* and the most extensive incursion into his life came in a cover story with the terse headline: '*RAP* Spies on Ratcliffe'. Over the course of a week, David Bartlett trailed him to various pubs in Norden and Bamford. Ratcliffe's alcohol intake was listed assiduously, usually halves of bitter and whisky chasers. The time he spent at the spring works was also clocked: 15 hours. While *RAP* felt Ratcliffe was worthy of condemnation and ridicule, it conceded, with grudging admiration, that he had a genuine love of Rochdale AFC and had remained loyal to the club for many years.

* * *

Everyone asked Walter Joyce about training and the response was always the same: it's going well. Training was easy. Given a few weeks, it was possible to get any group of fit young men able to do star jumps, press-ups, squats and sprints against the clock. Throw them a ball and they would probably be able to stroke it around with reasonable competency too, and maybe take a few strong shots at goal. They might even score a goal or two. Joyce knew that training, aside from getting everyone fit and familiar with one another, was no real indicator of talent, heart, guile, bravery or discipline. This only became apparent when an opponent was put before them, someone similarly young, fit and capable. Then it became a battle: you vs him, your team vs their team. Who had the most ability, the most desire? Who stuck at it, covered for their mates, encouraged their mates, put their foot and head in?

Joyce was playing catch-up after his delayed installation as manager and then the backroom appointments (Dennis Butler, Harold Holburt, Frank Campbell) and departures (Peter Madden). 'Hit the phone, Beryl, and see if you can sort us out with some friendlies,' he told his secretary. 'Who shall I ask?' 'Well, we're not going to get City or United at this late stage, are we? Anyone will do – the nearest non-league teams.'

Non-league teams relished playing against clubs from the Football League. Most of their players had, at some point, been affiliated to professional clubs and were driven to prove they had been mistakenly overlooked, while those that hadn't saw it as an opportunity to maybe earn themselves a trial or a few 'try-out' matches in the reserves of a professional club. Beryl did well and typed up a list for Joyce. 'Seven games in 16 days – exactly what we need,' said Joyce.

Rochdale managed to win only once (Stalybridge Celtic, 3-1) in those seven matches, all played away from home: Witton Albion (lost 2-0); Bangor City (drew 1-1); Burscough (drew 0-0); Droylsden (drew 1-1); Mossley (lost 1-0); and Witton Albion again (drew 1-1). Joyce told the press that 'he didn't want to make excuses' but did so anyway. His players were extremely young, he said; the average age of the team against Witton in the first match had been 18. Their opponents had fielded established sides. A 'nasty wind' at Burscough had made it almost impossible to play good football.

When it came to amateurs vs professionals, there was a typical match pattern. Amateurs showed the greater initial passion, kicking everything in sight, running themselves to a standstill, while professionals gradually drew the heat from the game, pass-pass-pass, followed by the odd touch of composure at crucial times, leading to a win by, usually, a three or four-goal margin. Rochdale had done none of this. In fact, anyone wandering into these non-league grounds, jacket over a forearm in the summer sunshine, would have had trouble discerning the level from which both teams were drawn.

Among his coaching staff, Joyce issued the habitual platitudes about pre-season friendlies. Results didn't matter. They were glorified training sessions with the added impetus of a higher tempo and greater physicality. They were opportunities to look at different team shapes and tactics, and to try out new players, or old players in new positions. Secretly, Joyce was concerned. One win in seven matches against supposedly inferior opposition was worrying.

* * *

RAP had expected an outcry – eggs hurled at Ratcliffe's Rolls-Royce, boos as he made his way across the car park to his hi-tech, office-cum-lair. Over a series of articles, in broad terms, it had revealed Fred Ratcliffe to be a moneyed, indulgent, small-town playboy, carousing in the town's more salubrious establishments (and further afield). He enjoyed this lifestyle while his workers were as good as welded to their lathes, underpaid and overworked. Surely this would ignite the revolution and get them off the shop floor and on to the streets.

Instead of anger, or at least disaffection, the pieces inadvertently elicited sympathy for Ratcliffe. The perception in many quarters was that these out-of-towners had acted as sneaks and bullies. Had these ten-bob gumshoes with an axe to grind nothing better to do than cower in pub car parks with their binoculars? Sure, he was a bit mean, but Fred had done a lot for the town, providing all those jobs. So what if he only worked 15 hours a week? Anyone else similarly close to retirement age might have relocated to Spain or the South of France. 'I feel sorry for the lad,' they said. 'Fancy following an old man around like that, trying to make a fool of him.' And, by the by, when did those posh boys from *RAP* ever put on a pair of overalls and get their hands dirty?

If *RAP* had overestimated the thirst for revolution in Rochdale, it had also underestimated the popularity of Fred Ratcliffe. They hadn't accounted for his quiet charisma, quick wit and flinty charm. 'I honestly can't remember anyone ever saying anything bad about Fred,' said Fred Eyre, ex-footballer and author of *Kicked into Touch*. 'He was at all the games and made sure everyone got a pie. You can't say that about most chairmen. He had an infectiousness and dynamism about him.'

Ratcliffe's financial support of Rochdale AFC and his wider affiliations in football had given him a broad constituency. He sat on various football committees, including the Lancashire Football Association. He did this to further Rochdale's cause, not for his own aggrandisement. He was the round-faced chap in the camel coat with pale blue eyes and a gap-toothed smile, far left on the press photo at the golf day at Everton, the sportsman's dinner at Manchester United or at a boxing night held by the Anglo-American Sporting Club in the Hotel Piccadilly, Manchester.

To supporters, the blue and white scarf he wrapped around his neck on matchdays made him 'one of them'. He shared the same hope and joy and pain and, when you did that, it didn't matter how wealthy you were, how you treated your staff or where you spent your holidays. At one time, he was asked to become a director of Manchester City but told them he had only one love: Rochdale. 'I was brought up on Rochdale AFC from the cot,' said Judith Hilton, his daughter. 'I don't remember a time when it wasn't part of our family's life. It was my dad's first love and something he talked about every day. When I told him I was getting married, he said it would have to be a morning wedding so he could get up to Spotland afterwards. I dread to think how much money he ploughed into it, though. If he had to pay the players' wages, so be it.'

* * *

Walter Joyce, Frank Campbell and Harold Holburt left the Monday morning training session to Dennis Butler; they had matters to discuss. They met in Joyce's office. 'They looked bewildered,' said Campbell. He was referring to how the players had seemed in each of the friendly matches. 'It was all harum-scarum,' he continued. 'As if the ball was a hot potato and all they wanted to do was get rid of it, get rid of it.'

Campbell often overstated, repeating the same sentence two or three times. He'd played for Cheadle Rovers in the Manchester League in the 1950s and was the optimistic, knockabout figure that managers liked to have in and around the dressing room and training pitch. He had a mop of straw-coloured hair and some of the players had commented that he 'looked like a bloody scarecrow'. He had a sense of fun and went along with the joke. 'We might do better in the next couple of matches. The lads will get a bit longer on the ball, more time to find their passes, find their passes,' said Campbell.

The last of the pre-season friendlies were against Leeds United and Bury, both at Spotland. The manager and coaches reached an agreement. 'Let's tell them to put all those other games completely out of their head, to imagine them as full-on training sessions and nothing more. And start the season proper against Leeds and Bury,' said Joyce.

The previous season, Leeds United had finished third in the First Division and were runners-up in the FA Cup and European Cup Winners' Cup. Don Revie had assembled a squad – Billy Bremner, Peter Lorimer, Eddie Gray, Joe Jordan et al. – that would become league champions in the forthcoming 1973/74 season. They had good support in Rochdale, which was reflected in the attendance of more than 3,000. Autograph books were at the ready but most fans were unaware that the Leeds team would comprise 'reserves and apprentice professionals' – the likes of Peter Tymczyszyn, Jimmy Mann and Derek Loadwick.

Rochdale won 4-2 and 'annihilated' Leeds, according to Stan Townsend. 'The 'Dale Style Will Bring Back the Fans' was the headline on his match report. The upbeat mood continued three days later when Rochdale beat Bury 1-0 in 'oriental' conditions (presumably extremely hot). Townsend wrote of the 'Spotland sparkle' and suggested it was 'another Dale hint of things to come'. Up in the stands, Fred Ratcliffe was enjoying these eulogies; it sold a few more season tickets. Another version of the pre-season campaign, however, might have been much less favourable – one win in seven matches against teams made up of part-timers; victory against Leeds United's youth team, and a lucky win courtesy of a disputed penalty against Bury, who had fielded a stand-in goalkeeper.

* * *

The baiting and biting of Fred Ratcliffe continued from *RAP*. He was labelled a 'mean old sod' for granting female workers a mere 95p per week wage rise at the company's Newhey factory; it still left them £2 per week below the union rate, had unions been recognised. Similar slurs were discharged at MPs, council officials, councillors, bosses, magistrates, head teachers, police officers and professionals.

RAP was on sale at most newsagents in Rochdale. The initial print run had been 1,500 but soon increased to

8,000, with each copy said to be read by up to four people – remarkable saturation for a new, self-funded, alternative magazine. 'They'll get fed up in a few months and pack it in,' was said often during the first few months of its existence. The naysayers were wrong. The magazine lasted 12 years, running to 112 issues; a remarkable feat of endurance for a team of volunteers, many with full-time jobs. In fact, Bartlett and Walker often used their wages to support *RAP* because, two years after being launched, it was running at a debt of over £600.

The magazine appeared to have a complete disregard for libel or privacy laws. Pubs, often named and pictured, were alleged to serve watered-down beer. One company, to save money, was said to have blocked off its fire escapes. Council officials 'weren't doing their jobs properly'. An employer (named) was reported to have been drunk while driving his car. Councillors were accused of being 'on the make' or 'on the fiddle'. They were routinely lampooned – Alan Taylor, the Liberal councillor for Central and Falinge, was made 'RAPmate of the Year', his head superimposed on to a reclining figure of a man wearing only a pair of underpants.

The privileged class was taunted ruthlessly and, if others wanted to join in, phone numbers and home addresses were routinely printed; these were in the public domain but difficult to source in 1973. When plots of land were sold at Norford Way, Bamford ('Rochdale's Rodeo Drive'), for homesteads set to cost between £20,000 and £50,000 each – exorbitant prices at the time – *RAP* listed each of the purchasers. Estate agents had their houses photographed so everyone could see the splendour in which they lived while 21 homeless families, including nearly 100 children, were billeted in emergency accommodation in the town. 'We were threatened a lot, usually people shouting down the phone at us rather than physically set upon,' said David Bartlett. One of these callers said he was going to throw acid in the faces of *RAP*'s editors, while another screamed 'you bastards' and slammed down the phone.

The lack of formal, legal response was puzzling considering accusations were made about the most powerful and well-connected people in Rochdale. Many bought *RAP* because they were shocked by the content and intrigued by its insolence: what are they going to say next? In the Spread Eagle, Dicken Green and every other pub in town, they were asking: 'Why is no one suing them? How are they getting away with it?' Many decided *RAP* was getting away with it because it was being allowed to get away with it. 'They're turning a blind eye on purpose, pretending it doesn't exist.'

'They' were Rochdale's aristocracy – the bigwigs and power-brokers who were ridiculed and pilloried in each issue. The freemasons (all 12 of the town's lodges, each comprising up to 40 men) had met with the Round Tablers, Rotarians and other well-to-dos at the Masonic Hall in Richard Street, close to Rochdale railway station. They had agreed on a policy: they weren't going to lend credence to *RAP*'s allegations by issuing a response. After all, *RAP* was beneath them, a grubby purveyor of gossip and the mouthpiece of malevolent Marxists. This communion of the accused may have been a folk tale. Some versions had them meeting at the grand Broadfield Park Hotel. Others, at an out-of-town venue 'somewhere near Blackburn'. Whether this narrative was apocryphal or not, the silence was curious and suggested some level of collusion.

One of many to adopt this standpoint was the town's MP, Cyril Smith. He was known as Big Cyril and stood at 6ft 2in, weighing nearly 30 stones. He'd won the Rochdale parliamentary by-election in October 1972 for the Liberal party and cast himself as a 'man of the people'. At first, *RAP* perceived him as a crude egotist, a small-town operator with ambitions above his ability, rather than a demagogue-in-waiting. Tony Smart, a lecturer at Rochdale College of Art, sent him up in his cartoon strip, Fatman, furthering the notion that Smith was principally a parochial publicity seeker. Over the years, *RAP* would redraw Smith, revealing a far darker and sinister profile.

* * *

The opening match of the season, against Brighton, was only days away. Walter Joyce was in his office, scribbling down the possible team and formation. Fred O'Donoghue, chief (and only paid) scout, knocked at the door. They exchanged greetings and O'Donoghue sat on the orange plastic chair in front of Joyce. He saw the frown lines on Joyce's forehead, the pursed lips. 'Everything okay, Walter?' he asked. Joyce responded, 'Can I ask your opinion on something, Fred?'

Joyce had taken quickly to O'Donoghue. He was without the cynicism and sly eye of most football men and Joyce viewed him almost as a 'civvy' – someone from outside the game, which he was in many respects. While working in the drawing office of the Engineering Department (traffic section) at Blackburn Council, O'Donoghue had volunteered his scouting services to Darwen FC, then of the Lancashire Combination. On his travels, he'd become inaugurated into the fellowship of football scouts, chatting behind the goals on park pitches or sharing a pork pie and a cup of milky tea in an anteroom at a non-league or lower-division Football League ground. He loved the camaraderie, gossip and, most of all, the chase – trying to secure a promise or, even better, the signature of a nascent talent who might later bring joy to thousands on Saturday afternoons.

O'Donoghue had combed the north-west for players on behalf of Liverpool before joining Arsenal's scouting team, for whom he'd found himself assessing a player at a night match at Spotland. Rochdale had only a handful of records to play before matches and at half-time, and one was '(I Can't Get No) Satisfaction' by The Rolling Stones. 'This is your song, isn't it,

Fred?' shouted the other Fred (Ratcliffe), to Fred O'Donoghue.
They knew each other from outside football. Ratcliffe's company
had sold springs and components to Blackburn Council for
many years. 'What do you mean?' asked O'Donoghue. 'I've
heard you keep recommending all these lads to Arsenal and
they knock you back every time,' said Ratcliffe. 'That's a bad
do, that is,' he continued. 'No wonder you can't get any bloody
satisfaction. You'd be much better off working for a club much
nearer home.'

That night, O'Donoghue hadn't been able to sleep. As much
as he was proud to represent Arsenal, he was aware that his
role was minor. He was tentative of endorsing players, such
was the club's high expectations of anyone sent to Highbury
for a trial. He was trying to fathom the code behind Ratcliffe's
comments. He knew he was a wily bugger and a man skilled
at playing others to get his own way. The next day, he phoned
Ratcliffe. 'Were you trying to tell me something last night?'
asked O'Donoghue. 'Of course I bloody was.' 'What?' 'Come
and be our chief scout and oversee the full job, not piddling
about doing bits and bobs for a club down yonder.' 'On what
terms?' asked O'Donoghue. Ratcliffe had expected the call and
had already prepared his offer, which was non-negotiable. 'We'll
not put you on the books but we'll pay you £3 a week for what
we'll call "telephone expenses". There'll be 6p for every mile
you do for us and we'll cover any repairs your car might need.
You'll not be the richest man in football, Fred, but you'll love it
here at Rochdale, and you can tell everyone you're a chief scout
in your own right.'

A chief scout was usually considered part of the backroom
team and put in place, or at least sanctioned, by the manager.
Neither Dick Conner, Rochdale's manager at the time, nor
his assistant, Peter Madden, had been consulted about the
appointment of O'Donoghue but were simply told by Ratcliffe
'here's your man'.

Before O'Donoghue had joined the club officially, Dick Conner phoned Ext. 322 at Blackburn Town Hall and spoke to him. 'What's he [Ratcliffe] paying you?' asked Conner. 'I think the sum could best be described as "miserly",' replied O'Donoghue. Conner laughed. When asked about his playing 'career', O'Donoghue told him he'd been a star winger with St Augustine's FC in the Preston Catholic League. 'Were you ever scouted by a bigger club?' asked Conner. 'Only once,' replied O'Donoghue. 'I think St Joseph's put in a bid of ten-bob and a packet of fags.'

Conner and Madden had since moved on but O'Donoghue sensed that he was liked and trusted by the new 'gaffer', Joyce; they'd had a few happy chats in that little office. 'Always willing to give you my opinion, Walter. And I won't charge you. What is it?' Joyce fell serious: 'I'm thinking of doing something drastic.'

* * *

A musician from Rochdale was caught up in a devastating fire at the Summerland Fun Palace on the Isle of Man in August 1973. Harry Greenwood had been among nearly 3,000 others at the futuristic 'indoor world', comprising a dance hall, theatre, swimming pools, amusement arcades, disco, roller-skating rink and several bars. The fire started when a lighted cigarette or match was discarded in a kiosk at the centre's miniature golf course.

Greenwood, a guitar player, was performing with the Don Taylor Trio in the Marquee Showbar. While on stage, he saw smoke rising from the floor. Soon afterwards, as people evacuated the building, Greenwood said 'flames shot as if from a gigantic blow-torch'. Earlier, a compère had appealed for calm, announcing that it was 'only a chip pan fire'. Greenwood was making good his escape when he realised the group's drummer, Malcolm Ogden, had returned to the bar for his cymbals. He raced to check on Ogden's whereabouts but ran into choking black smoke.

Back at Greenwood's home in Buckley View, Smallbridge, his wife, Mary, and daughter, Joan, had heard about the disaster on the television news but it was the early hours before he could find a free public telephone to inform them that he'd survived. His bandmate, Malcolm Ogden, aged 41, died in the fire along with 50 others; 80 suffered serious injuries. Many of the fire doors had been chained and locked, no sprinklers were fitted and the staff hadn't conducted a fire drill.

The centre, built at a cost of £2m, had featured a controlled 'sunny' climate: 'an environment where the sun always shines, where the weather can be guaranteed and where every activity connected with a seaside holiday can be enjoyed by all ages' – Isle of Man Development Company. Plastic was used in the structure, including transparent acrylic glass sheeting called Oroglas (later dubbed 'horror glass'). Oroglas should have been used sparingly, as recommended by the manufacturers, but the roof and two walls were constructed from it. When it became molten, burning panels dripped down from the roof. Afterwards, buildings throughout the UK were checked to see whether they contained Oroglas. The only one found in Rochdale was at the fire station.

4

Soft as Silk, Solid as Granite

WALTER JOYCE had run his idea past the rest of the coaching staff and received their full support. He'd expected this – they had been hand-picked because they shared a similar credo of football, after all. He wasn't sure how O'Donoghue would respond; he was on the edge of the circle. O'Donoghue listened intently. He discerned immediately the manager's belief and faith in what he was saying. He was adept at finding the perfect maxim for most situations and did so again. 'Follow your instinct, Walter. First thought, best thought, and all that,' he said.

Joyce was going to fill his team almost entirely with young players. He'd been impressed by their enthusiasm and athleticism in training and the last two friendly matches. They had run and run, closing down, shunting into tackle after tackle. They needed to show more composure on the ball and pick out better passes but that could be learned. In contrast, he'd been disappointed by some of the senior players. He detected complacency, as if they were playing within themselves, reluctant to embrace the upbeat mood of the youngsters. At times, he'd seen them take nips at the novices – mocking them for a misplaced pass, clattering them if they showed a piece of ingenuity on the ball – 'that's for trying to be a flash bastard'. In the dressing room, they had sometimes responded with sarcasm or an insult. 'Do you want me to come short to receive the ball or would you rather knock it long?' asked one of the young pros. 'I'd rather you fucked off and stop mithering me.'

Fred O'Donoghue warned that there would be a reaction. 'A few of the older lads are bound to see their arses [sulk] if you leave them out. But you know that, don't you?' Joyce nodded. 'I suppose you're going to do it gradually and ease the kids in?' said O'Donoghue. Joyce shook his head. 'Oh, fucking hell. Better get the tin hats out.'

* * *

TBA had been based for more than a century on a 72-acre site in the Spodden Valley, a ribbon of countryside running through an otherwise urban area about half a mile from Rochdale's Spotland ground. These days, 'Keep Out' signs are fastened to the metal fence that surrounds it. If anyone should wander down Spod Road, a dark incline behind the Royds Arms, the path is blocked by a swing barrier. Tarry for more than a few seconds and a security guard will leave his nearby hut and tell you it is private land, will you please move on.

At various points along Rooley Moor Road it is possible to see the falling-down structures on the other side of the fence: factory buildings, outhouses, storage units, pump houses, cracked roads and buckled car parks. Inevitably, 'urban explorers' have found their way in, holding aloft camera phones and torches, and uploading films to YouTube, under the tag 'Rochdale's Chernobyl'. The footage is eerie, a once-busy and noisy place now quiet, still. In the offices, dented filing cabinets have been tipped over and ring-binders spill out. Computer monitors and keyboards are on the floor among shards of glass, crockery, oily rags, fire extinguishers and items of clothing. Nature is clawing back the space. Trees pierce ceilings. Bushes camouflage mounds of smashed concrete and bricks. Buddleia is dotted here and there, its purple shoots fired off like stunted Roman candles.

The land remains heavily contaminated, which is why it is avoided, abandoned. Hence, the comparison to Chernobyl. And yet, until the 1990s, more than 3,000 people worked on the site, as machines almost as big as houses sent asbestos fibres spinning and swirling into the air and lungs. Residents in nearby terraced houses used to joke that every day was like Christmas because it 'snowed' so much. Asbestos dust lined the streets and they wiped it from their cars before making the first journey of the day; some even remarked how it prettified the area, especially fallen on the branches of trees, making everything fluffy white.

A century earlier, asbestos had been heralded as a 'magic mineral'. John Bell, a shipping insurance broker from Salford, introduced it into the UK. The nature of his job had made him well aware of the consequences of fires onboard ships. He'd heard of the fire-resistant qualities of chrysotile asbestos (sometimes known as white asbestos), which had been mined in Quebec, Canada since the 1850s when a forest fire cleared trees to reveal what became known locally as 'white gold'.

Bell, via family contacts, approached Samuel Turner, whose family owned Clod Mill, a small cotton-spinning concern employing five people, by the River Spodden in Rochdale. Bell asked Turner whether it was possible to weave asbestos to use as insulation. Turner, adapting cotton textile machinery, developed a process and supplied woven asbestos to John Bell & Son Ltd (later John Bell Asbestos Co.). When their agreement of exclusivity ended in 1879, Turner, supported by his brothers, John and Robert, entered the market as Bell's competitor; it was a walkover. TBA quickly grew to become the world's largest asbestos conglomerate and, in 1928, acquired Bell's business. The company was an early exemplar of global capitalism, where the many elements and subsidiaries – from mining to manufacture to marketing to delivery – were wholly or part-owned and controlled by TBA, with the Rochdale site as its hub.

Originally, asbestos was considered a lifesaver, providing protection from fire and heat, whether as a machine component or in everyday use around the home, even as a building material. It was said to be 'soft as silk, solid as granite' and had hundreds of uses, from a fabric weaved into curtains to a heat retardant in aircraft and vehicle engines. The company dreamed up 'Lady Asbestos' as its symbol, a figure similar to a Greek goddess, a giant holding a shield to protect civilisation from heat, acid and electricity.

* * *

The first match of a new season was ideal for making a statement, to both players and fans. After weeks of intensive training, shifting personnel (in *and* out) and a squad at full fitness, everyone accepted that this was the manager's ideal team, a distillation of all he believed in, a philosophy made flesh. The Rochdale team sheet was taped to the wood panelling on the dressing-room wall: Jones, Smith, Hanvey, Arnold, Marsh, Kinsella, Taylor, Briers, Atkins, Darling, Downes. To most people, this was merely a list of names, another set of footballers representing Rochdale AFC. Supporters of the club, however, had to do a double take, unable to believe what they were seeing. Or not seeing.

Joyce had left out four players who, between them, had made more than 1,000 appearances in the Football League. They were: Colin Blant (age 26, more than 150 matches and club captain); Gordon Morritt (31, nearly 250 matches and the club's player of the season in the previous campaign); Peter Gowans (29, almost 400 matches); and Keith Bebbington (30, over 350 matches). Both Gowans and Bebbington had slight injuries but would have been able to play if called upon. This wasn't the habitual 'shake-up' or 'rejigging' but, in lower-league terms, a revolution. Within minutes, there was banging at Joyce's door.

* * *

The Turner brothers, staunch Methodists, became pillars of Rochdale society. They served as aldermen on Rochdale Corporation and each had a spell as mayor; Samuel was knighted in 1914. They were viewed as philanthropic, paying workers the highest rates in town. Samuel Turner Jnr (1874–1955), son of Robert Turner, was TBA's chairman from 1929 to 1944. He endowed a school of industrial administration at Manchester Industrial Technical College and a dental school at the University of Manchester. He donated a pipe organ to Rochdale Town Hall, built by the renowned James Jepson Binns. In 1932, he bestowed the grand Denehurst House and its surroundings – a few yards from Rochdale AFC's ground – to the townspeople for use as a park. He still had enough personal wealth to have a yacht built to his own specification. *Halcyon* was described by *Yachting Monthly* as 'snugly rigged with Bermudan main and mizzen and a sail area of 2,275 sq. ft. that can be handled with a small crew'.

The threat posed to health by asbestos was known soon after it first became processed at an industrial level. In 1898, a factory inspector referred to it as 'an evil dust' and the first documented death of an asbestos worker from pulmonary failure was recorded in 1906. Afterwards, insurance companies in the US and Canada began decreasing benefits while increasing premiums for workers employed in the asbestos industry. By 1918, life insurance was withdrawn completely.

The first death in Britain accredited officially to pulmonary asbestosis was that of Nellie Kershaw, aged 33, who had spent nearly seven years working as a rover at TBA in Rochdale – a rover operated the machine that took threads from the carding machine and split it into fibres. Dr William Edmund Cooke, a pathologist and bacteriologist, examined her lungs posthumously and reported that 'they were peppered with numerous minute sharp fibres which had cut directly into her tissue causing thousands of tiny scars until eventually her lungs could no longer function and she died of suffocation'. TBA refused to accept liability for her injuries nor paid compensation to her bereaved family or contributed to funeral expenses because 'it would create a precedent and admit responsibility', according to Percy George Kenyon, works manager. Nellie Kershaw was buried in an unmarked pauper's grave at Rochdale Cemetery in March 1924.

In 1955, Richard Doll, the epidemiologist famous for establishing the connection between tobacco smoking and cancer, completed a study at TBA, which showed a similar link to asbestos. The research was carried out on TBA's behalf (presumably the findings were expected to suit the company) but he was refused permission to publish the report. Later, TBA persuaded its chief medical officer, Dr John Knox, to draft a paper undermining Doll's work. Knox, as part of his daily regime, regularly X-rayed employees and, when results showed early signs of disease, the worker was moved to 'less dusty' jobs at the plant, without being given a reason.

TBA circulated a confidential five-point plan in 1968 entitled 'Putting the Case for Asbestos'. Drafted by Hill & Knowlton ('One of the world's leading global communications companies' – its own claim), it was designed to help managerial staff field questions about asbestos cancer. It began, in capital letters: 'NEVER BE THE FIRST TO RAISE THE HEALTH QUESTION'.

* * *

Walter Joyce knew who would be first at his door, knock-knock, bang-bang. 'Come in, Colin,' he said. Few people called Colin Blant, Colin. It was either Blanty or Garth – named after the all-action, square-jawed, muscle-bound hero from the comic strip in the *Daily Mirror*. Blant was 6ft 2in and weighed 13 stone. While an apprentice at Burnley, the club had struggled to find shorts to fit over his thighs; occasionally they had to resort to cutting them down the sides. In the 'pen pictures' featured in match programmes, he was customarily described as 'no nonsense' or 'strong in the tackle'. He enjoyed the reputation; he felt he'd earned it. 'Colin Blant was a big man who didn't take very well to being told what to do,' said Stan Townsend. 'Walter could be very direct but more often than not he was right.'

Blant was hurting at being left out of the Rochdale line-up. And embarrassed. Club captain and the player who set the heartbeat of the team – dropped. 'What's going on, Walter?' he asked. 'I'm giving the kids a try,' he replied. 'I'm only 26.' Joyce held his gaze: 'Some of these lads I'm playing are 18 and 19.' 'Marshy isn't.' (Arthur Marsh, Blant's replacement in the team, was only seven months younger than him.) 'I'm not going to change my mind, Blanty.' Blant slammed the door behind him.

* * *

TBA was said to be, in employment terms, 'like a bath tap turned on without the plug in'. The round-the-clock operation was colossal and the site was effectively a town within a town, requiring a huge amount of manpower across a multitude of trades. Open days for prospective employees – advertised in Rochdale AFC's match programme and elsewhere – were held on almost a weekly basis. Buses were laid on from the town centre and leaflets handed out promising overalls ('laundered free by us'), subsidised meals and 'plenty of overtime'. Many Asians were employed at TBA, predominantly working nightshifts. Relations were generally good apart from altercations between ethnic groups during the Indo–Pakistan War of 1971.

Most of the employees were aware of the danger of asbestos dust but, at a time before information was easily available via the internet and social media, it appeared a vague, distant threat, especially as they could see that vast sums had been spent on gigantic extractor fans fastened to the ceilings, offering a reassuring hum as the harmful particles were drawn upwards to be filtered and collected in plastic sacks (most likely to be taken later to landfill sites). TBA also employed a man who wandered the site with what looked to be 'a juke box on wheels'. They were told he was 'sampling the air' and monitoring asbestos levels. Again, it made them feel safe.

Physical labour was the only gift to an employer from most people in Rochdale; few had an education of significance. Jobs were plentiful in the early 1970s but they weren't *good* jobs. They were mostly arduous jobs in unpleasant environments where breathing, the most basic human process, was often compromised by dust or fragments of asbestos or cotton fibres – hundreds had been left wheezing and coughing after contracting byssinosis in the cotton mills.

Those fortunate enough to work in cleaner, healthier settings – supermarkets, warehouses, shops and offices – had to clock in and out, and much of the work was dull and monotonous, over which they had little say or control. Staff at TBA knew, as most others did at workplaces elsewhere in town, that there was always a trade-off, a price to pay, but they had rent or a mortgage to cover, families to feed. They had heard of colleagues falling seriously ill, some dying, but they also worked with others who had been at TBA for more than 30 years and seemed healthy enough. In fact, different generations of the same families worked there and certificates for length of service were on the walls alongside photographs of staff receiving retirement gifts.

John Clarke started at TBA in 1965 as an apprentice maintenance engineer, aged 16. He was soon aware of the company's paternalistic approach, which stretched to encouraging staff to participate in sports and out-of-work activities, such as amateur dramatics. 'The company had its own groundsman to look after the football pitch,' said Clarke. 'There was a greenkeeper for the bowling green and proper lawnmowers – it was a hell of an undertaking. They had a policy that if you had an idea and could get a few people interested, then Turner's would match whatever you had raised. A few of us fancied having a go at rifle shooting and they gave us money towards it.'

One morning, Clarke was surprised to find a young man sitting on a stool in a cargo lift that served three floors. 'He was in there reading a book most of the time, pressing a few buttons now and again. He lasted about six months. I heard later that he was the son of one of the managers and had hurt himself after coming off his motorbike. I think the firm had made up the job especially for him, to help get him out of the house and mixing a bit. They did things like that,' he said.

* * *

Colin Blant had cobalt blue eyes and a smile that was difficult to discern: warm or cold, friend or foe? In the crude terms of the times, he was an archetypal 'hairy-arsed centre-half'. He enjoyed defending – trying to work out centre-forwards: which foot was his strongest, how fast were his feet, did he have the pace to push and run with the ball? He most enjoyed the 'challenge'. How much bottle did his opponent have? Make it clear, he'd be getting a 'tickle' early on – a sly jab in the ribs, a knee in the back of the thigh. Was the striker going to mutter and moan or start up with the gobbing off, saying he'd sort this out in the tunnel afterwards or have it out good and proper in the car park after the match – all that kind of nonsense? Footballers hated losing but Blant was worse than most. 'If he lost, he'd be in a horrendous mood after matches,' said his wife, Pauline. 'In the car after the match, he'd talk non-stop about who should have done what, what they'd done wrong. He was an absolute nightmare.'

Blant had been brought up in Taylors Buildings, among a row of back-to-back terraced houses in Rawtenstall, nine miles from Spotland. His father, Fred, was a keen sportsman and Colin's older brother, also called Fred, was a good footballer, too. They had both been invited to play for Rossendale United, a semi-professional club in the Lancashire Combination. 'Fred wasn't into football the same way as I was,' said Blant. 'As a kid, my mother and grandfather had taken me to watch Blackburn Rovers and Burnley on alternate weeks for many years. I was only young at the time but I enjoyed playing for Rossendale.'

The experience of playing at Dark Lane, Rossendale United's home ground, served Blant well. He came up against wily old pros on their last (slim) wage packet before retirement and seasoned non-league sluggers. He joined Burnley in 1964 at the age of 18, already able to 'look after himself' on a football pitch. He'd started as a centre-forward but, after a single season in the first team, was switched to centre-half. Whereas, as a striker, his role was to receive the ball, hold it up or turn and run for goal while a defender thrashed at his ankles, he could now do the thrashing. Over six seasons he struggled to secure a regular first-team place at Turf Moor but still made 53 appearances. He joined Portsmouth, where he was booked nine times in the 1971/72 season – a conspicuously high number at a time of charitable refereeing. While Blant was living in Portsmouth, his maternal grandfather, Tommy Eatough, who had first introduced him to football, fell ill. 'My mother was struggling to cope with it all and I decided to move back home,' said Blant.

* * *

As a maintenance engineer, John Clarke was one of few with access to all parts of the TBA site and saw how it was run on a strict hierarchical basis. 'There were six different canteens,' he said. 'The manual workers had to bring their own knives and forks and queue up. The next staff level up had tablecloths. The one after that, there was salt and pepper, and then waitress service. I was called out once to fix the potato peeler in the kitchen that served the directors' canteen. It was all oak doors and wood-panelled walls. I peeked in and there were bottles of wine on the tables. The chef saw me and shouted, "What are you doing here?" I told him no one would be getting any spuds if he chased me off.'

Exposure to asbestos dust varied across the site with the 'W Block' the most excessive. In the 1930s, raw asbestos had arrived at TBA in trucks at the company's private railway sidings close to Shawclough Station. Workers, known as 'snowmen', would shovel it into containers. By the 1970s the system was mechanised but there was still a great deal of dust in the air. Occasionally a 'grab-bag' burst in the W Block and a blizzard of dust would be unleashed, scattering workers in search of fresh air.

The same as all workplaces, there were occasional laughs. 'We had this safety officer and he was the image of Harry Worth, the comedian,' said Clarke. 'This particular day, he was showing us the effectiveness of safety shoes. He wedged the protected toe bit under the leg of this big oak table and was asking people to sit on it. After a few had done so, he pointed to this daft lad and asked him to come forward. Straight away, we all knew it was a mistake. This lad jumped up and landed on his backside causing the table to jerk forwards. Poor Harry took the full weight of the table and all the people on it. He had to be rushed to the medical room!'

Within a year of starting at TBA, Clarke developed a chronic sore throat and couldn't speak in the morning without first having a glass of water. After seven years, he left to work as an engineer at Whipp & Bourne Ltd, Castleton, Rochdale. He felt tired and unwell for several months but improved markedly after his tonsils were removed. 'I'll never know if working at TBA affected my throat or not,' he said. 'I was young and naïve when I worked there and didn't really think about such things,' said Clarke, now aged 72.

* * *

In the summer of 1972, Blant had met with Dick Conner, Rochdale's manager at the time, at the Owd Betts pub on the remote road running across Ashworth Moor on the outskirts of Rochdale. Blant agreed the personal terms to join Rochdale, who paid a £7,000 transfer fee to Portsmouth. He was made vice-captain on the understanding he'd lead the side if Reg Jenkins was injured.

Blant had soon revealed both sides of his personality to team-mates – 'hard on the field, soft off it'. At Christmas that year, he represented the players in an unusual dispute. In previous years, each player had received a turkey from the club as a Christmas gift but they were told the gesture had been withdrawn. Blant was nominated to express the players' discontentment even though, as he told them, his mother, Annie, had already purchased *their* turkey. The turkey bonus wasn't reinstated and Blant was fined two weeks' wages – he was unsure on what basis this was permissible, although his team-mates joked that he owed the club 'a few bob' for all the fines it had paid on his behalf for the bookings and sendings-off.

He'd been looking forward to the start of the season, more so when he heard that Reg Jenkins wasn't being retained; he'd expected to now be made captain. He knew that Portsmouth to Rochdale was a retrograde step but captaining a solid, mid-table Third Division team (which was how he perceived Rochdale) at the age of 26 and living among family and friends was a splendid way to spend your life. Now, all this might change.

* * *

Anyone associated with *RAP*, whether an editor or a news stringer from the factory floor, was often waylaid by someone pleading clemency on behalf of the bosses. 'They've had to work their way up,' was a regular entreaty, along with 'they've invested a lot of their own money, you know'. Others claimed that 'they worked long hours' or 'they take their work home with them – *we* don't'. The one that drew the most fervent response was 'we all get the same opportunities in life'.

Both David Bartlett and John Walker, *RAP*'s founders, relished in telling the tale of the Batemans, especially Ralph Melton Bateman, Rochdale's local boy made (very) good. They wanted Rochdalians to contrast their lives with the bounty of the Batemans and associates. They were among a handful of such families, Midas figures who owned the mills and works. As *RAP* saw it, they epitomised the advancement gained by being educated, wealthy, privileged and well connected.

In the early 1970s, the asbestos industry was still teeming in riches, with TBA's annual profits exceeding £10m; it was 'dirty money' as far as *RAP* (and many others) was concerned: 'He [Ralph Bateman] has said nothing about the risks workers face in dangerous industries such as the one that spawned him,' read one editorial.

Bateman was born in 1910, one of three sons and a daughter of the GP and Justice of the Peace, William Hirst Bateman, who had spent 48 years as a doctor in Rochdale; the Bateman Centre at Birch Hill Hospital bore his name. Ralph's mother, Ethel Jane Scrimgeour, had read mathematics at Cambridge University at a time before women were awarded degrees.

Dr William Hirst Bateman was the first Bateman to cultivate a relationship with TBA. He'd been a 'medical officer' at TBA while holding down the same position, albeit part-time, at Rochdale Urban District Corporation (as it was then known). In the late 1930s, TBA's medical staff (in practice, Dr Bateman) routinely attended post-mortems of workers, although 'he was not allowed to wield the knife'. He could, though, take away specimens for analysis. Bateman was succeeded at TBA in 1949 by his good friend, Dr John Frederick Knox, born in Belfast, who had arrived in Rochdale initially to support Bateman at his GP surgery. Knox was appointed as a 'factory medical officer' at TBA but, on his retirement as a GP, became 'chief medical officer' and then a medical consultant for the company until he retired fully in December 1968. He died while playing golf four years later. Meanwhile, Bateman had moved to Keswick in the Lake District after being made a freeman of the borough in Rochdale for 'the many ways he had served his community'.

The three sons of Dr Bateman – Ralph, Geoffrey and Donald – were educated at Epsom College, a boarding school for sons of men from the medical profession. They later studied at University College, Oxford. On his freshmen photograph of October 1928, Ralph Bateman was pictured next to Lancelot Bernard Liddell, with, close by, Eric Montagu Price Holmes, Norval Arthur Gray Burbridge and Redvers Baden Cordukes – three young men with 14 names between them; most in Rochdale got by with two. Ralph Bateman married in 1935 and lived in Prestbury, Cheshire – 'well away from the asbestos infected area from which he has made good', as *RAP* pointed out. Bateman, as chairman, received £41,000 from TBA in 1973 and drew considerable amounts from directorships at Stothert and Pitt (dock cranes and construction plant), Rea Bros (industry), Furness Withy (shipping liners) and Crosby Woodfield (industrial machinery).

Geoffrey Hirst Bateman, Ralph's elder brother by four years, also received a knighthood, for services to the medical profession. He was a distinguished ear, nose and throat surgeon at St Thomas', London. In 1931 – the same year Ralph had started at TBA as a management trainee – Geoffrey married Margaret Turner, daughter of Samuel Turner, the son of Robert Turner, one of the founders of TBA. Geoffrey and Margaret lived in Chelsea, before, on his retirement, moving to Sussex, where he played golf and tennis and took a holiday every May in Scotland to fish for salmon.

Donald Scrimgeour Bateman, the eldest brother and also a GP, died, aged 39, while serving as a wing commander in the RAF. His plane hit a radio mast shortly after take-off in Benghazi, Libya in 1944. Two years before his death, Bateman had written a biography of the noted abdominal surgeon, Sir

Berkeley Moynihan. The Bateman sister, Winifred Helen, was an architect and magistrate.

* * *

If Colin Blant hated losing, he hated not being in the team even more – it made a mockery of all the training, the effort, the dedication. How could you call yourself a professional footballer if you didn't play? As a young player, he'd been patient at Burnley (much the same as Joyce) and he'd had the courage to move to Portsmouth when it felt to be on the other side of the world, such was the distance from Lancashire.

Here he was now, unable to get into Rochdale's team when, three years earlier, he'd been playing in the top division and, a year ago, they were chanting his name at Fratton Park, a place where they knew their football and he'd been accepted and celebrated for being a heart-and-soul footballer. He asked to see Walter Joyce again. 'Put me on the transfer list, will you?' 'But we might need you in a few weeks,' said Joyce. Blant shrugged. He knew the team was in flux – it always happened when a new manager came in. He knew too that, as an experienced pro, it usually went one of two ways: the new manager embraced you, trusted you, confided in you, made you a quasi-coach; or they viewed you as a threat, someone who might question their tactics or team selection, their credentials even. If you fell into the latter category, it didn't really matter what you did on the pitch or how hard you trained or encouraged others (especially the young lads) – you were going to be bombed out. 'I won't be a mardarse,' he promised Joyce. 'I'll not be running to the press, but I want to play first-team football, either here or somewhere else, and I'll do all I can to make sure I do.'

* * *

The asbestos industry was profiled in the *World in Action* documentary, *Killer Dust: a Standard Mistake*, broadcast by

Granada Television. It revealed a murky world of obfuscation, deceit and collusion where victims of asbestosis and related diseases often died in destitution while their bosses received honours and riches. More than 20,000 people were still working in the industry in the early 1970s, including those in Rochdale. In a crude bid to receive sympathetic treatment, TBA had supplied the film crew with plentiful food and drink and its public relations team pestered the production staff, trying to prejudge the tone of the documentary.

Between 50 per cent and 60 per cent of TBA workers were revealed to have lung scarring, 10 per cent of whom had asbestosis. A sample of 290 workers showed that of the 28 who had died in a given period, seven had lung cancer, three asbestosis and three mesothelioma – a disease associated with asbestos. The night-black joke in Rochdale was that it took three days to cremate a TBA worker because they were so heat-resistant.

TBA's own atmosphere tests showed that a single worker encountered eight million asbestos fibres per week and there were airborne particles present in Rochdale town centre, about a mile from its site. Professor Irving Selikoff, a world expert in asbestos-related illnesses, said that the TBA workers were 'in serious risk of dangerous and fatal diseases'. Hilton Lewinsohn, TBA's medical officer, conceded that the company could do more to protect workers' health by making it compulsory to wear protective clothing. Smoking was banned on site and cigarettes were no longer sold in the canteens. Alan Dalton, the director of *Killer Dust*, said, 'With very few exceptions, doctors and scientists have not played a great part in the prevention of asbestos diseases. The aim of industry is production and profit for a few, not health and safety. And those who pay the piper call the tune.'

Another documentary, *Alice – a Fight for Life*, made by Yorkshire TV, featured the harrowing last few weeks in the life of Alice Jefferson, a 47-year-old who developed malignant pleural mesothelioma 30 years after working at Cape Insulation's Acre Mill asbestos plant in Hebden Bridge, West Yorkshire. Both programmes had a compelling influence on public opinion – as television documentaries often did at the time – and were major levers in the close-down of the asbestos business, albeit nearly 20 years later. *RAP* extended a typically strong opinion: 'Consider these facts [those revealed in the documentaries] the next time you pick up the local rag and see the advert showing those smiling faces inviting you to "join your friends at TBA". Think on the possibility that the new overall they give you could soon be exchanged for a shroud.'

* * *

Harold Holburt understood Walter Joyce better than anyone else at the club. 'We all knew there would be an issue with him wanting to sideline the older players but once he'd made up his mind, there was usually no going back with Walter,' he said. The pair had been friends since school days when they attended Counthill School in Moorside, Oldham. 'Walter was from a very typical working-class family,' said Holburt. 'His dad was a milkman and his mother worked in a mill. His brother, Michael, was a butcher and had a shop in Springhead [Oldham]. He had a sister, too, called Mavis, and I think she was a good athlete.'

Holburt was struck by Joyce's determined nature, whether they played football on wasteland at the bottom of Alderson Street where the Joyce family lived (a row of terraced houses now demolished), or for Oldham and Lancashire Boys. 'He was very, very competitive in all he did. It didn't matter whether it was football, cricket or snooker, he had to win. He went about everything with total aggression and was outstanding at all sports. The only thing he didn't have was pace. I could give him a ten-yard start in a 100-yard sprint and still beat him!' said Holburt.

Much the same as Dennis Butler, Holburt had suffered a serious injury, although this time it was the 'career ender' that all footballers feared. He was 21 years old and playing left-back for Oldham Athletic reserves away at Barrow, marking the fleet-of-foot Scottish winger, Alec Glover. Holburt could see that Glover was set to run at him with the ball and instinctively turned side-on to give himself more chance of halting his progress. It was raining. The ground was heavy and cloying. While his upper body turned, Holburt's feet held firm in the ground. His knee buckled and he knew immediately that it was badly damaged. On the journey back to Oldham, the swelling was so bad that he had to cut off the leg of his trousers.

The coaching staff at Oldham advised Holburt (known as 'Aitch') to 'run off' the injury and he spent several weeks struggling up the terraces and pulling at sandbags attached to ropes – 'sandbag' training was practised extensively in football in the 1950s and 1960s. Four months after sustaining the injury, he had an X-ray, which showed he'd torn the anterior cruciate ligament. He had several operations and returned to football at amateur level but the knee would often 'go' and he'd have to be substituted.

Holburt worked as an accountant at Osram Ltd, the electric-light manufacturer in Shaw, Oldham, and in his free time trained to become a coach with the Football Association (FA). He was seconded to Fitton Hill Youth Club in Oldham and forged a link that lasted several years, during which its football team won the league and cup double. Walter Joyce heard of Holburt's success and invited him to help with the youth teams at Oldham Athletic and then Rochdale.

* * *

A heatwave visited Rochdale in August 1973. Children did what generations of Rochdalians had done whenever the sun warmed the streets, drying the dirt to dust. They put a tatty towel under their arm and headed to the rivers, reservoirs, millponds and canal.

A main congregation point was at Lock Bridge, where the canal slinked below the busy Oldham Road. A radio was placed against the factory wall running alongside the canal and, between dips and dives into the water, teenagers were singing along to Gary Glitter, Donny Osmond and Suzi Quatro. They splashed and swam and shouted in the wide pool of water sloshing against the lock gates. On the other side of the lock, where the water was a mere trickle, all kinds of detritus was visible poking out of the deep, dark slop: bedsteads, bicycle frames, fence posts, broken bottles and dead animals. This scene served as an X-ray of what was probably also on the other side, invisible beneath the grey-black water.

The *Rochdale Observer* dispatched a journalist who reported that the children were 'dicing with death'. Readers were reminded that two years earlier 'the town had been shocked by the drowning of a little immigrant boy'. There had already been two injuries at the site – teenagers suffering cut feet from broken glass and metal. The journalist interviewed what he referred to as a 'water babe', asking why he didn't swim at the public baths instead. 'Why should I? It's free here,' he answered. Audrey Mulcahy of Welbeck Road, a 'mother-of-four', said, 'It's a nightmare keeping them away from the canal. I am telling them constantly, especially in the school holidays and on hot days. So far, they have obeyed me but there is always the fear they will forget. The canal should be filled in.'

Will Kay, engineer for the Rochdale Canal Company, said the canal had to be kept open to provide water for local industry. Chief Superintendent T. F. Rankin, head of the Rochdale Police Division, said, 'Obviously it is a highly dangerous situation and one which could lead so quickly and easily to tragedy. If there are quite a large number of children in the water, one could disappear without anyone knowing. Then, sadly, it is too late.'

* * *

Another to encounter Joyce's combative nature was Trevor Butterworth. A Rochdale supporter since a boy, he owned a sports shop in the town centre and supplied kit and equipment to the club. He was, the same as Joyce, in his mid-30s in 1973. Although they barely knew one another, a challenge was issued; it was as if Joyce was pleased to find someone of a similar age and fitness against whom he could pit himself. 'He told me to pick five sports, any sports, and said he'd beat me in all of them,' said Butterworth. 'I knew he was a fitness fanatic but went along with it. I can't remember on the agreed sports but two of them were definitely squash and table tennis.'

They met at Rochdale Squash Club and Butterworth soon found himself in a frantic match, struggling to keep up with Joyce. 'I tore the cartilage in my knee and by the end of the game it had ballooned up to twice its normal size. I'd obviously over-exerted myself and the next morning I found myself in hospital having an operation,' he said.

Whenever he visited Spotland on business, Butterworth dealt with Fred Ratcliffe. 'I always found Walter to be a bit brusque,' he said. 'I had the impression he was a hard man. He gave off that kind of air. I was never thanked by him for anything I did for the club but that didn't matter; I wasn't doing it for that reason. Rochdale was my club and I'd do anything for it.'

On one occasion, Butterworth was asked by the directors to call at the newly opened Tesco superstore and visit Michael Tarpey, the manager. Butterworth's shop supplied match balls to the club and he presumed he was about to be offered a contribution towards their cost from Tesco. 'A Mitre ball could cost up to £40 back then, which was a lot of money,' said Butterworth. 'When I got to Tesco, Mike wasn't in. His secretary passed me a pile of invoices from their suppliers and said I should phone them up to see if they'd donate some money.' He did so and, over the course of the season, instead of the usual patrons of local tradesmen and shops, Rochdale's match balls were sponsored by, among others, Crosse and Blackwell, Heinz and Findus.

Another time, Butterworth, who had become a 'Mr Fix-It' for the club, was preparing to head to Spotland on a windy, rain-lashed night when he received a phone call from the ground. 'A bulb has gone on one of the floodlights,' he was told. 'Don't worry,' he said. 'There'll still be plenty of light from the others.' 'No, it's gone.' 'Replace it in the morning,' he said. 'No, you don't understand. It's come out of its socket and landed on the terraces. It could have knocked some poor bugger out if it had happened during the match.' Butterworth advised them to cordon off the area and put a police officer nearby to ensure fans kept away. The next day, the floodlights were checked and engineers reported back that they hadn't been examined since they had been installed three years earlier.

* * *

Posters calling on recruits for the British Army were pinned to the walls at Rochdale Labour Exchange on Station Road, across from the railway station. They caught the eye and the imagination, especially on dismal days when the sun struggled to rise tall enough to send light through the windows. 'See what today's army offers you' was the text above three handsome young soldiers making their way through palm trees, everything lit golden with end-of-the-day sunlight. 'Good Jobs. Good Money. Good Times' had two smiling soldiers studying a map, the landscape behind them fringed by a cobalt sea. 'Join the Professionals' illustrated the rich diversity of army life, with soldiers in frogmen gear, karate outfits, snow wear, etc.

After walking to the exchange, through streets penned in by mills, past housing estates with barking dogs and kicked-down fences, this lifestyle on offer was enticing. And when they got back home that same day, the army was there again, this time on television. 'Reckon you could keep a clear head in a crisis?' was the voice-over as the soldier jumped from a helicopter, rifle in hand. Those young men expressing an interest in 'joining' were invited to an interview and a day's training where there was talk of them being based in Cyprus, Hong Kong, Brunei, Kenya or Germany. They were told there was also a chance they may serve in Northern Ireland.

Chance? Most knew where they were heading. Other soldiers had told them it was a dead cert. The British government had sent troops into Northern Ireland in August 1968 as a 'limited operation' to restore law and order after prolonged violence in the Bogside area of Derry/Londonderry. The Troubles, as it became known, had escalated and was raging during the early 1970s. More than a hundred British soldiers had been killed in 1972, and 500 wounded. On 30 January 1972, Bloody Sunday, 13 unarmed people had been shot dead (another died later in hospital) by the British Army during a proscribed anti-internment rally. Swathes of the province were deemed 'no-go areas' with barricades across roads.

Most of the soldiers recruited in Rochdale served alongside the 22,000-strong force in Northern Ireland with the Royal Regiment of Fusiliers. A snapshot of their lives was provided by the local media, invited by the army's public relations team to file pieces on 'the boys from home'. The selection of Rochdalians included Fusilier Brian Whitbread, aged 22, from Whitworth, on his third tour of duty, who thought 'the army is great, be it in Belfast or Berlin'; Sergeant William McDonald, aged 26, who wanted to train as an officer at Sandhurst; Fusilier David Kirby, aged 18, from Spotland, an ex-pupil of Redbrook Secondary Modern School who viewed it as 'a job of work to be done'; Fusilier Peter Steriker, aged 18, a former mill worker, who had become 'fed up and considered the army a good swap'; Fusilier Stephen Whitworth, aged 20, of Littleborough, a fan of Rochdale Hornets, who said he wanted to join the Catering

Corps; and Fusilier Pat O'Brien, aged 26, from Castleton, who had just become a father to Kimberley.

The soldiers spoke of their time riding in 'pigs' (Humber Pigs, armoured troop carriers) carrying Armalite rifles. They lived in barracks in Anderstown, nicknamed Silver City because of the corrugated-iron palisades. They said they often had stones thrown at them by youths who were alerted to their arrival by the quick flashing on and off of bedroom lights.

Another soldier from Rochdale, Barry Scowcroft, a lance corporal, received serious injuries in September 1973 while guarding an army Land Rover parked at the Royal Victoria Hospital, Belfast. Gunmen sprayed bullets at the entrance of the hospital and Scowcroft was hit in the chest. He was treated at the same hospital and his life lay in the balance for several weeks. He received a disappointing welcome on his return to Rochdale. Despite being on the council house waiting list for eight months, Barry and his wife, Joyce, were told none was available. The couple and their two young children moved in with his mother in Castleton, where they lived cramped in a single bedroom.

5

A Sash of Blue and Yellow

SEASON TICKETS weren't selling well. Fred Ratcliffe had expected a change of manager to galvanise interest but very few people were making their way across the car park towards the general office, cash in their coat pockets. He'd been asked for official figures by the press but had swatted away the request. 'A few hundred,' he grunted. He called Angus McLean into the boardroom for a few nips of whisky and a chat. Most days, McLean opened up at Spotland. He was a friendly sort, with a cheery wave and greeting for the early-morning people he passed – the paperboy racing back to the newsagents with his empty bag, the milkman leaving a crate of five or six bottles by the main entrance. 'Do you think we'll do better this season?' they'd ask him. They weren't sure exactly what he did at the club but, in his smart suit and Brylcreemed hair, it looked important. 'We'll give it a go,' he replied.

McLean was liked and trusted by the players but viewed principally as an office wallah, the bloke who sorted them out with tickets for away matches and photocopied team sheets on matchdays. The depth of his football experience and knowledge was largely unknown, unspoken. He'd been appointed as assistant manager/secretary a year earlier but, now in his late 40s and with more than three decades in the game, he knew the precariousness of a managerial role, so had concentrated on his secretarial duties; he hoped it would keep him in a job for longer. He'd 'upped sticks' (as he called it) many times, watching on with his wife, Hilda, and young daughter, Una, as their belongings were carried once more in to or out of a Pickfords van. 'Are you feeling better now, Gus?' asked Ratcliffe. McLean had spent a few weeks in Birch Hill Hospital over the summer with a stomach bug. 'Aye, I'm fine now.'

Ratcliffe often sought him out. McLean guessed that this was because Ratcliffe considered him to be of a similar age, although he was 15 years younger; it might have been the suit. McLean preferred to chat with a player up in the stand after training, or sitting on the knackered plastic chairs in the laundry room, sipping milky coffee. 'What do you think, Gus?' the player would ask. 'The gaffer thinks I should have covered the run that led to their goal but I'd bombed on trying to help the forwards.' In his soft Welsh accent, McLean would counsel: 'Considering we were 1-0 up, I'd have sat-in and closed off the space. The lad would have probably knocked it square then, waiting for support until they could push on with greater numbers. By leaving the barn door open, you tempted fate, made it easier for them.' Sometimes the players were astonished by this level of tactical acumen, the insight he could provide.

Although McLean's parents, Joseph and Martha, were Scottish (as the surname suggested), he was born in Queensferry, Wales. His father had been a blast furnace re-liner and had moved around the UK to work at various foundries. He died when Angus, their youngest child, was five years old, leaving Martha to raise six children. McLean, broad-shouldered and standing over 6ft in his mid-teens, was the archetypal 'strapping' lad and a natural fit as a centre-half, although he later also played full-back. After a handful of games for Aberystwyth Town, he'd signed for Wolverhampton Wanderers in 1942. He spent 11 years at Molineux among players such as Billy Wright and Bert

Williams, who formed the great Wolves team of the 1950s that won three league championships and two FA Cups. He was later player-manager of Aberystwyth Town, player-coach at Bury, coach at Hull City and caretaker-manager at Wigan Athletic. His last job before arriving at Spotland had seen him succeed Brian Clough as manager of Hartlepool United.

The Rochdale players went easy with the piss-taking. McLean could take a bit of ribbing about his bushy, bedspring eyebrows but he was a man with integrity, always good for a quiet chat. He didn't make it known, but on a six-week tour of South Africa with Wolves in 1951, he'd been offered a role coaching young players. He turned it down because of his distaste of the apartheid regime introduced by the all-white National Party three years earlier.

The poor season ticket sales were rankling chairman Ratcliffe. 'I think we could give them away and they still wouldn't come,' he said. 'Times are hard,' said McLean. 'You read in the papers every other day about all these strikes that are looming.' Ratcliffe suddenly pulled a face, holding out the glass tumbler in his hand. 'This whisky is bloody awful. Fairy piss.' McLean had to suppress a smile: 'Don't you remember? You asked me to water it down so it would go further, saying no one would know because they always have water or ice in it anyway.' Ratcliffe was affronted: 'I didn't mean to do that with *my* drink. Bloody hell, Gus.' Ratcliffe quickly returned to his original theme: 'I mean, what else is there to do in Rochdale?'

* * *

The answer to Fred Ratcliffe's question was that, actually, there was rather a lot to do in Rochdale. The offerings on television did little to fasten people to their settees, with only three channels available. On any given weekend in 1973, the choice comprised, among others, *Dad's Army*, *A Man Called Ironside*, *Mike Yarwood*, *Startime 73*, *Sez Les*, *M*A*S*H*, *The Saint*, *The Golden Shot* and

Follyfoot. Homes were still awaiting the arrival of multi-channel television, video recorders (later replaced by DVD players and film subscription services), PCs, mobile phones, laptops and iPads. The culture of home shopping, phone-in meals and low-cost alcohol carry-outs had also not yet been established. Without these, life in 1973 was lived more communally. People *went out* to pubs, clubs and cinemas. They played bingo. They attended evening classes at schools and Saturday morning classes at the art college. Rooms were in constant use for meetings, whether political or religious. Youth clubs were well attended. Huge numbers took part in sport – amateur football was thriving – and classes were held all over town for martial arts.

The football club hosted a nightly gathering, for a few months at least. The DJ, 'Big Al', held a disco at the social club at Spotland from 9pm to 2am *every* night and 9pm to 11pm on Sundays; remarkable opening hours for an out-of-town venue in a residential area. Live groups appeared three nights a week. Rainbow Cottage ('ITV's *Golden Shot* band') from Wigan were regular performers. Posters were put up around town advertising the disco with, in small print, the memo: 'By the way, a message for the dollies: membership is free. For the fellows, it's only a pound.' The disco lasted a few months before David Wastling, a resident of nearby Mons Avenue, drew up a petition signed by 19 residents objecting to 'the volume of noise caused nightly by over-zealous disc jockeys and visiting pop groups'. Neighbours often called at the main office and were usually met by Angus McLean, who informed them that the social club was rented out to a third party, the Richmond Group, 'to whom they should address all correspondence'.

In the 1940s, Rochdale had 17 cinemas but only three remained in the early 1970s – the Odeon, the ABC and the former Palace Theatre in Great George Street, which, since 1968, had specialised in showing Asian films. Cinema attendance in Britain had fallen appreciably from its heyday of 1946 when 1.64 billion visits were made, to 134 million in 1973. The number would fall to its lowest in 1984 (54 million) during the video-market boom. The Odeon and ABC, in August 1973, were showing, respectively: *Battle for the Planet of the Apes* and *Young Winston*, and *The Life and Times of Judge Roy Bean* and *The Wild Bunch*. Both cinemas had Saturday morning clubs for children. The ABC's 'Minors Matinee' offered DJs and magicians interspersed with cartoons, the adventure serial, *Secret of the Forest* and the main picture, *The Big Job*, a comedy about a bank robbery starring Sidney James – admission 5p (plus everyone got a free badge). The Odeon was showing *A Stitch in Time*, in which Norman Wisdom, as Norman Pitkin, caused mayhem in a hospital – admission 10p (also included a plastic cup of orange squash and a biscuit). Both cinemas showed adult films. One of these, *The Other Canterbury Tales*, was described by *RAP* as 'strictly for the fawn raincoat brigade'. Others of the same ilk included *Sex After Six*, *Versatile Lovers*, *Sextroverts*, *Super Dick* and *Naughty Knickers* – 'a naughty sex romp film in which a lot goes on and a lot comes off' – the *Rochdale Observer*.

The social and working men's clubs in Rochdale did appreciable business. Over a weekend in August 1973, the choice of cabaret was varied. Brian Ford was appearing at Dane Street Social Club, where 10p admission included three free games of bingo. Forthcoming at Dane Street was 'Paddy' – 'a Scots lassie that can really sing'. Wandering Walter ('the comedian you've all been waiting for') was at Whitworth WMC. Featherstall WMC hosted The Gaytimers, a 'top comedy drag show'. The Smooth Water Showband was at Kirkholt WMC, where Shane Fenton (on the cusp of becoming Alvin Stardust, notching chart hits and starring in road safety television adverts – 'Be Smart. Be Safe') was 'coming soon'. The Kingfishers, Vi Donaldson and Tommy Walker were sharing a stage at Lowerplace Liberal Club, where Cyril Smith was to be 'guest of honour'. Another frequent performer at the club on Oldham Road was Ross McManus, father of Elvis Costello. The Boomerang Club in Castleton boasted 'Top line Manchester DJs and go-go dancers' and it sometimes combined both forms of entertainment with 'Melanie, the topless DJ'. Salacious entertainment was also offered at, of all places, Wardleworth Conservative Club – and at breakfast time. A 'Striparama Stage Show' was held on a Sunday morning at a cost of 25p, featuring 'girls girls girls'.

* * *

Walter Joyce watched the minibus full of players head to Sparth Bottoms for training. He wanted to clear his head and made a slow walk around the edge of the Spotland pitch. Albert, the groundsman, was painting out markings. 'Okay, boss?' he shouted. 'Just having a think,' answered Joyce. 'Careful you don't do yourself some damage!' Joyce was thinking that he shouldn't have mentioned Blant's age and gone on to him about prioritising kids. It was always best to tell it straight to footballers: I don't fancy you in my team, you're not for me. Was it that far gone with him and Blant, though? Might he bring him round, stir up more enthusiasm and commitment now he'd had the bitter taste of being dropped? Joyce might need Blant once winter had set in and you could pick up points and wins when someone like him was clenching his fists, putting in the tackles.

Rochdale was a speck on the sporting world, forgotten for most of the time, but to those that cared, who came every week, scarves around their necks or tied at their waist, badges on their bobble hats, it meant the world. They would see this first-team selection as a statement: a new, young manager putting his branding on the club. But was it ill-considered to topple a figurehead such as Blant – a declaration made for its own sake? Or was it an expression of self-confidence and shrewdness? Joyce completed his lap of the pitch. Too late now, anyway. He'd done it, made the decision, informed Blant (and the others) and, right or wrong, it was only one match, with another 50 or so to follow over a long season.

Back in his office, the phone rang. It was Stan Townsend. 'Is it right that you're not playing Blant against Brighton?' he asked. How did news travel this fast, pondered Joyce? Who was telling whom about what? Joyce was still learning press-speak, how best to camouflage truth but hide it in plain sight. 'It's not so much that I've dropped Blant,' he said. 'It's more that I've selected Arthur Marsh instead. Over the pre-season, he's shown a little more zest. Blant told me he was disappointed about being left out, as I expected he would. We had a talk but, apart from that, I've nothing more to say.' Townsend asked Joyce to speak more 'generally' about his off-field staff and playing squad. 'They have all got young ideas and believe the same as I do, that youngsters should be given every encouragement,' said Joyce. 'We want to make Rochdale the best in the division. We want players to run for each other, to use each other's skills to develop space. Everyone is training hard, concentrating on developing movement off the ball.'

Townsend was a canny reporter. He made a metaphorical body swerve back to Blant without actually using his name, still asking 'generally'. 'Players will have to live up to the demands for 100 per cent effort or face the possibility of being dropped,' said Joyce. 'Last season, I'm told it was all too evident that an element of complacency had drifted into the players' attitudes. We must expect maximum effort from every member of staff.' As if he'd realised what he might have revealed, Joyce, unbidden, returned directly to the subject of Blant: 'Colin is a likeable lad and did an excellent job last season.'

* * *

Although a few years away from the disco craze ignited by the film *Saturday Night Fever*, dancing was extremely popular in Rochdale. Four 'schools of dancing' were based in and around the town centre – Williamson's, John Birtles', Syd and Glenys Carr's and Turner's, which is still open after 70 years in business.

In a bid to entice the emerging aspirational class of the 1970s, pubs began serving food outside the usual crisps and packets of nuts fastened to a card behind the bar (Big D peanuts had a pin-up girl waiting to be revealed beneath the packs). Business lunches were introduced. Wicker screens were placed strategically around pubs for a more upmarket appeal. A patch of linoleum was set into the carpet to form a stage or dancing area. Cabaret evenings and dinner dances were held most nights and the dish of choice was often fried chicken on a bed of chips placed on a serviette in a plastic basket. Musicians and entertainers referred to these venues as the 'chicken-in-a-basket circuit'. Smokies, a 'discothèque and restaurant', was popular with the Rochdale in-crowd, although it necessitated a drive to Oldham: 'Smokies is synonymous with elegance and sophistication, and provides for those who deserve and associate with the superior pleasures in life.'

Fewer than half the UK population had a driving licence in 1973; the number has now grown to 74 per cent. The main vehicle of choice was the Ford Cortina Mark III, which, after 1972, was the country's most popular car for nine years. The second best-selling car was the Ford Escort, followed by the Morris Marina and Vauxhall Viva. The motif accompanying adverts for Humbers reflected the purchase as a lifestyle choice: 'Drive a Humber – be a somebody'.

Football, rugby and cricket pitches in Rochdale were busy every weekend, depending on the season. The council's parks department had sufficient staff to tend these pitches and the policy of selling off land for housing or retail hadn't yet been established. On any given weekend, nearly 60 football teams and almost 700 players participated in five distinct leagues – Rochdale Amateur, Littleborough Sunday, Middleton Sunday,

Sunday Schools' and the Rochdale Sunday. Teams were formed at work (Alderglen, Fothergill & Harvey, Whittles, etc.); pubs (Blue Ball, Lark, Woolpack); churches (St Gabriel's, Spotland Methodists, Torchbearers); working men's clubs (Wellfield, Milnrow); or were stand-alone clubs (Whitworth Valley, Rochdale Athletic). Sports bags at their feet, players gathered at meeting points – in pub and club car parks, at the Town Hall Square or outside Electric House (the showroom in Smith Street), waiting to scramble into the back of Ford Transits or Bedford CF vans heading to away matches.

* * *

Cliques were endemic and unavoidable in all squads of footballers. The aim of the coaching staff was to meld them as much as possible, especially on matchdays. No other workplace was similar, where a 17-year-old could earn more than a 35-year-old but have only played a handful of matches, or where someone of low self-esteem or intelligence could be exalted as a hero, a man among men, for an hour and a half every Saturday. Or, alternatively, someone of high self-esteem and intelligence could be the subject of mockery and ribaldry on that same pitch.

Before Walter Joyce had arrived at Spotland, the senior pros hadn't viewed themselves particularly as a clique – they recognised it as a pejorative term – but as merely a group of colleagues who enjoyed each other's company. Only now, through what they were hearing and how they were feeling, did they sense that they were being banded together, judged as one. 'I think he's after the lot of us,' Colin Blant told Bill Atkins. 'How do you mean?' asked Atkins. Blant responded, 'Anyone over the age of about 25 has had it – he's going to try to build the club from the bottom up.' 'He can't do that – he's going to need some experience, someone to bring the young lads on.' 'I'm not sure, you know.'

* * *

Local newspapers were thriving in the 1970s with a prodigious breadth of stories. They had a near monopoly of local news coverage and were well staffed with a wide circulation.

Many of the news pieces in the *Rochdale Observer* reflected a latchkey culture. Children were often 'run over' by cars while playing out or when 'nipping to the shop'. Vandalism was rife, especially acts of arson. Most weeks, a garden shed, storage hut, stable or even a house was set alight. Children went 'missing', usually to be found a few days later, often at the home of a relative or friend. Fires were common, perhaps because smoking was more prevalent and there were fewer safety checks on energy appliances and items of furniture; families were regularly pictured amid their burnt-out belongings. Severe industrial accidents – workers burned by acid, lorries backing into (or over) people in yards, limbs caught fast in machines – were regular occurrences. A former Rochdale player, Joe Richardson, aged 32 at the time, was killed in such an incident when he was struck by a lorry carrying 15 tons of coal after it collided with a stationary brewery wagon in Haslingden. Bomb hoaxes were common, possibly influenced by the Troubles in Northern Ireland. There were more fatal car crashes (wearing a seat belt wasn't compulsory until January 1983) and suicides; maybe it appeared this way because inquests were covered in extensive detail.

People staring out of newspaper pages looked older than their stated age. 'Leisure wear' had yet to arrive, which would see teenagers and 40-somethings in similar T-shirts, sweatshirts and joggers. Many young men had long, feather-cut hair, usually with a moustache. Most sported stack-heeled shoes. Few had beards (apart from schoolteachers) and there were barely any 'buzz cuts', shaved heads ('chrome domes' as they were known locally) or, alternatively, evidence of the use of hair gel. Men over 30 routinely wore a suit, their hair side-parted and flattened down. There were plenty of 'comb-overs'. The jumpers, on boys and girls, had stars on the front or squiggly lines similar to interference on a television. 'Pretty' and 'attractive' girls were photographed in sashes, usually after being nominated as carnival queens at factories or working men's clubs. Rose queens were elected to represent individual churches or chapels. Blacked-up white women, sometimes referred to as 'mammies', were pictured lifting their palms to the camera at fetes and open days; *The Black and White Minstrel Show*, watched by up to 16 million viewers each week, ran on BBC1 until 1978. Newspaper photographs were often teeming with faces, whether pensioners about to board a coach to Blackpool or infants on their first day at school. Few people carried cameras, so there was a social cachet in being featured in your local paper – it increased sales, and newspapers supplemented income by selling black-and-white photographs at the front counter.

* * *

Outside of football, the friendship between several senior pros at Rochdale had been forged at dog tracks, specifically the Albion Greyhound Racecourse in Salford and the Owlerton course in Sheffield. Both Dick Conner and Peter Madden had been regulars, especially at Salford, and were often joined by Colin Blant and Dick Renwick. Blant was especially keen and owned three racing greyhounds. 'Colin loved going to the dogs,' said Pauline, his wife. 'I'm not sure how it used to happen and how I allowed it to happen but he used to have one of them sitting in the front seat when we drove home from the track, while I was in the back!'

Walter Joyce had learned of these nights out; little remained unspoken or unknown within a football club, although there was, of course, no reason why a few colleagues enjoying downtime together should remain a secret. He kept quiet, however, so that Colin Blant, Dick Renwick, Bill Atkins and Rod Jones were left second-guessing on how their camaraderie was viewed.

This was nothing new to them; it happened at every club with every manager. They didn't take it personally (although it was, paradoxically, highly personal) because your 'face fitting' (or not) at a club often felt as random as the spin of a bottle. Managers were almost impossible to read. All players had been at clubs where a manager had ignored them for weeks or blasted them continually in training, but then they had been told he planned to 'build a team around them'. Likewise, they had been told session after session how brilliant, how vital, how bloody wonderful they were, only to be stuck on the bench or sent with the reserves to play at Barrow or Carlisle in a snowstorm.

Still, they looked for clues, a word said here and there, a gesture, to at least give them an inkling as to how and where they stood. If it wasn't good (i.e. they were unlikely to be picked), they each knew the horrible rigmarole of what came next: phone a few pals, find a club, move the family somewhere else in the country (hopefully relatively nearby) or find digs on a dark, dusty estate in Aldershot or Colchester, somewhere no one ever went to, aside from footballers.

Colin Blant had more of a reason than the others to be concerned about another move forced upon him. He'd bought a newsagents business in Heywood from his brother, with a view to life after football. Everyone that knew him, his love for football, his pride, was aware that he wouldn't be prepared to languish in Rochdale's reserves, content to pick up a wage.

* * *

Shops and stores had traditionally clustered in or around town centres but in the early 1970s retail outlets began to be established in outlying areas, often close to dual carriageways. Comet opened in Well I' Th' Lane, Deeplish, selling a wide range of electrical goods – televisions, dishwashers, tape recorders, fridges, etc. On special discount was a Bush 26-inch colour television at £339; most people still rented televisions at the time because they were so expensive. Radio Rentals in Yorkshire Street offered a Baird colour 19-inch television (with stand) for £1.48 per month, promising 'all your money back if you're not satisfied'.

Asda was the first superstore in Rochdale, followed by Tesco in December 1973. The purpose-built site in Silk Street, Sudden, covered 30,000 sq. ft. and sold 6,000 grocery lines. The manager, Michael Tarpey, aged 27, used PR-speak (most likely supplied by an agency): 'As a family man myself, I am well acquainted with family shopping problems and well equipped to help others solve them.' These outlets were on a mission to initiate a new way of shopping. Tesco provided a free bus to the store, leaving Rochdale Town Hall every 30 minutes on Thursdays, Fridays and Saturdays. Anyone buying six gallons or more of petrol received a ticket for a free car wash. These inducements were in addition to prices that smaller supermarkets and corner shops couldn't match – loaf of bread 12p, packet of cornflakes 15p, 'home-produced' chuck or blade steak 46p and, in the home 'n' wear section, cotton-covered foam-filled pillows at 39p each.

Until the late 1960s, most petrol stations were of basic construction – often a small hut/office containing a till and oil-smudged papers with perhaps a calendar on the wall and, outside, one or two manned pumps. The first off-motorway 'service station' arrived in Rochdale in 1973. Speedwell Garage opened in Milnrow Road with full-page adverts taken out in local newspapers. Terry Whitworth, Speedwell's managing director, announced that the station included a canopy, two blender pumps with four grades of petrol (supplied by ICI, at 34p per gallon) and a shop. 'Whether you come to buy a new Renault or a half a gallon of petrol, you can be sure of a cheerful and courteous greeting,' he promised. As an example of this geniality, the advert carried a photograph of two chuckling women, Marlene and Sandra, who were 'on hand to serve you'.

* * *

The players were asked whether they'd had a good wash and brushed their teeth. Frank Campbell hurried them along, clapping his hands as their studs click-clacked on the concrete between the dressing room and the pitch. 'Come on, lads. Give us your best smiles. Make your mams proud.'

It was team photo day, the day they would remember all season, the day they would think back to and recall the warm fresh air, the larking about, the thick grass and, most of all, the optimism. They were positioned in front of the Main Stand, the big lads standing at the back, mediums sitting on a bench and four young apprentices on their knees at the front. By virtue of being in the middle of the middle row, a ball was planted at the feet of Bobby Downes. 'How come you get to have the ball, Downesy?' 'Because I'm the only one who knows what to fucking do with it!' They each gave their names to the photographer. 'Leopold Skeete.' 'Leopold Skeete?' mocked a team-mate. 'Who's that?' 'Me! That's who that is.' 'I thought you were called Leo.' Skeete shook his head in disbelief.

They looked the same as any other football squad photographed in the early 1970s: feather cuts, sideburns and Zapata moustaches. Unlike their modern counterparts, there were no tattoos and they were much thinner, built for running rather than wrestling. The only feature differentiating them – the 24 players chosen to represent Rochdale AFC through the 1973/74 season – from almost every other club, was the shirts they were wearing. Since their formation in 1907, Rochdale had worn shirts of three distinct colours (in effect, the club's branding): black-and-white stripes, blue, and white. In 1973/74 they were to wear a very conspicuous kit – all white with, on the shirt, a sash of blue and yellow running from the left shoulder to the waist. The sash had been a feature of club strips in South America, although nearby Manchester City had adopted it a couple of years earlier; this was thought to have influenced Rochdale's decision.

This striking kit meant that, unlike previous and future generations of Rochdale teams, these particular players wouldn't be lost in a smudge of blue or white but would remain forever distinct. On that team photo day of August 1973, a few of the players remarked how trendy they looked, how chic. But this wasn't to be the sash of the champion, hurriedly draped over the shoulder at the finishing line; it became the insignia of one of sport's most inglorious losers.

* * *

Rochdale had a long-established Irish community, many of whom became anxious as the IRA carried out the relentless bombing campaign during 1973 and 1974. The original Irish settlers had been invited to work in the town by John Bright, the wealthy mill owner, Quaker, MP and social reformer. He provided houses for them at Mizzy Buildings, Larkhill Place in Healey and in the district of Wardleworth, which became known as the Irish Quarter. Rumours spread among locals about the alleged amorality and bedraggled state of these incomers. They kept pigs, they heard, with whom they played and slept. They were said to participate in 'clogging', where men would strip to the waist and kick each other while wearing clogs. The first to kick his opponent unconscious was declared the winner and bets paid out accordingly.

John McKenna, a man of Irish descent – furthermore, a member of a 'secret political society' – committed a brutal murder that became part of the town's folklore for decades. McKenna, a 25-year-old plasterer, attacked his pregnant wife, Anna, while drunk, banging her head on stone tiles and 'leaving her with a mass of fearful black bruises' according to the police report. News of the murder spread quickly and, within an hour, hundreds had gathered at the house in Dawson Square, near the town centre. Police officers had to stand firm across the door to stop them forcing entry, so desperate were they to see the corpse.

McKenna fled to Liverpool, where his parents lived, but was arrested within a day or so.

He was found guilty of murder and sentenced to death by hanging. While at Strangeways Prison awaiting execution, McKenna was visited several times by a local priest, Father Corbishley. McKenna asked the priest to pass on his worldly possessions, a suit and a pocket watch inscribed 'John McKenna, Plasterer, Rochdale' to his brother, Charles. He also requested that his daughter, 'a very intelligent girl of about five', be placed with Charles, who planned to travel to the United States in search of work. Father Corbishley told the *Rochdale Times* that McKenna 'had spoken in terms of gratitude of the kindness he had received from the authorities at Rochdale'. He was hanged on 27 March 1877 by William Marwood, the executioner famous for his 'long drop' method, whereby the prisoner's neck broke instantly, causing him or her to asphyxiate while unconscious.

The press was invited to witness the hanging and it had a profound effect on an uncredited journalist from the *Rochdale Observer*, who had reported on the episode from the outset, even attending the post-mortem. In closing his piece, he wrote:

> Are we as a community indirectly responsible for this enormity? I am afraid we are. Certain classes are allowed to herd in cellar dwellings, amid the most vile and indecent surroundings. No effort is made to get this low class to take an interest in nobler and more purifying amusements than sitting in the beer house till they become dead drunk, fighting, dog racing, tossing, other forms of gambling, and ruinous vices. Until something is done for this class, which has no elevating power in itself, we must expect to have a plague spot in our community, a horde of savages to make society insecure and fill our gaols

with criminals, to be maintained at great cost by the nation.

Soon after McKenna's death, neighbours in Dawson Square (now demolished) claimed to see the ghost of Anna, walking the cobbled streets crying, 'Please don't kill me.'

6

Moto-Psycho Nightmare

ANDREW HARRISON was 15 years old in 1973 and, the same as most Rochdale supporters, anticipated the sound of the *Rochdale Observer* dropping through the letterbox on Wednesday and Saturday mornings with news about Rochdale AFC. He read the back page on Saturday, August 25 and phoned his grandad, Clarence Holding, immediately. 'Have you seen the paper? Blant's been dropped,' he said. 'Has he? I wonder why that is,' replied Clarence. 'Joyce says he wants to build a team of young players,' said Andrew. His grandad fell quiet for a moment before responding, 'Not sure that's such a good idea.'

Clarence had first taken Andrew, then aged six, to Spotland in 1964. 'I loved it straight away,' said Andrew. 'Everything about it – the smell of the turf and Wintergreen coming from the dressing rooms. Night matches under the floodlights were especially great. I loved the buzz, the excitement. I used to walk from Heybrook where we lived and catch one of the football special buses facing the town hall.'

In his teenage years he'd adopted what he called 'the uniform of acceptance' – the clothes young supporters wore on the terraces. These included Skinners jeans (advertised as 24-inch parallel leg, heavy blue denim or drill cloth in white, navy or black, selling at £3.95 per pair, plus 25p postage. Girls were advised to 'order one size larger'); loafers (slip-on shoes, originally designed as a slipper but increasingly worn outdoors to 'loaf around in'); or Doc Marten oxblood quilon 1461 shoes with yellow stitching; and Harrington jackets ('as worn by James Dean') – a lightweight, waist-length jacket made of cotton, polyester, wool or suede with designs often incorporating traditional Fraser tartan or checkerboard-patterned lining. Andrew affixed a Lancashire red rose to the lapel. To complete the outfit, a pair of red socks was obligatory.

The band most associated with the look and given almost universal approval was Slade, who, by the summer of 1973, had scored five number-one hits, including: 'Mama Weer All Crazee Now' and 'Cum On Feel the Noize'. 'I liked to dress that way,' said Harrison. 'But I wasn't a bovver boy; I'm not a fighter. It was just that almost everyone under the age of about 20 dressed that way back in the 1970s.'

He was a regular visitor to the 'soccer shop' at Spotland, a small space at the rear of the Main Stand where the dropping down of a wooden counter, before and after matches, revealed that it was open for business. Items on offer included rosettes, scarves, tiepins, ashtrays and gonks – novelty toys with small, spherical bodies, a furry texture and two googly eyes (Wikipedia). Scarves weren't usually worn in the traditional way but more often tied to the wrist or tucked into the side of flared trousers. Replica shirts weren't available in the 1970s. They had been introduced by Umbro in the late 1950s but only in child sizes and were worn when *playing* football, rather than as a fan's statement of allegiance. Famously, a handful of adult Newcastle United supporters were photographed in replica shirts at the 1974 FA Cup Final against Liverpool but this was considered 'fancy dress'.

As he pulled on his matchday clobber, Harrison was excited about the new season, keen to see the new signings but also perplexed that Colin Blant, one of his favourite players, wasn't going to be in the team.

* * *

Over the years, the Irish in Rochdale had integrated with locals until a surname was often the only indication that someone had originated from elsewhere. The IRA's activities in the early 1970s, however, had stirred tensions and suspicions from a century earlier. In March 1973, bombs planted outside the Old Bailey and Whitehall left more than 200 wounded. The targets were widespread and included train stations, Royal Mail sorting offices, shopping centres, pubs and even postboxes. These attacks were often carried out by 'sleeper cells' – groups living in secret among a targeted community waiting for instructions or an opportunity to act. This meant that anyone known or assumed to have Irish connections (most of whom were innocent of any wrongdoing, of course) was placed under suspicion.

Several families in Rochdale endured police raids in the dead of night. Six officers arrived at the home of Mike Thornhill in Kirkholt at 4.30am. They made his four-year-old daughter get out of bed while they searched the house for several hours, even opening Christmas presents and tipping out the contents of his wife's make-up bag. Mr Thornhill, from Cork, said, 'I'm a staunch republican but I'm not an IRA man. But it's treatment like this that drives people to join organisations.'

Tommy McGrath was having treatment for a heart condition in hospital when his house was raided. He'd left his three children, the eldest being 17, home alone for the night; their grandmother was set to arrive the next day. He said police had shouted through the letterbox, 'Get up you Irish bastards and wash yourselves, we want to talk to you.' They questioned the children for two hours. Another man whose house was raided on the same morning was a member of the Rochdale branch of Clann na hÉireann, a support organisation for Sinn Féin among Irish emigrants in Great Britain. Police searched cupboards and drawers, read letters and papers, and scrutinised photographs. They found a sheet of paper with shorthand written on it and asked whether it was Gaelic. They left, taking 'suspicious materials' with them – a booklet published by the TUC (Trades Union Congress) and a diary containing names, addresses and phone numbers of friends and relatives.

At each raid, special branch officers had shown a search warrant signed by a JP on the pretext of 'acting on anonymous information that there are explosives on the premises'. Peter Atkinson, secretary of the Rochdale Communist party, spoke out against the police's tactics: 'It seems incredible that these Gestapo-type raids can be authorised on the basis of such vague evidence. The fear, shock and worry caused to innocent people cannot possibly be justified. If the police are allowed to get away with this kind of action without the severest criticism, then many political, religious and racial groups may well find themselves subjected to the same treatment in the near future.'

* * *

Rochdale took to the field on the opening day of the season in their new strip. The editorial in the match programme was effusive: 'Yes, the Dale are going continental! So, whatever happens, you will be watching a NEW LOOK ROCHDALE this season!' This buoyant tone was matched by Walter Joyce in his manager's notes: 'I want Rochdale to win promotion THIS SEASON! But I've got to admit it's a tall order.'

Brighton, as Joyce had expected, were a strong team. They moved the ball quickly and their game was channelled to Ken Beamish, a wily forward from Liverpool who had been signed by Pat Saward, Brighton's manager 'because he had the devil in him'. Beamish and fellow striker Barry Bridges linked well and Brighton took the lead before half-time, with Bridges slotting home. Rochdale were awarded a penalty but Malcolm Darling struck the crossbar. Minutes later, a shot by Darling was parried by the goalkeeper, Brian Powney, but Darling followed it up and scored the equaliser.

Joyce was pleased after the match, patting the players on the back as they left the pitch. He followed them in. 'You've done well today, lads,' he told them. 'There's a few in that side who can put it about a bit but you've lived with them, held your own. Play like that and we'll be more than fine this season, I promise you.'

* * *

The streets of Rochdale were distinctly unsafe in the summer of 1973, with foe drawn from the animal kingdom on the loose – dogs, rats and a monkey. A pack of more than a dozen fierce dogs was roaming the Kirkholt estate. A resident said, 'We are woken up in the night by these dogs and can no longer enjoy a peaceful Sunday afternoon because of the barking.' A 13-year-old paperboy was bitten and had his shirt torn. A butcher said a dog went into his shop and snatched a breast of lamb from the window. A spokesman for Rochdale Corporation offered scant solace to residents who said they were afraid to leave their homes: 'There had been a plan to create a dog catching service but to keep the rates down we have had to cut back on spending and shelve this idea. At the moment we have no facilities for dealing with the problem of stray dogs.'

Enid Ashworth of Thornhill, Ashfield Valley, reported that a young boy had killed a rat outside her front door and neighbours had seen 'a great big rat' scurrying around. 'We have complained about it but I don't know what else we can do. Some of us are frightened to death,' said Mrs Ashworth. She said the infestation was because the bin room was locked at night and rubbish left outside. Mr Harold Syson, Rochdale's Housing Director, acknowledged the issue: 'The problem of rats has arisen on occasion.'

Stuart Ratcliffe, son of Fred, wasn't the only person in Rochdale to own a monkey. Cheeky, a six-year-old macaque, belonged to the children's entertainer, Bunny Baker of Greave Avenue, and was kept inside a cage in his garden. Mr Baker was about to take the stage at Hamer Youth Club when staff at the venue received a call informing them that Cheeky had escaped. Before Mr Baker could reach home, the monkey attacked Mrs Norah Barnes, who had been making her way to a bus stop. 'It gave me a terrible bite in my left leg which started pouring with blood and then it bit my right leg. I fell down and was laid in a pool of blood. I couldn't get up,' she said. As he tried to recapture the monkey, Mr Baker received cuts to his hands. 'He went berserk,' he said. 'I could see the danger and went for him. We had to kill him. It didn't mean to hurt anyone.'

* * *

As the players dressed after the Brighton match, Walter Joyce turned to Frank Campbell, who was crouched, dipping a sponge into cold water and holding it against the knee of Paul Brears. The 18-year-old midfielder, a player Joyce and Campbell had worked with in the youth set-up at Oldham, had taken a 'whack' 25 minutes into the first half. A few Rochdale fans said they weren't surprised at his lack of resistance to such tackles, describing him in almost Dickensian terms as 'weak and under-nourished'. Within the club, he was known as a lad who 'kept himself to himself' and was happy in his own company. At one training session his absence hadn't been noted until he was spotted reading a book up in the stand. 'How is it, Paul?' asked Joyce, pointing to the swollen knee. Before Brears could answer, Campbell replied. 'He'll be right, boss. Just a knock.'

Brears stood up and turned to unhook his day clothes from the peg. While Brears was looking elsewhere, Campbell attracted Joyce's attention. He grimaced and shook his head; Joyce knew what this meant. Brears had damaged his ligaments. The 'best' knee injury was caused by a clean impact, either bone on bone with another player or from the side – a solid kick from an opponent trying to clear the ball but striking the knee instead, for instance. These caused bruising and were sore for a week or two but healed quickly. The 'worst' was any contact that also included the knee twisting, causing damage to the ligaments and cartilage. Brears had heard older pros talk about their knees 'ballooning up' and then later, after the inevitable operation and months of rehabilitation, how they felt to have a small 'bag of spanners' where their knee used to be.

He limped towards the players' lounge, trying to return a smile at every issue of 'get well soon' or 'hope you're okay, lad'. He'd recently bought a Triumph Spitfire and insisted he'd be able to drive it back to his home in Oldham. After the weekend, he was put under the 'magic lamp' (infrared heat therapy) for a couple of days but by the middle of the week the pain was unbearable. He was admitted to hospital and underwent surgery to have the cartilage reattached. Joyce told the press he'd be back after a couple of months but those 25 minutes on that dust-dry August pitch would be the only ones he'd spend playing football all season.

* * *

Haight-Ashbury was 5,000 miles from Rochdale but the revolution it inspired, via London of the mid-1960s (*Time* magazine, April 1966 – 'London: The Swinging City'), had a marked impact on the town's cultural life. The blueprint of a nonconformist, progressive outlook – free love, widespread drugs use, equality for all, anything goes – had become a global movement, from the sunlit boulevards of California and side streets of Soho to the gable ends and ginnels of south-east Lancashire. Those professing to be 'switched on' were labelled, either by themselves or the media in different parts of the world, as hippies, flower children, heads, drop-outs, stoners, freaks, bohemians, beatniks or peaceniks. The doctrine of birth-school-work-death handed down from parents was being challenged by a generation that wanted more of everything that was creative, spiritual, sensual and exciting. A large sector of the youth of

Rochdale had banded together to form a community of the like-minded and it was flourishing in 1973.

They congregated at pubs where jukeboxes were stocked with 'cool' music and the landlord or landlady had no issue about how their clientele was dressed. Albums were de rigueur, with few hippy-endorsed bands releasing singles. This meant those groups that did issue the odd single – Hawkwind ('Silver Machine'), Black Sabbath ('Paranoid'), Deep Purple ('Black Night') and Jethro Tull ('Living in the Past') – were on heavy rotation. The Coach and Horses in Lord Street was a popular hang-out and many Rochdale 'heads' travelled to Heywood, to The Dressers Arms or The Seven Stars, where Be-Bop Deluxe, Judas Priest and Supertramp played early in their careers. Rochdale's blind guitarist, Tony Crabtree, was a regular performer at these and other local venues. Many formed their own groups – Dead Sheep, Howard the Duck, Screaming Warthog, among many more – or bought acoustic guitars, fancying themselves as Bob Dylan or Joni Mitchell. They shopped at outlets selling 'the gear', whether clothes or the paraphernalia of drugs use or similar 'mood setters' – incense sticks, crystals, resins, scented candles, patchouli oil, Buddha figurines, etc. Rochdale developed a reputation for its preponderance of drugs and dependable trade network, which led to users and dealers from much bigger towns and cities making regular visits.

Barry Fitton was a principal 'head', one of the first in town to wholeheartedly embrace hippy culture. He'd been brought up in a council house in Kirkholt, where he was often beaten by his father. He suffered similarly at school where 'being a chubby guy in glasses' led him to become a 'bullies' punch bag'. In 1969, in his early 20s, he'd travelled through Pakistan and Afghanistan, giving impromptu readings of his poems in exchange for a meal or bed for the night. Bearded, long-haired and usually wearing a floppy leather hat, he looked the part; he was sometimes mistaken for two godheads of the international hippy scene, Jerry Garcia and Allen Ginsberg. Another easily spotted in the town was Pete Bird, aka Pete No Danger. He'd drink in the Burns Tavern, Bamford, before either walking or boarding a bus to the town centre. His drunken state and tatty clothing might have been alarming but to set people at ease he frequently bellowed, 'No Danger.'

Hair was worn almost universally long in bohemian circles, principally as a reaction to the close-crops forced upon many during army life; National Service had ended only a decade earlier. In Rochdale, a hairdressing war was under way with each salon outbidding their rivals from a few doors along the street. Astra at Drake Street boasted of the arrival of Kenneth Silva (probably not his real name) to their team, pictured on posters with extremely bouffant hair. He'd come to Rochdale 'direct from his successful tour of the USA', where he was a personal stylist to the cast of the stage show, *Godspell*. He'd also 'dressed' the hair of 'world famous stars including Robert Wagner, Natalie Wood, Irene Demich [more likely, Irina Demick, the French actress], etc., etc.' Kauffman International (Salons) Limited in Yorkshire Street announced a half-price sale with haircuts at £1.50. Clients were encouraged to 'book now and avoid disappointment' if they wanted a cut by Collette or their 'international stylist', Brenda, 'who specialises in cutting'. Across town at Juniper Hair Fashions in School Lane, the business was under new management and offered a pragmatic slant: 'car parking nearby'.

* * *

Rochdale raced into a four-goal lead before half-time at Spotland against Hartlepool United in the first round of the Football League Cup. Up in the press box, Stan Townsend hardly had time to write down the names of the scorers before the net was bulging again; his pre-season prophecy was coming true. Afterwards, he wrote: 'Hartlepool were completely bemused by the lightning Rochdale attacks which began to rip them apart at the seams. They floundered and panicked in midfield leaving huge holes for the home side to explore at their discretion.' Walter Joyce didn't understate: 'In the first 40 minutes we played some of the best football that has ever been played on this ground,' he said. The match ended 5-3.

Although Rochdale had started the match brightly and won, 14-year-old David Gartside, sitting with his grandad, Norman Gartside, in seats E15 and E16 of the A Stand (the Main Stand was sub-divided, A and B, and, with 800 seats, had the lowest seating capacity in the Football League; the roof was made from asbestos), responded differently to Stan Townsend and Walter Joyce. He sensed all was not well. 'It was the way we so easily conceded those goals in the second half. I thought there and then, "We're going to have a problem this season,"' he said.

Gartside had been introduced to Rochdale by his grandad, a fruit and vegetables wholesaler who had long held a season ticket at Spotland. Typically, Rochdale had lost the first match David attended: 3-0 against Orient in August 1969. 'I was devastated. I'd never heard of Orient before and assumed we'd win,' he said. 'I remember the strong smell of Woodbine. Nearly everybody smoked then. There were always seven or eight of those blue invalid carriages [Invacars] parked up really close to the pitch.'

He was often more enraptured by the goings-on around him than the football; his grandad insisted they were in their seats 45 minutes before kick-off, as if to make the most of this badinage. 'Bovril was the chosen drink and the place stunk of it. This tiny man sat near to us and absolutely hated referees. All through the match he'd shout at them, "You dozy hen!" One fellow had a radio plugged in his ear and a match programme in his hand. He was peering at the match programme, taking his glasses on and off, fiddling with his ear and the radio. He must have barely seen any of the game. It really was like *One Flew Over the Cuckoo's Nest*. Having said that, I felt I was among friends at

Spotland and we all shared the common desire of wanting to see Rochdale win,' said Gartside.

* * *

RAP functioned as a notice board for Rochdale's cultural and artistic factions. Concerts, events, openings, get-togethers and happenings were all listed within its pages. Every Monday evening, the Rochdale Film Society (entrance fee 40p) showed left-field films at Rochdale Art Gallery. Among its offerings in the late summer of 1973 was *Fat City*, directed by John Huston – a 'bleak, mordant, slice-of-life boxing drama that doesn't pull its punches' and *W.R.: Mysteries of the Organism* by Serbian director Dušan Makavejev, a film 'exploring the relationship between communist politics and sexuality'. At Rochdale College, Professor Dennis Welland of the University of Manchester was giving a speech on the 'Poetry of the First World War', while, at the same venue a few days later, the social historian, Professor Harold Perkin, was due to lecture on the Rochdale Pioneers. At Rochdale Library, Joseph Cooper, chairman of the BBC television panel game *Face the Music* was hosting an evening dubbed 'Face the music of Schumann'.

Much of Rochdale's alternative scene emanated from Rochdale College of Art, which had been transformed by Leo Solomon, a charismatic and visionary figure. Before he was appointed principal in July 1953, there had been discussions about the college's possible closure. On his first day in the job, there were nine full-time students, 90 part-time and two members of staff who worked limited hours. Solomon asked the full-time students, soon numbering more than 200, to supply him with passport-sized photographs to help him remember their names and faces. 'It's no use being a demagogue in an ivory tower when you are dealing with young, intelligent people whose future is in your hands,' he said. 'Students want to be aware that a personal interest is being taken in them and their work.'

His great ally was the town's former mayor, Charlie Crowder, chairman of the education committee. Crowder's father had died when Charlie was four years old and, to help support the family, he'd worked in a mill rather than take up secondary education. 'My home background had the effect of making me want something better for other people,' he said. Before Cardiff-born Solomon came to town, other councillors had referred to the art college as 'Crowder's Folly', but by the early 1970s it had almost 200 full-time students, 550 part-timers and 26 staff, covering all aspects of art, from traditional painting to silver-smithing. The foundation course was particularly eminent and attracted students from throughout the country and sometimes abroad. 'I wanted to build up the cultural climate in Rochdale,' said Solomon. He succeeded.

* * *

One of Rochdale's goals against Hartlepool had been scored by Alan Taylor, a winger who had been one of Fred O'Donoghue's first recommendations to the club. O'Donoghue had been struck by Taylor's pace and capacity to 'rat' defenders, constantly snapping at their ankles and hurrying them into clearances. Initially, O'Donoghue had been doubtful of his judgement because Taylor was struggling to make Morecambe's first team in the Northern Premier League. Earlier, he'd been released by Alan Ball Sr when he was manager at Preston North End; Ball had nearly 25 years' experience in the game and seldom let good players slip his grasp. Ball felt that Taylor, weighing nine and a half stone, was too slight to thrive in lower-league football.

O'Donoghue took several trusted pals to see Taylor play, including the ex-Darwen player Sean Gallagher, and Stan Howard of Chorley. They each reported back positively, both mentioning his speed, particularly from a standing start. Angus McLean was also impressed, although he only saw him play for 20 minutes; Taylor was taken off injured while playing for Morecambe against Scarborough.

The deal to sign Taylor was negotiated in the former coaching inn, the Bull and Royal, in Preston town centre; Taylor, aged 19, lived a few miles away in Bolton-le-Sands, near Carnforth. A significant number had gathered around the table with the player, including his father; Morecambe's chairman, Harry Baines; *three* Morecambe directors; and the delegation from Rochdale – O'Donoghue, Conner and McLean. Baines made great play of the fact that Everton had inquired about Taylor and had invited him to Goodison Park for a month's trial. McLean told them that bigger clubs often did this but it rarely led to a permanent transfer. 'Have they offered any money to either Alan or Morecambe?' he asked. 'No,' they chorused. 'Well then, take that as an indication of how interested they are,' he said.

Morecambe accepted a transfer fee of £2,500 to be paid at £500 per month over five months. Taylor agreed to leave his apprenticeship as a mechanic to become a full-time footballer. Dick Conner was completing his last piece of significant business while Rochdale's manager. He told the press, 'We've had him watched four or five times during the last two months and we liked what we saw.'

* * *

The Rochdale Sculptors was formed by Peter Wolstenholme, a lecturer at Rochdale College of Art and winner of the *Daily Telegraph*-sponsored Young Sculptor of the Year award. His first accomplice was fellow lecturer and soon-to-be *RAP* cartoonist, Tony Smart. Both men had arrived in town, from Sheffield and London, respectively, to work at the college. This was a feature of life in the 1960s and 1970s – university graduates, chiefly from middle-class backgrounds, were prepared to locate to wherever they found a job, especially in the creative field. 'I came up on the overnight train from London for the interview, getting into Manchester at 7am, maybe earlier than that, and then catching a train to Rochdale. I remember going past all these dark satanic mills. It was raining and I'd never seen such a place as that. I should have known from Lowry paintings, I suppose,' said Smart.

Such was their attire and laid-back disposition, lecturers were often indistinguishable from students. 'I just wanted a permanent job based around art and one that I liked,' said Smart. 'I don't know what I was expecting but it was better than being a postman or working in a cemetery. The fact that the job was in Rochdale was intriguing more than anything. Peter [Wolstenholme] arrived a year or so after me to teach pottery and was saying that nobody ever goes to art galleries, or hardly anyone. His idea was to have art on the street where people could bump up against it – not a war memorial but something a bit more interesting.'

The group grew to include Barry Hobson, Walter Kershaw, Brian Woods, Danny Milne, Christine Pearson and Robin Forrester. Their sculptures appeared regularly along the Esplanade – a wide walkway across from the town hall. They often slept out in a tent fixed to the pavement to guard exhibits such as Moto-Psycho Nightmare, The Four Horsemen of the Apocalypse, Dolly Dickie Dodo and Our Gracie's Place – a pyramid made from baked bean cans. Some joked that more time and thought went into the titles than actually making the sculptures. One of the pieces, The Man in the Iron Beast, was attacked by vandals while displayed outside Heywood Civic Hall. Afterwards, the group held a mock funeral to mark its passing.

The group was funded by the Arts Council and North West Arts and based at first in a disused chapel in Durham Street, Deeplish, before moving to Hunter's Lane in the town centre. It had a clear mission statement: 'These vital visual arts are increasingly the products of contemporary life and may reflect or reject it. Some are humorous, others cool. Maybe they provoke thought as much as judgement: what is of greater importance to you, the people of Rochdale, is that they are made locally – not Rome, New York, or London. A sculptural renaissance has happened here.'

Much of the work was designed to agitate and didn't disappoint. Walter Kershaw, who later became a renowned painter of urban murals, received censure from *The Guardian*. His exhibit, 'Prime Cuts' – a female mannequin painted in 'meaty' colours as a skit of a butcher's chart – was deemed 'hideous'. On publicity photographs, the group's only female member, Christine Pearson, clipped a flesh-coloured cast over her clothes, which gave the appearance that she was naked from above the waist. Cyril Smith, then a local councillor, said it was an 'absolute disgrace', especially considering she was a 'mother of three'.

* * *

Rochdale had played with flair and intent against Hartlepool but they showed another quality at Walsall in a 0-0 draw. In football terminology, they dug in, closed down, stayed tight, covered the runs and shut out their opponents. They barely created a scoring opportunity but, at a time when a win was rewarded with only two points, an away draw was coveted, especially if a goal hadn't been conceded. 'We're doing alright, aren't we?' said Joyce. Dennis Butler recognised the wider implication of the statement; Joyce was referring to his decision to trust the younger players, leaving out experienced pros. 'So far, but it's early days,' warned Butler.

Only Graham Smith and Dennis Butler, as long-serving members of staff, were able to contrast the players forming Rochdale's current squad with those who had won promotion four years earlier. Butler, in particular, felt the standard had dropped appreciably. 'The talent wasn't there in the early 1970s.

We looked and looked but we couldn't pick up young players with enough talent. You can coach them all you want and get them fitter and stronger but you can't bring out what is not there,' he said.

Another factor, he felt, was that the abolition of the maximum wage for footballers in January 1961 had led to an influx of accomplished players into lower-league clubs. When the maximum wage had stood at £20 per week, bigger clubs had 'stockpiled' players and many had up to 50 professionals on their books – this was why several amassed hundreds of appearances in reserve-team football. When clubs were suddenly faced with wage demands commensurate with a player's age, experience and ability, squad numbers were cut, meaning scores of well-coached, professionally minded players were released to join clubs further down the leagues. 'We had some very good players in that promotion team,' said Butler. 'But by 1973 the lads being released by the top clubs were much younger and largely untried. We were also having trouble finding players from non-league which had always been a good source.'

* * *

The counter-culture fostered by the art college and Rochdale Sculptors led to the opening of several 'head' shops. Barry Fitton, back after living nomadically for several years, took over a 'space' (the term was in popular usage at the time) with other poets at 6A Hunter's Lane, the home of the Rochdale Sculptors. The shop was called Axis and income was used to cover overheads and make donations to cat rescue charities. They sold books and leaflets, spanning treatises such as Jeff Nuttall's *Bomb Culture* to advice for new adopters of a macrobiotic diet.

Fitton was living in Bellshill Crescent on the council estate at Belfield with his new wife, Joyce, described by acquaintances as 'a mad American'; the marriage didn't last long. 'She was tall and thin and a typically laid-back Californian chick,' said a friend. 'Back then, Belfield was quite a place. People had coal in the bath, that sort of thing and a lot of gypsies were living there, so you got shire horses roaming free or tied to fences.' In the evenings, Fitton and his accomplices worked on a poetry magazine, also called *Axis*. Proof pages were spread out across his kitchen table as the team debated on where best to stick down poems by the likes of Brian Lomax and Keith Armstrong or short pieces of fiction, often sent anonymously. 'Magazines were piled up all over the house. The place was part-hippy, part-poverty. They had spent a fortune on this really special paper that was like silky card – there was no way they were ever going to make any money from it,' said a contributor.

The magazine, selling at 12½p, was touted around pubs, works' canteens and working men's clubs. These same poets, under the moniker of Axis Experimental Poetry Theatre, had appeared at the White Lion pub in Drake Street as part of a fringe event to the Rochdale Festival in August 1971. Fitton, who later settled in Amsterdam, remained a conspicuous and charismatic figure in the town. 'I once went back to Rochdale and, for some reason, found myself at a party full of young people. When I say young people, I mean 25 and under, you know. And I was sat talking to this guy and he said, "Who the fuck are you?" and I said, "I'm Barry Fitton." And he says "What? I thought you were just a story that everyone talked about!"'

The running of the Axis shop was taken over by John and Jean Clegg, a married couple who also ran the Rochdale Film Society. Peter Campbell, better known as Cammie, was also a partner. An eminent poet and 'head', he was known for his 'idiot dancing' at gigs – in hippy circles, losing self-consciousness and submitting totally to the music was considered a state of distinction. The shop's name was changed to Beautiful Stranger and 'sold all underground mags (*Oz, IT, Frendz, Mole Express*), Indian and hand-made clothes, posters and all things nice'. Cheesecloth was a popular fabric and Beautiful Stranger stocked shirts, blouses and skirts 'at low prices'. The Rotton [sic] Carrot in Cheetham Street publicised itself as 'your local South Sea bubble!' Faded dungarees were on sale at £4.99, along with knitwear by Lord Anthony and Benjamin Capitol. On a theme, the Oxfam shop in Baillie Street offered 'Tibetan shoulder bags, African heads, Indian sandals and Mexican cushion covers'.

* * *

The season was only three matches in and Rochdale had two draws and a win; too soon to talk of runs or suggest it might stand as a barometer for the rest of the campaign. All the same, a letter appeared in the *Rochdale Observer* written by H. Ashton of Houghton, Preston:

> I have been reading in your newspaper good reports of the pre-season games and from the reports it would seem the club are in for better times under Walter Joyce's new-look approach to a good youth policy. It has been something that has been wanted at Spotland for a long time. Here's hoping that it pays off and the crowds at Rochdale will return and enjoy some good attacking football.

'Which one of your mates wrote that?' asked Dennis Butler. Joyce laughed but, secretly, it had delighted him. Whether a solitary letter or not, he took it as a distillation of what he hoped many fans were thinking: they were buying into the philosophy of pass-and-move, playing it to feet and investing in youth.

In a good mood, Joyce summoned Fred O'Donoghue to his office. 'Shall we stage a public trial match and get some kids up here to see if any of them have got what it takes? Isn't that how we found Paul Fielding?' he asked. O'Donoghue told Joyce that Fielding, a former pupil at Kingsway High School, Rochdale, had been spotted playing for both the town team and Lancashire

Boys. 'He played for Lancashire alongside a scouser called Peter Reid who's signed for Bolton. The pair bossed the midfield,' he said. Joyce returned to his original idea: 'Come on, Fred, let's give it a go. You never know who might be out there.'

* * *

The most significant boon to the town's alternative scene was the opening of Black Sedan record shop at 17 Fleece Street, a backstreet in the town centre. Two friends, Pete Day and Mike Turner, already had another record shop of the same name in the student quarter of All Saints, Manchester, which dubbed itself 'Manchester's Leading Rock Specialists'. Although only in his mid-20s, Mike Turner had travelled the globe as a top-level swimmer. Over a three-year period (1966–68), he'd won medals at the Empire Games, Jamaica; World Student Games, Tokyo; and the Olympics, Mexico. He had the idea for Black Sedan while undertaking a master's degree in mechanical engineering at Manchester University.

Andy Sharrocks was a regular customer at the Manchester shop and, on leaving school at 16, had written to Turner seeking a job. 'He told me they were opening a branch in Rochdale, if I was interested. The shop was on the second floor and I heaved the racks up through the storey window and catalogued all the records,' he said. The walls and windows were painted black and joss sticks lit throughout the day, wafting sweet scent down the stairs and on to the street. 'It was meant to be an experience, walking up two flights of black stairs into this dimly lit shop,' he said. On opening, the shop offered, among others, albums by Soft Machine, Tangerine Dream and Iron Butterfly at £2.19 each.

The building in Fleece Street quickly became a hub for Rochdale's bohemian set. Dave Smith, later a principal organiser of the Deeply Vale Festival – he'd discovered the site while out riding on his BSA Bantam motorcycle – moved his shop, The Magic Mushroom, from Oldham Road to the first floor at 17

Fleece Street; it sold clothes made from cast-off denim. Dave Edwards, another Deeply Vale founder, tried to establish a health-food café on the ground floor but was thwarted because he was legally obliged to provide toilet facilities but the only one available was accessed through the kitchen.

After work each evening, Sharrocks, Smith and Edwards decamped to a commune they had set up in a terraced house in Oldham Road, Balderstone. Also living there was Andy Burgoyne, who designed the striking posters for the Deeply Vale Festival and later set up Peopleprint, a community-run print shop. Sharrocks fronted the band, Accident on the East Lancs. The 'good vibes' centred on Fleece Street were short-lived. Police became suspicious that drugs were being used and sold on the premises and made regular visits. Black Sedan moved to the ground floor and, according to some customers, became 'straighter'; the other two ventures closed down.

Shelagh Hudson, an Australian friend of Mike Turner and a fellow swimmer, moved from Liverpool to manage Black Sedan, assisted by Moira Matthews. 'It was the kind of place where you would make friends with customers and share good music,' said Shelagh. 'We wanted to sell discounted records, albums mainly, rock and associated genres – music we liked and could chat about. Customers recommended music to *us*. I remember this nerdy bloke switching us on to Philip Glass. There was another fella who only ever ordered Johnny Mathis albums, probably the only ones of his we ever sold.'

Most mornings, Shelagh walked across town from her home in East View, Mitchell Street, to open the shop. Occasionally she'd forget the keys and have to gain access through the adjacent loft at the tobacconist's next door. 'That entire corner of shops on Fleece Street and Drake Street shared loft access, so as long as I remembered where all the alarmed pressure pads were inside the shop, I could open it up from inside. Working there was the best job ever,' she said.

* * *

More than a hundred lads trudged on to the Spotland car park, football boots in their duffel bags, sidestepping the potholes. Fred O'Donoghue scribbled down names in a tiny jotter, crying out, for god's sake, heavens above, every time he broke the tip of his pencil. 'Where the bloody hell does Fred [Ratcliffe] get these from?' O'Donoghue was chatty and cheeky, ready with a quip or a put-down, sometimes at his own expense. He'd gone to sea at 19 as a junior engineer in the merchant navy and could tell a story or five; it was the Irish in him, he said. He was the man who had missed out on Kevin Keegan. As Liverpool's scout for the north-west, he'd been sent to watch him playing for Scunthorpe United at Stockport County. He reported back that 'he left no impression whatsoever'. Soon afterwards, Liverpool, presented with more favourable scouting reports, signed Keegan. 'You can only report back on what you see and, on the day I watched him, he did bugger all,' said O'Donoghue.

As the lads lined up, he wanted them to know that, although he was now 45, he'd once been the same as them: raw, keen, young. Between puffs on his cigarette, he spoke about his days as a teenage boxer ('it bloody hurts getting punched') and his time assembling planes at the English Electric factory in Preston. He picked out a lad at the end of the line: 'Muckpot, has your mam ever been to Blackburn?' 'I don't know,' he answered. 'Tell her not to bother. She'll only get lost when she gets there.' O'Donoghue told them how he'd worked at Blackburn Town Hall and helped design the one-way system running through the town centre. 'We made such a pig's ear of it, you can go round and round Blackburn forever, if that's your thing,' he said.

The joshing was cover; it set them at ease so he 'could see their bones' – by which he meant see them for what they really were, whether they were confident, dedicated, set for the fight. He'd already worked out most of them in the car park: how they walked, or their body language. The swaggerers would be good

133

for a bit of tricky footwork, skipping past a few lads or putting in a solid whack of a hard tackle, but that would be their all. The scrawny lads flicking their bloody hair out of their eyes, shoulders hunched, had probably been sent by their dads. There was a lot of it about, always had been – dads boasting about how they would have made it and were all set to sign for Arsenal or Huddersfield Town but they had been clattered playing for the Golden Lion on a mudbath of a pitch. Their knee or ankle had gone and now the career-that-should-have-been was being lined up for their son, this timorous soul lost in a parka, eyes fixed to the floor.

* * *

Rochdale's other record shop was Bradley's, which had opened at the corner of The Walk and Yorkshire Street in the late 1950s. Family-owned, Bradley's had outlets across Yorkshire and Lancashire, catering mainly for chart-based music. The popularity of *Top of the Pops*, watched by 15 million viewers each week, had led to a buoyant market for singles. Among the best-selling singles artists of 1973 were Donny Osmond, David Cassidy, Slade, David Bowie, Wizzard and The Sweet. Bradley's also stocked left-field albums, many of which later crossed over to mainstream appeal. *Tubular Bells* by Mike Oldfield, *Goodbye Yellow Brick Road* by Elton John, *Tales from Topographic Oceans* by Yes, *Houses of the Holy* by Led Zeppelin and both *Aladdin Sane* and *Pin Ups* by David Bowie were all released in 1973. 'Hippies would sit on Bradley's window ledge on a Saturday afternoon. We'd go in and ask Janet, the manageress, to put King Crimson on the shop's record-player, really loud,' said Andy Metcalfe, a regular customer.

Louie Whiteley was among others sharing wall space outside the shop. His real name was Alan but, in tribute to Bob Dylan, he'd become Louie after it featured in the lyric of *Highway 61 Revisited*. Stan Faulkner, a softly spoken hippy, was known to have the longest hair in Rochdale (male or female) – it almost reached the back of his knees. A lot of cannabis was smoked, passed around and sold, as they observed the straights passing by who sometimes stopped to advise them to 'get a wash' or 'cut your hair'. Throughout the day, the music became louder and the head-tapping and foot-stamping more vigorous as 'Cat Food' or '21st Century Schizoid Man' blasted out from the shop doorway.

Among the wider youth, glam rock was at its most popular in 1973. David Bowie had introduced an outlandish and androgynous element in the late 1960s and this was co-opted by, among others, Marc Bolan, who wore satins and glitter. A performance by T. Rex of 'Hot Love' on *Top of the Pops* in February 1971 was said to have led the teenage evolution from a general 'hippy' look to 'glam rock'. Other artists and bands similarly classified included Sweet, Slade, Mud, Mott the Hoople, Roxy Music and Gary Glitter. The associated garb – stack-heeled shoes, vivid and tight clothing, feather boas, shoulder pads, face paint, long centre-parted hair, etc. – was also adopted by established acts such as Elton John, Rod Stewart and Queen.

* * *

The public trial, as O'Donoghue had envisaged, was a fruitless exercise, although both he and Walter Joyce recognised that a football club scouring its local community for talent was a good story for the press. Such was the efficacy of football's scouting system, only a fraction of players slipped its grasp. Across the country, a network of PE teachers, youth club leaders and managers of junior teams was ever vigilant to alert Football League clubs of any nascent talent, young lads who could 'run rings' round the rest.

While he was surprised that almost 100 had turned up to the trial, even if it had been 1,000, O'Donoghue wouldn't have expected to find a single player worthy of a place in the first-team squad. He was often asked why this was the case. He had a ready answer. 'It's all about balance,' he'd say. 'How a lad holds himself before and after receiving the ball. And he has to have the pass ready before the ball even comes, his brain thinking one step ahead. He's got to know where to stand to receive a pass and where to run to, to take players with him and create space for others. They've got to be brave too, physically and mentally. They have to *show* for the ball, even when they're having a shit game and the last three or four passes have been misplaced. When a civvy watches a game, he thinks the best players are the fancy-dans or those with a hard shot or a tough bugger who can shove opponents out of the way. My eye passes over them. They're fine for park football but no good in the professional game – they'd get shown up for what they are, made to look daft.'

Joyce, sitting up in the Main Stand, had watched the impromptu match called at the end of the trial, where O'Donoghue had asked what he considered the best 22 to form into two teams. At the end, they were clapped off the pitch by O'Donoghue and told to 'go and get a wash, lads'. Joyce made his way down on to the strip of cinder that ran the full length of the pitch. 'Nothing there for us is there, Fred?' O'Donoghue shook his head. 'Sorry, Gaffer – we'll have to work with what we've got.'

* * *

The race to a vibrant, space-age, hi-tech future was an infatuation during the 1960s and early 1970s. A world of robotics and cantilevered living, as foretold in sci-fi films and comics, suddenly appeared within reach. Town planners and councillors in Rochdale decided upon a foray into this future with an extensive development scheme of Brutalist architecture, where colossal, monochrome slabs of concrete would meet the housing needs of the town.

Rochdale had a high demand for social housing, with approximately half of its population living in rental accommodation, often in run-down areas due for demolition. The £3.5m development of Ashfield Valley, approved in July 1966, was viewed as the ideal way to meet a pressing need in the quickest possible time. The area, running parallel to the Rochdale Canal, was a swathe of scrubland and marshland containing little aside from hen huts and Jacky Brook, a stormwater overflow that occasionally carried sewage. A total of 1,014 flats to house more than 3,000 people would be contained in a series of blocks with two-storey structures, gradually dropping to a maximum of seven-storey at the valley's deepest points. The multistorey deck accesses to each block, walkways in the sky, were considered a unique design feature, expected to cause a stir in architectural circles.

The contract was awarded to Skarne, a Swedish company and driving force in new construction methods using concrete. Between 1965 and 1974, it undertook the 'Miljonprogrammet', building a million new dwellings in Sweden, a country with a population at that time of under eight million. The 'Skarne system' involved casting prefabricated concrete panels, which were transported to sites for assembly. The design, dubbed 'the architecture of democracy', was said to emulate a socialist utopian ideal where there was uniformity, with everyone living in near-identical flats; the only difference was the number of bedrooms in each. This theme made it particularly appealing to Labour-run councils such as Rochdale, whose councillors imagined Ashfield Valley as a new slant on the Garden City movement of the early 1900s.

* * *

All through the week and on the morning of the match, the players had been told what to expect. Tranmere Rovers were a tough side; they liked to mix it. 'Win the fight and you'll win the game,' Joyce had repeated, clapping out the rhythm of the words to bring home the message. 'They'll let you have the ball

all over the pitch but, as soon as you get near their box, expect to get smashed,' he added.

One of the players waiting for them out there was Ron Yeats, Tranmere's player-manager who had previously captained Liverpool for almost a decade. On signing for Liverpool, Bill Shankly had told the press, 'The man is a mountain, go into the dressing room and walk around him.' At 6ft 2in, the Aberdeen-born centre-back had the nickname Colossus, and in football parlance was known as a 'craggy Scot'. The score was 0-0 at half-time. Joyce reminded the players again: 'What have I told you, lads? Don't get involved in the rough stuff. That means no pissing about. Get the ball out from your feet and work at those one-twos.'

Just five minutes into the second half, Peter Gowans, Rochdale's winger, was caught 'pissing about' in his own penalty area. Ambushed by two Tranmere players, he prodded the ball back to goalkeeper, Rod Jones. The pass fell short and Eddie Loyden nipped in to score: 1-0, game over. 'It's those bloody sideburns. He's like a horse with blinkers on,' shouted a fan from the stands. (Gowans sported a luxurious set of mutton-chop sideburns, which had instigated numerous nicknames, including Elvis [Presley] and Charlie [Charles Dickens]. Sometimes, the players also referred to him as Mungo, after Ray Dorset, the singer with the pop group, Mungo Jerry.)

In his match report, Stan Townsend made a prescient observation: 'Rochdale seem to have lost the flair for putting the ball where it matters most – in the net. Hartlepool felt the blast of their power, so why has it suddenly been tucked away like some terrible plague?' Walter Joyce had already detected a weakness in the team: 'I'm a great advocate of having someone, if not all of my players shouting encouragement or telling colleagues where the opposition is. We are failing to do this and allowing other sides to take the initiative. The sooner the lads realise this, the better.'

Teams that had players who didn't talk and shout and bawl to one another on the field and didn't offer impromptu counsel – 'man on' or 'time' or 'settle' – were perceived to be missing one of the sport's most vital components: character. If you weren't expressing your appreciation or disappointment to a team-mate, did you care enough? On a practical level, the talking improved the team's performance; it alerted players to the whereabouts (or otherwise) of opponents. Walter Joyce had made quite an admission.

* * *

Work began on the Ashfield Valley site in April 1967 and the first batch of 50 flats was let 14 months later. By the end of 1968, all 26 blocks had been constructed, although 'installed' was more accurate because the building components arrived ready-assembled. Built in the traditional way, from either breeze blocks or brick, the project would have taken much longer to complete, with commensurate higher manpower costs. The blocks of flats were named alphabetically: A (Appleby) to Z (Zennor). No one could think of a suitable word beginning with X for the 24th block, so it was named Exford.

Within months, residents began to report that they were unhappy on the estate. They said the harsh grey structures and regimented feel made it more akin to an army barracks or prison. A national newspaper referred to the estate as 'the Alcatraz of the North'. As the original tenants moved out, their replacements were low-income families, unsupported mothers and the elderly. The council was legally obligated to house 'problem tenants' and Ashfield Valley, soon the least desirous of the council's stock, became a catch-all for this sector. Between April and October 1973, social workers took on a hundred new cases from the estate.

Vandalism and drug-dealing was rife. Teenagers were fighting on the decking. A horse was tethered at the entrance of one block. Homing pigeons were flying in and out of another.

Drunks were sleeping in the corridors. Lifts were either broken or being used as toilets. Tenants were illegally subletting flats, the keys handed over in the tap room of pubs. There were calls for the council to provide the estate with its own school, family advice centre, community centre, health centre and, most of all, police station. A better solution, according to David Trippier, a Conservative councillor and resident of Bamford, would be a return to corporal punishment for the vandals and miscreants. Mike Smith, minister at the nearby Zion Baptist Church, said, 'The problems are the fault of the minority. It's become a huge transit camp because antisocial types are being sent there. The council should build special accommodation solely for them.'

Sweden, with its more progressive society and doctrine of Lagom – 'not too much, not too little … just right' – might have set down a utopian dream of Skarne communities, but in Britain, Ashfield Valley in particular, it was a disaster. *RAP*, as ever, had a very direct view: 'Children reared in this kind of concentration camp will suffer from it for the rest of their lives. Many of those responsible now privately admit that the estate was a mistake. What they're not prepared to do is take any action to deal with it.'

* * *

Plymouth away was the disaster Walter Joyce had feared. The previous season, Rochdale had lost 6-0 at Home Park; this time they did only slightly better, losing 5-0. The wider football community always noted such a margin of defeat: it was a stuffing, a hiding. Most professional teams could work hard and organise themselves to at least minimise a loss but when it got to four, five or six without reply, questions were asked – had there been a sending-off or a spate of injuries that had compelled the manager to fill the team with kids? Without mitigating circumstances, the assumption was crude and damning: it was a team of bottlers, or worse – they were inept. 'I'm going to put some of the old heads in for the next match, against Shrewsbury,' Joyce told his coaching staff.

He insisted he hadn't abandoned his faith in young players; it was a temporary measure to 'see them over a bump'. Bill Atkins (age 34), Colin Blant (27) and Len Kinsella (27) replaced Paul Fielding (17), Leo Skeete (24) and Arthur Marsh (26) for the match at Gay Meadow. Shrewsbury Town had lost their opening three league matches but beating Rochdale 2-0 was 'as easy as plucking feathers off a chicken' – Stan Townsend. The defeat meant Rochdale swapped places with Shrewsbury at the bottom of the table and, for the first time, the headline in the *Rochdale Observer* revealed a pessimistic tone: 'Long, Hard Drag Faces Goal-Shy Rochdale'.

* * *

A man's body was discovered in the bin room of one of the blocks on Ashfield Valley; he'd been dead for about six months. An insurance collector was attacked and robbed. If tenants revealed that they lived 'on the Valley', they were unlikely to be considered for jobs. Television rental shops, gas showrooms and furniture stores refused to supply goods there or, on the rare occasions they agreed, charged large deposits. George Cartshore, one of the estate's caretakers, resigned from his position. 'The problems are getting worse and close to crisis point,' he said. 'Out-and-out thuggery has reached terrifying proportions. More and more flats are standing empty and some blocks have deteriorated into an appalling and dangerous condition.' A resident said, 'This place is a dumping ground for has-beens and never-will-bes. It's a shame because there are some good people on the estate but we're treated like a leper colony.'

The flats were riddled with condensation and mould and it was agreed to spend £3.3m to 'bring the estate to a level of decency'. Councillor Edward Collins, council leader, deemed this 'a fearsome amount of money'. The massive programme was immediately condemned as a failure. 'The repairs have not worked because of the simple fact that people do not want to live at Ashfield Valley. You don't modernise houses or flats for people *not* to live in them,' said Councillor Richard Farnell. Demolition had been long planned but began in May 1989. By August 1992, only three of the 26 blocks were still standing (these were refurbished and let mainly to older tenants).

The scheme had been part of an extensive 'regeneration' of Rochdale. Numerous compulsory purchase orders had precipitated vast development projects, all of a modernist/ Brutalist idiom, utilising concrete and plastic – Falinge Flats (1970), Freehold Flats (1971), the complete revamp of the town centre (1978), a municipal office block (known as 'the black box') and new bus station (1978), Ashfield Valley (1968), the Seven Sisters tower blocks (1966) and several new dual carriageways. They each contributed to changing the face of Rochdale.

The bus station, the municipal offices and Ashfield Valley barely lasted two decades before demolition. Both Falinge Flats and Freehold Flats have been subject to extensive modernisation, and plans have been tabled to bulldoze the Seven Sisters. If each of these and the other projects were considered incongruous to the character of the town, they were also an economic catastrophe.

Many have pondered on decisions made by councillors and officials in the 1960s and early 1970s. Those of a benevolent disposition point to the idealism and optimism of the times. Municipal leaders might have been dazzled by a trip to the Skarne headquarters in Stockholm (when few people boarded an airplane) but this was 'due diligence', accepted on a 'no strings attached' basis. The presence of one particular man on the scene, though, gives credence to charges that there might have been routine conflicts of interest. Cyril Smith was mayor in 1966 and served on Rochdale Council until he became an MP for the town in 1972. On his death in September 2010, the public learned of his conniving nature, his duplicity and willingness to camouflage self-gain and self-interest as civic duty. 'Someone's telling bloody lies,' was one of his favourite sayings.

* * *

John Bond, manager of Bournemouth, was able to sign players considerably outside the wage and transfer budget of Rochdale. Among these were Harry Redknapp (ex-West Ham United) and Jimmy Gabriel (ex-Everton and Southampton), two relatively well-known players who had appeared in the top division. Bond, a big man often seen smoking a big cigar, had also brought in Brian Clark from Cardiff City for a fee of £70,000; he had a creditable goals-per-game ratio of one in every three.

As expected, 'star-spangled' Bournemouth dominated the match at Spotland and there were boos at half-time as Rochdale appeared to be 'doing a Plymouth', losing 3-0. A gung-ho spirit fell upon the home team after the break and, with a minute remaining, they found themselves just a goal behind. Paul Fielding took a corner and the ball fell to Keith Hanvey. He mistimed the header but, as the ball dropped towards his midriff, he drove his knee forward and arrowed the ball into the net. The referee blew immediately for full time. Fans in the Sandy Lane End clapped their hands and sang their song: 'Up the Dale, Up the Dale, Up the Dale'. Take that, John Bond – a good measure of northern grit.

* * *

Among the records sold at Black Sedan were those by Rochdale groups, Saraband and Tractor. Saraband were fronted by former primary schoolteacher Barbara Yates, and originally known as The Honeydew. On their album cover they were pictured in a sun-slatted forest. Yates, hair bobbed, was leant against a tree in a lacy minidress and knee-high cream boots, while the lads sported mainly purple, neckerchiefs at their chins and belts fastened *over* their pullovers. This hippy theme was fortified by songs such as 'Outward Bound' and 'Magic Caravan', and by the hip-speak on the sleeve notes, where Stewart Mawdesley, guitarist, was described as 'a genial goon'.

Tractor was a duo comprising Jim Milne and Steve Clayton. They had signed to Dandelion Records, the label co-owned by Radio One DJ John Peel (real name John Ravenscroft), who had close ties to Rochdale. After his National Service, he took up weekly bed-and-breakfast accommodation in Deeplish in 1959 while working at Townhead Mill. His father, Robert Ravenscroft, a wealthy cotton merchant, had organised the placement with a view to his eldest son taking over the family business. Tractor were known initially as The Way We Live. Peel suggested the name change and two albums were released on Dandelion – *A Candle for Judith* (as The Way We Live) in 1971 and *Tractor*, a year later.

Much the same as the Black Sedan shop, Tractor became a hub for Rochdale's fringe culture. John Brierley, an unofficial third member, recorded them at a studio set up in his parents' home in Edenfield Road, Spotland, close to the football ground. 'John built it virtually from old washing machine parts in his bedroom and attic. If his mum and dad were up, he used their bedroom for recording vocals because the acoustics were better,' said John Peel.

Brierley established Cargo Studios at Kenion Street in Rochdale town centre, where hundreds of bands, mainly punk and new wave, including Joy Division and The Fall, recorded seminal tracks. Chris Hewitt became Tractor's manager and a key player on the local music scene, as owner of Tractor Music (a music shop and rehearsal space) and, later, as co-organiser of the Deeply Vale music festival. Hewitt, a former pupil at Hulme Grammar School, Oldham, began working as social secretary at Rochdale College and booked Tractor to play the college's

Christmas Party of 1972, tickets priced at 30p. Rochdale was without a regular gigging venue, so concerts were held on an ad hoc basis. Hewitt brought Skin Alley and Pink Fairies to the college in 1972 while, at a similar time, the Champness Hall, a Methodist art deco building, hosted Barclay James Harvest, Quintessence and the Incredible String Band.

On a wet, windy evening in August 1973, the 'terminally hairy' Edgar Broughton Band performed on land adjacent to Hollingworth Lake, a reservoir in Littleborough, on Rochdale's boundary with Yorkshire. The group (most famous song: 'Out Demons Out') had forged a reputation as a 'people's band' by playing free, impromptu concerts on flat-back lorries. They played for about 20 minutes to an estimated 200 fans. The performance was filmed by Granada TV for its early-evening series, *OK* ('Rock ... news, films. Rock, events, people. Rock again, information, and more rock').

The filming had been scheduled originally to take place at Hanley Forest Reclamation Park but Stoke Council decreed that the 'music of the Edgar Broughton Band is not conducive to the social atmosphere of our town'. Councillors also expressed fears that fans 'might cause saplings to be trampled'; they had no such concerns in Rochdale. Another group with a similar vibe were Hawkwind, whose spaced-out music and pro-freedom lyrics made them a touchstone of the bohemian generation. Their concerts were a 'gathering of the tribes' and, when they played at King George's Hall, Blackburn in December 1972 on their *Space Ritual* tour, Chris Hewitt hired a Bedford VAL six-wheeler coach. Seventy-two 'freaks' in denim and cheesecloth clambered aboard but only 50 made the return journey. 'They're probably still out there, wandering about on the moors between Rochdale and Blackburn,' said Hewitt.

7

A Socially Divided Society

AFTER THE Bournemouth match, Walter Joyce was greeted with smiles and thumbs-up gestures from fans sitting at the round wooden tables in the players' lounge. He thought it but didn't say it: where was this support at half-time when we were on our knees and needed it the most? Those boos, those fucking boos, had riled him. They could shout whatever they wanted at *him* from the darkness of the Main Stand, call him all kinds of names. He could take it, no bother, but, come on, give these young lads a break, give them a chance. They had just held moneybags, swanky, show-offs Bournemouth to a 3-3 draw, for god's sake. The press lads were talking about 'turning a corner' and asking whether he'd finally found 'the magic formula' that would lead to the first league win of the season. He was obliging, issuing his own platitudes in response – things were looking up, the signs were encouraging.

When all the players and punters had gone home, the coaching staff met up in Joyce's office. He poured them each a tipple of whisky in a plastic cup. 'They've been talking up there [in the players' lounge] as if we're going to kick on and win the league now. But it doesn't work like that, does it?' They shook their heads. This was the difference between civvies and football pros. The civvies were lost to the moment, all fired up on hope, but the pros knew better. They each knew the philosophy behind a storming second-half comeback and how it held little, if any, bearing on future performances. When a team was so far behind, 3-0 or similar, it became daring and fearless, reverting to 'car park football' – racing forwards, leaving opponents unmarked, quick-quick, everything in pursuit of a goal. Mostly, this approach failed and teams were 'picked off' with adroit counter-attacking, so a 3-0 became a hammering, became 'a Plymouth'.

Bournemouth had been caught by surprise, not sensing that Rochdale were capable of playing such direct and enterprising football. Joyce and his coaches knew that no matter how hard they tried, whatever they said, what inducements were offered, this mentality couldn't be instilled into the team for every match; it had been an instinctual response. Maybe, thought Joyce afterwards, the boos had actually helped and drawn a sting from his team that he hadn't previously detected. This idea pleased him. 'Who's up next?' asked Frank Campbell. 'Southport, here,' said Joyce. 'They're as fucking bad as we are! We're bound to stuff them,' laughed Campbell. 'Come on, you know it doesn't work like that.'

* * *

A regular childhood visitor to Rochdale and a lifelong advocate of its alternative culture was the comedian Victoria Wood. She'd joined the Rochdale Youth Theatre Workshop in the summer of 1968. David Morton, a graduate of the prestigious Central School for Speech and Drama, had set up the workshop a year earlier in an upstairs room at Heybrook Primary School, fitted with lighting, sound rigs and tiered seating. Morton held two evening classes each week and full days during the summer holidays. Wood, at 15 years old, travelled over by bus from her home in Bury and later said it provided 'salvation' and was 'the happiest period of my life, where I learned more than anywhere else'. She began with a small role and also painted the set in *The Rising Generation* by Ann Jellicoe, a bizarre post-apocalyptic play where women had formed a new race in outer space.

The appointment of David Morton was further affirmation that a handful of motivated and inspiring figures could galvanise the cultural life of a town, the likes of Leo Solomon, Barry Fitton, Chris Hewitt and the catalysts behind *RAP*, Rochdale Sculptors, Tractor and the Black Sedan shop. Morton was steeped in the theatre, starting as a young teenager with a touring variety troupe and later appearing regularly on television. At 6ft 6in, with a heavy beard, he formed an imposing, charismatic outline for teenagers and straddled the difficult divide between authoritarian and confidant. Another of his protégés in Rochdale was Mary Jo Randle, who, after a stint at RADA, appeared in numerous television dramas. 'I joined when I was 13 and spent the whole summer doing theatre and after that became obsessed. David was like a Pied Piper figure,' she said.

Cyril Smith was another who, ostensibly at least, contributed a great deal to the social and cultural life of the town. He was chairman of Rochdale Youth Services – in the early 1970s, Rochdale had 35 youth clubs with more than 2,000 members. He was also a keen patron of the Rochdale Youth Orchestra. At this juncture, little was known of any possible ulterior motives. On his death in September 2010, David Morton, the same as many others, was fulsome in his praise: 'Sir Cyril was a key figure in making so much possible. He took great interest, asked demanding questions about approaches and regularly attended concerts and performances of plays. Because of Big Cyril's interest, young people too were aware of his enthusiastic interest and support. They, like me, will forever remember Cyril for helping us to share some great and rewarding experiences.'

* * *

Frank Campbell stood at the players' entrance, waiting to greet each new arrival. 'Left or right, injured or fit, which is it to be?' he sang.

Those choosing the 'right' were pointed towards the treatment room, while the others made their way to the dressing room to get stripped and ready for training. Most of the squad had minor afflictions, tight hamstrings and bruised shins, but six or seven had twisted their ankles or knees or had pulled muscles in their groin or thighs; they would be out for at least a month. 'Can't we fire some cortisone into the buggers?' asked Walter Joyce. 'We can, gaffer, but we know where that will lead, don't we?' responded Campbell.

Hydrocortisone was recognised across football as a 'miracle cure'. Players who could barely put their weight on a sore ankle to walk, for example, would later be running freely, careering into tackles. The hormone was injected directly into the seat of a trauma and masked soreness and pain, misleading the player to believe he was without injury. The downside was that without this constant reminder of discomfort – in effect, the brain warning the body – further, often extensive, damage was inflicted to the original injury.

The playing career of Dennis Butler had been sustained with regular injections into his knee, almost on a match-to-match basis, but he found, as many others did, that once the steroid had dispersed from the injury site, he was left in greater pain and with more soreness than before having the injection. Another Rochdale player who regularly had cortisone injections, to treat a strained muscle in his groin, was defender Graham Smith.

'It's Southport, not the bloody cup final,' added Campbell. By this, he meant that if it were a particularly important match, it might be worth getting out the 'old horse tranquilliser' (as the players had nicknamed it after seeing the size of the syringe) but, otherwise, its regular use merely prolonged recovery.

* * *

Radicalism wasn't wholly embraced in Rochdale. Keith Mason, in a letter sent to *RAP*, complained about an 'extravaganza of filth' on the shelves of Rochdale Library. He was referring to the novel *The Wild Boys*, by William Burroughs. He wrote: 'Intellectuals presumably call it erotic content, but on almost every page joyless, painful acts of homosexuality are described with the metaphoric freedom made famous in this man's earlier work.' He said it was 'an emblem for the manufacture of young male brutality', and closed: 'There are certain people with degrees sitting placidly behind the desk at Rochdale Library … they should know better.' Absent from the library was *Gay News*. The magazine's publishers, the Gay Liberation Front and Campaign for Homosexual Equality, had offered a free copy of each fortnightly issue to libraries in the UK. On a vote of 40 to 16, Rochdale Council rebuffed the offer; some councillors cried 'filth' during the debate.

A controversy broke out in the pages of *RAP* that was reflected elsewhere in society during the 1970s. 'Sauna Corner' of 117 Yorkshire Street had taken out adverts to publicise its panoply of services, among them manicures, eyebrow shaping and dyeing, electrolysis, facials, 'suntan treatment', skin peel, waxing, slim club, yoga, physiotherapy, speech correction and 'DIY hairdressing'. The extensive list ran alongside a photograph of a woman wearing a bikini, tousling her hair. The Rochdale Women's Liberation Group (RWLG) was affronted: 'Is it really necessary to print adverts which blatantly exploit women? It teaches women to be ashamed of their bodies and tells them where, for a nominal fee, they can go to change themselves miraculously by waxing, dyeing and electrolysis, into the plastic image portrayed in the advert. It perpetuates views already held by the ignorant.' The letter closed with a request: 'Can we ask that the word "Liberation" be printed in full? The abbreviation "Lib" has become a derogatory term used by TV and the Press.'

The discourse continued over several issues. Sheila Hemmings of Freehold, Rochdale wrote that she was a staunch supporter of women's rights but accused the group of 'pettiness'. She wrote: 'They claim they want to release women from male domination but seek to replace it with a domination of their own. Isn't it time the Liberationists got rid of their "burn your bras" image and realised women do not have to deliberately make themselves unattractive to fight for equality?' The RWLG remained defiant: 'When the day comes that people are considered as human beings and not pieces of meat to be judged, there will be no need for places like Sauna Corner.'

The *Rochdale Observer* epitomised the institutionalised sexism of the times. Women in various states of undress, either as cartoons or real-life models, were featured in adverts for supermarkets, tyres, fridges and even quilted bedspreads. In news pieces, women were referenced by their hair colour and often described as 'attractive' or 'pretty'. Beauty competitions and pageants were held routinely at factories and working men's clubs. The main item in the paper's 'Milnrow and Newhey' section of August 1973 showed Pat Rostron sitting awkwardly on a chair, hands clasped to her side with skirt hitched up a foot or so above her knee. Under the headline of 'Eyes on Legs', it read: 'Mrs Pat Rostron of Milnrow has won a weekly Miss Lovely Legs competition while staying at Pontin's Blackpool Holiday Camp at Lytham St Annes. Pat is a 25-year-old brunette housewife.' As another indicator of times changed, Pat's full address was featured, including door number.

A peculiar letter appeared in the *Rochdale Observer* seeking consideration for another supposedly under-represented sector of society – widows. A woman calling herself 'Dancing Widow' wrote: 'I am a widow and go out with a few more widows. We are sick and tired of people on the telly telling us how to enjoy life.' She said she'd attended dances 'to keep feeling young and, above all, fit'. Unfortunately, she said she wasn't welcomed because she was a widow. 'We get what I'd call sly smiles,' she wrote. 'They seem to think we are just after men. Heaven knows, we don't want anybody's husband. We want to live a life with something in it apart from boredom. Are we allowed to do this? No, unless we want to get talked about. Do we get any partners? Oh dear, no. They treat us as if we're something from outer space.'

* * *

The spate of injuries meant that Colin Blant was selected to play at centre-back against Southport, and Dick Renwick, a 30-year-old full-back, was named as substitute. Renwick was renowned as another tough player. Jackie Graham, the Scottish midfielder who had played with him many times when they were both at Brentford, said Renwick 'used to count how many stitches he'd put into people!' He'd lost a little pace and a Rochdale team-mate said of him, 'He was the sort who, when he crossed the halfway line, needed a taxi to get back.'

Walter Joyce hadn't abandoned his commitment to youth. He dropped goalkeeper Rod Jones (age 28) after he'd conceded ten goals in three matches and replaced him with Mike Poole, aged 18, who had previously been signed as a schoolboy to Coventry City. 'I like the energy and enthusiasm Mike has shown in training,' said Joyce. He also introduced Jim Burt, a midfield player, into the team. The 23-year-old was on a six-week trial at Spotland after being released by Northampton Town. He'd earlier been an apprentice at Leicester City, where he suffered a broken leg. Such 'trialists' were often taken on in the 1970s on match-by-match contracts. Most, much the same as Burt, had been released by professional clubs but others were semi-pros or even, occasionally, Sunday league players. Over the years, several of these played for Rochdale, usually during injury crises; it showed that the required level of fitness and strength was quickly attainable back then – such an elevation would be impossible in the modern game.

Rochdale drew 2-2 with Southport. Once more, they had failed to win but afterwards the directors and fans were in forgiving mood, even Fred Ratcliffe. 'They gave it their best, considering it was a makeshift side. They'll soon improve, I'm sure, when all these blasted injuries have cleared up,' he said.

Joyce did the after-match rounds, nodding and smiling and shaking hands. The surfeit of injuries was a constant theme; even the directors' wives were inquiring about particular players, calling them by their first names and acting familiar, almost as if they were family members when, most probably, thought Joyce, they didn't know one from another. Secretly, Joyce wasn't having any of it: blaming injuries for drawing a match they should have won. It was civvies and pros again. Every pro knew that injuries always racked up in mid-September, a month or so into a new season. Players were keen and fit during pre-season training and in the kick-about friendly matches but, as soon as it mattered, when players stretched and lunged and it became life and death in *proper* matches, muscles twanged, bones got bashed and footballers got hurt. Every team was depleted and patching up (or injecting) the wounded so that they could get out there, playing through the pain. Joyce was sure that if he'd have asked Alan Ball Sr, Southport's manager, he'd have fished out his own injury list from his back pocket: 'Don't talk to me about bloody injuries, Walter. Look at this lot.'

Joyce was beginning to wonder whether this run without a win – it now stretched to seven league matches – ran deeper, much deeper, than a few players being unavailable to play in a particular match.

* * *

The television series *Kung Fu* and a profusion of martial arts films inspired a craze that swept the UK in the early 1970s. In Rochdale, as elsewhere, men, women and children filled church halls and scout huts as they learned the reverse neck choke, tiger claw strike and butterfly kick. The actor, David Carradine, starred in *Kung Fu* as Kwai Chang Caine, a Shaolin monk who traversed the American Old West in pursuit of his half-brother, Danny. The hushed candlelit scenes imbued with stagy mysticism were a slow-slow heartbeat to sporadic acts of ferocity, closing with a courtly bow by the victor. 'Chopsocky' films (overblown storylines, outlandish special effects, bizarre music and numerous fight scenes) had been made in Hong Kong since the late 1930s but films such as *5 Fingers of Death* and *Blood of the Leopard*, made in 1972, led to one of the most profitable films of all time: *Enter the Dragon*.

Bruce Lee, the film's magnetic star, died in July 1973, aged 32, a month before the film was premiered in the United States. His early death lent him iconic status, and the BBFC's (British Board of Film Classification) decision to give it an 'X' rating – meaning cinema viewers had to be over 18 to see the film – added to its verboten appeal. Stephen Murphy, BBFC's secretary, demanded cuts (kicks to the crotch, neck breaks and broken bottles used as weapons) and reported:

> I consider that the film exploits violence purely for the sake of entertainment. Such a presentation of violence without any qualifying context is potentially harmful to teenage boys, to whom the BBFC recognises such films will be very attractive. While the highly choreographed fighting is viewed as a 'fantasy', the level of aggression, sadism and violence in the film could only be accommodated at the adult level.

As he passed this ruling in October 1973, posters of Bruce Lee, snarling, claw marks across his chest, were already on the walls of thousands of teenage boys' bedrooms.

Both cinemas in Rochdale, the Odeon and ABC, often showed kung fu films at the same time. One particular week in January 1974, martial arts aficionados could gorge on *Fist of Fury* at the ABC, starring Bruce Lee, and, at the Odeon, *Ten Fingers of Steel* with Jimmy Wang in the lead role. The plot lines were almost identical – foreign aggressors pursued (routinely Japanese), assaulted (by Chinese hero and his cohorts) and honour restored (to the village, town or sacred temple).

Fears expressed by the BBFC appeared justified in Rochdale, where several 'kung fu attacks' were carried out by youths. Douglas Clegg, the father of a boy who was 'kicked about the head and body' by an older boy, wrote to *RAP*:

> I suggest that the growth of Kung Fu programmes/ films and now classes in the martial arts are yet another step towards the acceptance of violence in our society. We deplore violence in Northern Ireland yet there is little doubt that our children are becoming far more violent towards one another. I find it frightening to see children kicking and chopping as a matter of course.

The overall standard of films shown in Rochdale failed to meet the approval of 'Mr PC Fitton' of Balderstone, who wrote a letter of complaint to the *Rochdale Observer*. He said both cinemas screened 'anything which contains cheap, smutty laughs, people being beaten to a pulp, or perverts romping around in the nude for two hours'. He despaired of fellow citizens: 'Unfortunately there must be a market for this kind of product but it is sad to think there is so many people in Rochdale with brains the size of a pea.' He called for more films of the calibre of *O Lucky Man!*, *Dr Zhivago*, *Paint Your Wagon* and *The Madwoman of Chaillot*, instead of 'some tripe called *The Erotic Adventures of Zorro*'. He closed with: 'The watchword with Rochdale's two cinemas seems to be: if in doubt what to show, show a film where people have their necks broken, their bodies mutilated and their girlfriends raped. It's a horrible, tragic train of thought.'

* * *

Most football clubs at all levels had one or two players referred to within the game as 'old before their time' or 'man-boys'. These were players who had developed early and, by their mid-teens, had the physique of grown men. They stood out in schoolboy football because their stature enabled them to intimidate and dominate smaller opposition. In a professional environment, where most players were equally as strong, they faded quickly. A handful, however, maintained that early flush of confidence and self-assurance, on and off the pitch. Walter Joyce had seen this in Keith Hanvey, who, although only 21, had already experienced the highs and lows presented by football. 'Keith has everything going for him. He is young, has lots of ambition and that is what I am after,' Joyce told the press.

Hanvey, born in Newton Heath, Manchester – hence his nickname of 'Newton Heath Keith' – had lived a gilded childhood. He was head boy and captain of all the sports teams at Briscoe Lane Junior School and played football and cricket for Lancashire Schoolboys. He passed ten O levels without trying particularly hard. His first real challenge came when he was invited to play for Manchester Boys. 'It hit me like a bombshell. I hadn't had to concentrate at school or at sport; it just came natural. Suddenly, I came across all these lads who were fitter and stronger than me,' he said.

He worked on his fitness, completing solo training drills on wasteland near the Princess Parkway in Manchester, and began attending sessions on an ad hoc basis at Manchester City's training ground in Park Road, Cheadle. He progressed to the reserves and, after playing at Molineux against a Wolves team that included John Richards and Dave Wagstaffe, he was told to report to Joe Mercer, City's manager, the next morning. 'He

said to me, "Keith, we want you to be a Manchester City player."
I signed a two-year deal on £27.50 a week. I couldn't believe it
and said, "Are you really going to pay me this much every week?"'
said Hanvey.

While playing for City's 'A' team at Liverpool, he suffered
a broken fibula. He received £108 from his insurers, which
City asked him to pay on to them. Hanvey's solitary first-
team appearance for Manchester City was in controversial
circumstances. The Texaco Cup, with sponsorship of £100,000
from the American petrol company, was a competition for
clubs in the UK and Ireland who had finished high in their
divisions but failed to qualify for Europe ('a cup for also-rans').
City entered reluctantly and, in a first-round, second-leg tie at
Airdrieonians in September 1971, they fielded nine reserves,
including Hanvey; they wanted to ensure first-teamers weren't
injured. City lost 2-0 and were made to forfeit their entry deposit
of £1,000 and banned from the tournament for two years.

Hanvey picked up another injury playing for the reserves
at St James' Park, Newcastle. He collided with winger Stewart
Barrowclough, and knew immediately that it was serious. 'I had
broken my right femur. All the muscle had been damaged and I
had a haematoma, too. Later, they found out that the bone had
calcified,' he said. He was out of the game for a year, spending
days in the treatment room, where he struck up a friendship with
Colin Bell. Hanvey recovered and, to regain match fitness, was
loaned to Swansea City for six months. He lodged with several
other young players at the home of a member of the coaching
staff. 'Before I went to Swansea, a good night out for me was a
couple of bottles of Mackesons. I was all that way from home
and felt as if I'd been let loose. One night, I had 15 pints of
beer,' he said.

Roy Bentley, the ex-Chelsea striker, was manager at Swansea
when Hanvey joined but he was replaced in November 1972
by Harry Gregg, the former Manchester United goalkeeper.

Gregg had a fearsome reputation and Hanvey was expecting to face his rancour after he spotted Gregg in a pub when he was out drinking. 'Nothing was said the next day at training,' said Hanvey. 'And I started to wonder whether I'd imagined seeing him or that maybe *I'd* seen him but he'd not seen me. Anyway, we got in the bath after the next match and Gregg waited until I was on my own in there, stripped off and jumped in. He started punching me in the stomach, knocking buggery out of me.'

On Hanvey's return to Maine Road, he was told by Johnny Hart, the club's new manager, that he would not be included in the first-team squad and wasn't guaranteed game time with the reserves. Hanvey also learned that his father, James, who worked at a sweet and tobacconists shop, had been diagnosed with cancer; he died in September 1973. 'I'd lost a little bit of my ambition, with all that was going on,' he said. 'I was grateful to Walter for taking me to Rochdale. He was a super guy. Spotland was a shock after Maine Road but Rochdale was still a professional club. The pitch was often muddy or frozen but it was a homely place and I liked the people in and around it.' He signed for between £35 and £40 per week, depending on appearances and results. 'I wanted to get games under my belt and play at a reasonable level on a regular basis,' he said.

* * *

Industrial relations had simmered across Britain from the late 1960s into the early 1970s. Miners, long considered 'the aristocracy of the working class', had staged unofficial strikes in 1969 and 1970. Officials from the National Union of Mineworkers (NUM) argued that wages had fallen significantly behind inflation and, in 1971, had asked for a pay increase of 43 per cent. The National Coal Board (NCB), the statutory corporation appointed by the government, offered 7 per cent.

An official strike had been called in January 1972, the first undertaken by miners since the General Strike of 1926. Flying pickets travelled to industrial sites, which led to railway workers refusing to transport coal, while staff at power stations declined to handle it. A miner, Freddie Matthews, was killed while picketing at Keadby Power Station, near Scunthorpe. A non-union lorry driver had mounted the pavement to pass the picket line; 5,000 attended the funeral. In the aftermath, picketing became violent, with greater disruption and resentment. Power shortages led to cuts lasting nine hours per day and householders were asked to heat only one room. A state of emergency was declared in February 1972. Lord Richard Wilberforce chaired an inquiry and, within a week, reported that miners should receive a rise of 27 per cent because 'we know of no other job in which there is such a combination of danger, health hazard and discomfort in working conditions, social inconvenience and community isolation'. They returned to work; the dispute had lasted seven weeks.

The strike and its outcome had a pervasive effect. The Conservative government, led by Prime Minister Edward Heath, had been advised not to break the blockade of power stations and risk further violence and loss of life. He'd mooted the idea of calling in the army or assembling a civil guard. Members of the cabinet viewed it as 'a victory for violence' and Douglas Hurd, Heath's private secretary, said that by the end of the dispute 'the government was wandering around the battlefield looking for someone to surrender to'. This perception of humiliation was said to have determined the hard-line approach to organised labour adopted later by Margaret Thatcher's government. In the meantime, workers in towns throughout the UK, including Rochdale, had seen the prize secured through direct and sharpened industrial conflict.

* * *

Rochdale fans were unaware of Hanvey's backstory. They had only a broad summary provided by the club in match programmes: big lad, ex-Manchester City, loan spell at Swansea, defender. Joyce, though, knew it all and liked it all. He wanted more players similar to Hanvey, who had been beaten up by football but had enough about them to pick themselves up, battle on, still dreaming. As Joyce saw it, Stewart Barrowclough, Harry Gregg and Johnny Hart had all done him a favour: they had put armour over a footballer who was already big-hearted and strong in mind and stature.

In this situation – five matches without a win, bottom of the division – who else in that dressing room could he call on? The kids were all effort and enthusiasm but without guile. The older pros – well, he hadn't fully worked them out yet, how much they were listening and their level of commitment. And the lads shipped in from non-league – they were all elbows and knees but struggled to get their foot on the ball and see a pass. Joyce was realising that Keith Hanvey was as good as it got at this level.

On Hanvey's part, he was pleased to be back in the Manchester area, close to friends and family. He'd played in every match for Rochdale so far and was enjoying being fit again and having a settled position in a team; in his five years in football he'd not had this before. He hated losing but, looking about him, he felt there was enough talent in the squad to soon start winning matches.

* * *

The mood of industrial unrest spread to Rochdale. Laundry staff went on strike in a dispute over wages and this meant hospitals had to limit their intake of patients. About 60 members of the Civil and Public Service Association went on strike at Rochdale Labour Exchange. Mr C.P. Shaw, the exchange's manager, said only a dozen members of staff had remained in work. 'There could be a delay in paying out unemployment benefit until we get rolling again,' he said. Civil servants working for the DHSS in Lonsdale House in the town centre held a one-day strike

Rochdale's first-team squad, 1973/74

Gateway to ignominy

Main Stand, Spotland

Welcome to Rochdale,
Walter Joyce (left) and Fred
Ratcliffe

Fred Ratcliffe leads the annual pilgrimage to The Shay, Halifax, to raise funds

Tense moment, Rochdale directors view another defeat

Lair of the gods. The boardroom at Spotland. Note: bust of Fred Ratcliffe looking down

Pies and pastries this way – the tea room at Spotland

ROCHDALE A.F.C.

SEASON............................

ADMIT THE BEARER TO
PLAYERS LOUNGE

...............................Director/Secretary

No Admission without This Card
Not Transferable

A chance to meet the stars

*Leo Skeete, aka
Leopold*

*Rare programme
for the infamous
Cambridge United
match*

The bath at Spotland. Ronnie the rat not pictured

Better days. Mike Brennan with team-mate, George Best, in the United States

DON TOBIN
MIDFIELDER

Carolina Lightnin' 1981-83
ASL Championship 1981
ASL All-Star 1979, 1981
MVP ASL Championship 1981
Lightnin' All-Time Most Assists
Everton 1971-73
Sligo Rivers 1977-78 (FIA Cup Final)
MISL Wichita Wings 1980-82
MISL LA Lazers 1982-84
USL Rochester Flash (1984); Tulsa Tornados (1985)
AISA Canton Invaders (84-87) Memphis Rogues 1989
AISA All-Star, MVP, Championship 1986
ASL Tampa Bay Rowdies 1988-89
NC Soccer Hall of Fame - Hall of Honor

Don Tobin career card. No mention of Rochdale

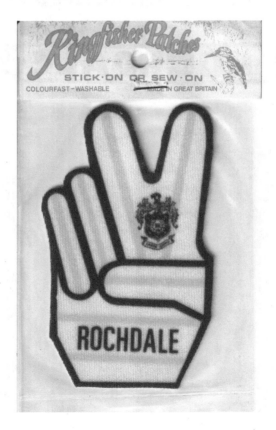

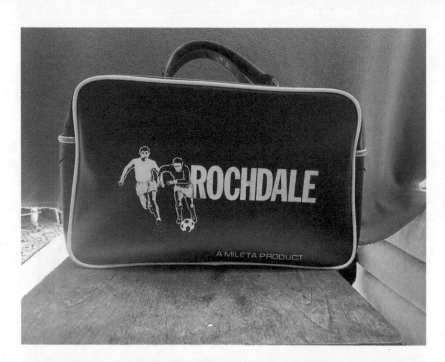

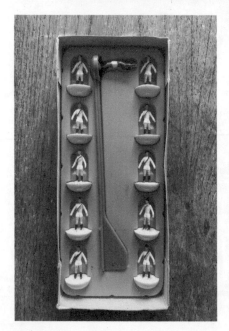

over the government's policy to limit pay rises, which had been introduced to stymie rising inflation.

A wider protest was organised by the TUC on Tuesday, 1 May 1973 when 1.6 million workers supported the May Day strike. Many took to the streets carrying banners, shouting 'Heath out'. The strongest support came in the Midlands. Ruth Elliott, an ITV news reporter, roamed Birmingham city centre with a camera crew as 20,000 workers marched past the famous Rotunda building. The impromptu interviews with marchers and passers-by crystallised the state of the nation. 'You're bleeding idle,' shouted a red-faced lady to the marchers, adding: 'According to you lot, you think you're bloody big heads but you ain't got a ha'porth of what I've got in my little finger.' Another woman, sitting in her car while the march passed, said (while nodding repeatedly): 'My god, they should be working to help the country instead of trying to bring it down and inconveniencing everyone else.' The microphone was placed before a middle-aged man waiting at a zebra crossing with his wife. 'It should have been a General Strike, I should think,' he said. 'It's about the only way to get this government out. They're no good to no one, surely not.'

Rochdale's engineering companies were most affected by the May Day strike. Kenneth Bradshaw, managing director of David Bridge & Co., manufacturers of rubber processing machinery, said, 'All the manual workers are out but the electricians are still working.' Henry Sampson, a director of Thomas Robinson & Son, a machine-making firm, said 'about 75 per cent' of the manual workers hadn't turned in for work. The strike had greater support at Whipp & Bourne, marine switchgear manufacturers, where 90 per cent of the 700-strong workforce was absent. The John Bright Group and TBA were phlegmatic about the impact. 'We're carrying on as usual,' said Mr T.R. Crowther, company secretary at Bright's, while Harold Slater, chief personnel officer at TBA, said, 'For all practical purposes we are working normally.'

In support of the strike, Rochdale Fire Brigade said staff would only attend incidents of a serious nature. More than 150 drivers went on strike at the Bass Charrington brewery in Bury, over a dispute about loading methods and bonuses. More than 250 pubs in Manchester and east Lancashire had to close, although the Robin Hood in South Parade, Rochdale town centre managed to stay open for a few days serving wine, tea, coffee and sandwiches. Among several with 'closed until further notice' taped to their doors were the Lancashire Lass in Norden, The Mayfield in Belfield, The Gale in Whitworth Road and the Lord Howard in Kirkholt.

* * *

If a spate of injuries was a distinct feature in the season of a football club, another was the moving on of disgruntled players, usually occurring at the same time of mid to late-September. Only the very best players, maybe the club captain and 20-goals-per-season striker, ever felt assured of their place in the team. The rest were ever fretful, trying to read the manager's body language or interpret a snap remark ('well played, son' or 'bit slow there') to see if it provided an indicator of whether they would be in his team or not. The exchanges took place every day between worried players. 'He doesn't fancy me.' 'How can you tell?' 'He won't look me in the eye.' 'He doesn't look anyone in the eye!' 'Okay, why did he put me with the yellows yesterday [those in yellow bibs] – that was a try-out for the reserves.' 'It wasn't. A few of his pets [favoured players] were in yellow as well.' 'Don't know what it is, I can just sense it.'

Most footballers were paranoid; it was a routine state of being. If you were out of the team, you wished the worst on whoever was in your position – misplaced passes, tackles bottled, scuffing shots, even an injury. And if you were in the team, you were always looking over your shoulder to see who was coming up behind you, ready to lift that sacred shirt off your back. Punters spoke of team spirit and there was a rendition of it – everyone steaming in on an opponent if he clattered a young lad, for example, or standing ground in a tunnel punch-up, but, largely, players were ambivalent to each other; it was the way of the sport. You played for the team but, most of all, you played for yourself.

Players sought to justify this single-mindedness by claiming it was to ensure they received appearance money and a win bonus because it 'fed the family' or 'paid the mortgage'. In truth, the wage differential between a playing, winning footballer and another on the periphery of the team wasn't particularly consequential. Footballers were selfish and ruthless because of their ego and pride. A football club was a fiercely male environment, where they were naked next to each other every day in the bath or showers and the same stood for their personalities: it was all on show. If you lost your place in the team or were bollocked by the manager in front of others, the hurt was primal. You were a kid again, told off when you didn't deserve or understand it. So, to save yourself from this unjust searing pain, you set every facet of your being to self-protection – and that largely meant staying in the team at all costs.

Within the space of six days, Rochdale parted company with three experienced players. They had given up on second-guessing Walter Joyce and putting in that 'extra yard' in training. They had decided it was all in vain, futile. He didn't fancy them and that was the end of it; time to move on. The coaching staff was disappointed. To their mind, these players had set against Joyce from the start and purposely undermined him. In football vernacular, they had 'seen their arses'.

* * *

A controversial film and a new genre of fiction dubbed 'Youthsploitation' gave dominion to the belief that times were becoming more violent in the early 1970s. *A Clockwork Orange*, directed by Stanley Kubrick, was based on the dystopian novel by Anthony Burgess. The heavily stylised, colour-saturated film centred on the Korova Milk Bar, where, according to the main character, Alex (played by Malcolm McDowell), the drug-spiked 'milk plus' ... 'Sharpens you up and makes you ready for a bit of the old ultra-violence.' The most disturbing scene saw his gang force their way into the isolated home of writer, Frank Alexander. They kicked him repeatedly before raping his wife, while Alex sang 'Singin' in the Rain', the song made famous by Gene Kelly in the musical film of the same name.

Within weeks of its cinema release in January 1972, pockets of young men were spotted in towns and cities wearing the outlandish garb of Alex DeLarge and his 'droogs' (accomplices), Pete, Georgie and Dim – white shirt, half-mast trousers, braces, bowler hat, 'bovver' boots and a cricket codpiece worn over the trousers. The most ardent devotees went so far as to carry a cane and have grotesque lashes attached to one of their eyes. The look was adopted and modified by football hooligans who, in a similar vein, also wore overalls and butchers' coats.

The Labour MP and journalist, Maurice Edelman, wrote a piece in the *Evening News* (now defunct London broadsheet) in January 1972 titled, 'Clockwork Oranges Are Ticking Bombs'. Edelman, a good friend of Anthony Burgess – the novel, *Honey for the Bears*, was dedicated to him – predicted that the film would 'lead to a clockwork cult which will magnify teenage violence'. The furore was such that Home Secretary Reginald Maudling demanded a private screening. Police, solicitors and journalists began to link the film with atrocious acts of violence, including a 14-year-boy from London charged with the manslaughter of a classmate; a 16-year-old boy killing David McManus, a 60-year-old homeless man in Bletchley, Buckinghamshire; and a youth murdering a 50-year-old man in Newton-le-Willows, Lancashire.

Stanley Kubrick said the film had become a media scapegoat. He claimed the crimes would have occurred anyway and films couldn't make people act in a way they weren't already capable of doing. Protestors indignant about the violence in *A Clockwork Orange* assembled outside Abbots Mead, Kubrick's eight-bedroom mansion in Borehamwood. Both he and his wife, Christiane, were warned by police to take heed of their safety. He also feared being sued by a bereaved family or an injured victim. Under great pressure, Kubrick asked Warner Bros to withdraw the film from British cinemas; it had already played for almost a year and had lodged itself into the psyche of the nation, including a group of delinquents from Rochdale.

* * *

Gordon Morritt, one of the three players leaving the club, felt he had good reason. He'd gone from being player of the season to third-choice goalkeeper, behind Mike Poole and Rod Jones. He signed for Darlington and teamed up once more with Dick Conner, Rochdale's former manager; players leaving to rejoin former managers at their new clubs was a regular occurrence within the game.

Bill Atkins, after starting the first three matches, had lost his place in the Rochdale team and, at 34, was keen to play as much football as possible before retiring. He'd heard and read much about Joyce's belief in youth and had told trusted team-mates that 'his face didn't fit' with the manager. At 6ft 2in, Atkins was a typical lower-league striker, able to hold the ball up or turn and surge towards goal himself, if necessary. He had an impressive goalscoring record, even when playing for poor teams – averaging a goal every three matches. He was a boon to any team because he became the 'out ball' when under pressure. They could send it in his general direction and he used his strength to take it back under control. He'd already prepared for retirement, buying a baker's shop in Keighley; he'd moved there when he signed for Halifax Town in 1965.

Atkins followed Gordon Morritt to Darlington, where the promise of a first-team place was a better proposition than the subs' bench at Rochdale and an occasional match, with afternoons helping his wife at the shop. Keith Hanvey wasn't disappointed to see him leave the squad. 'He thought he was too big for the club. I don't think him and some of the older players had the best of attitudes. Walter was getting frustrated with them,' he said. After Atkins's departure, Joyce told the press, 'We play better with one big man upfront, not two. I rate Leo [Skeete] a better prospect than Bill.'

* * *

A rape took place in Rochdale that was clearly influenced by *A Clockwork Orange*. 'A Song that Filled Girl with Fear' was the headline in the *Rochdale Observer*. The 17-year-old girl, from the Netherlands, was on a two-month trip to Britain with her 19-year-old boyfriend when they pitched a tent for the night at the scout camp at Ashworth Valley on the Rochdale/Bury border. They were approached by five youths, each carrying sticks with motorcycle grips, similar to those used in the film. The girl was raped by one of the youths in the tent, while her boyfriend had a knife pressed to his throat and sticks jabbed into his stomach. As the attack took place, the gang members sang 'Singin' in the Rain'. When the ordeal was over, the pair ran to a nearby farmhouse to seek help.

The youths were arrested and appeared before Manchester Crown Court. The judge, Sir William Morris, said, 'The evidence in this case must fill the mind of any decent person with a sickening sense of revulsion. The girl had a terribly agonising decision – whether to see her boyfriend hurt or to have her body violated.' The ringleader of the group, aged 18, was jailed for five years. Three defendants were sentenced to four years' imprisonment and a fifth was sent to a detention centre for six months.

* * *

The other experienced player to leave was Scottish winger, Malcolm Darling, widely considered to be one of Rochdale's best players. He'd played in Division One with Blackburn Rovers and, at 26, was at the age generally agreed to be optimum for a footballer. The previous season, Notts County had bid £10,000 for him and it was rejected. Fred Ratcliffe had been phoned several times by Jimmy Armfield, manager of Bolton Wanderers, and they wrangled over the transfer fee for two or three weeks. They finally agreed on £14,000 which Walter Joyce said was 'too good to turn down'. He added: 'Malcolm wasn't turning in the performances for us that I would have liked.'

* * *

A spate of novels began to appear in the early 1970s based on shocking portrayals of various youth subcultures, some of them clearly concocted by publishers: skinheads, boot boys, knuckle girls, suedeheads, smoothies, glams, speed freaks, terrace terrors, bikers and even 'dragon skins' – skinheads adept at martial arts. The genre was forged by New English Library and the prodigious Richard Allen (real name, James Moffatt – his editor chose the pseudonym). Moffatt wrote 290 novels under 45 pen names, averaging 10,000 words per day.

Moffatt, in his late 40s at the time, had volunteered himself to his agent, Victor Briggs, as a prospective teen-pulp author. 'It was ridiculous. He was no more a skinhead than Greta Garbo,' said Briggs. Moffatt's 'research' had been chatting to a group of drunken East London skinheads in a pub before dreaming up the close-cropped psychopath, Joe Hawkins, who kicked and punched his way into 18 books. *Skinhead* (1970), the first, was written in six days and, the same as all Moffatt's work, the initial draft was the final draft; he refused to rewrite or edit copy. It sold more than a million copies. He gorged on episodes of racism, violence, gang warfare and rape. 'It's a business – it's the way I make my money. I write to live,' he said.

Skinhead culture was originally multiracial, co-opting much of the fashion and music of Jamaica, but Moffatt's protagonist, Hawkins, mandated the neo-fascist version, which took hold in the 1970s: 'He leant against the bar between two coloured men. The stink of the blacks made him sick … "Spades" or "Wogs" didn't count. They were impositions on the face of a London that would always be white, Cockney, true-British.' – *Skinhead*. The books – and there were hundreds in a genre that became known as 'Youthsploitation' – were extremely popular, especially among the working class. Much the same as *A Clockwork Orange*, they were perceived as holding a cracked mirror to a socially divided society, which had fomented a restless generation, rebelling against authority and setting upon brutal infighting, often of a gratuitous nature.

Trevor Hoyle, an author from Rochdale, was inspired to write a novel within the genre after seeing a fan arrested during a match at Spotland. 'He was frogmarched around the pitch by a policeman with his arms up his back,' he said. 'He was growling at the crowd and they were spitting at him. It was an ugly sight and I remember thinking, "Christ, this is a violent reaction." I wanted to know more about people like him and started hanging around with a group of skinheads.'

The resultant book, *Rule of Night*, featured Kenny Seddon, a football hooligan and skinhead. He prowled Rochdale's rainy fluorescent-lit streets, smoking Players No. 6 and hunting down greasers to fight or girls to chat up. Hoyle wrote it 'as found', with no sentimentality or condescension, which was the foremost appeal of *Rule of Night* and similar books. Youths, primarily in urban areas, many of whom didn't habitually read books, were attracted because they saw themselves or people they could recognise within the pages. Many felt disowned by their families and schools, and demonised by police. They had formed gangs to approximate the support denied them by their parents, who were often violent or absent. They were contemptuous of 'hippy' culture, which seemed dreary and dreamy and focused too heavily on the United States; this was why the Union Jack was so prevalent among the various cults – they considered long hair, beads and whimsy to be 'unBritish'.

* * *

Bobby Downes, at the age of 24 and having played more than 150 league matches, was one of few players in the Rochdale squad at the midpoint of his career. He'd been around the personnel of football clubs – players, coaches, managers and directors – since he was 14 years old and had a clear perspective on what was happening at Spotland. 'Walter was a nice fella but the older lads weren't having it,' he said. 'From the off, he was viewed as a youth team coach and was having trouble with the hardened pros who were sometimes openly defying him in front of others – moaning that the sessions were crap. They weren't prepared to give the kids any advice and were shouting at them, blaming them for this and that. Walter was used to working with younger lads and he had these older players shaking their heads in front of him, obviously not buying into what he was telling them.'

At the age of 18, Downes had been released by West Bromwich Albion without playing for the first team. He spent two seasons at Peterborough United, where he struggled to establish a regular place. He joined Rochdale in 1969 and was a consistent performer, usually playing left-wing. 'Back then, football was a hard game. The first time you received the ball, you knew you were going to get smashed by the full-back. In my first-ever game for Peterborough, I dribbled past one of their lads and afterwards he came up to me and said, "If you ever do that again I'll break your leg so that you'll never be able to play again." You can't then hide on the pitch for the rest of the match but, when you've been told that, you keep an eye out for him. The thing was to get to them first, to try and put them off *their* game,' he said.

Downes had been 'done' by Rodney Marsh while playing for Rochdale in a League Cup tie at Manchester City in September 1972; he suffered a broken fibula. Afterwards, Marsh visited him in hospital. 'He turned up without any socks on. I'd never seen that before and assumed it must be a trendy thing to do. He didn't really apologise but told me I was a young lad [Marsh was five years older] and it was something that happened in football and I'd more or less have to get used to it. He said he'd had a clout that had left him deaf in one ear.' (Marsh was referring to a broken jaw and skull he received while playing for Fulham against Leicester City in 1963. He'd collided with John Sjoberg, the Scottish defender, and spent ten months out of the game.)

Downes, much the same as Keith Hanvey, was another player enjoying a 'decent run' in the team – free of injury and a regular first-teamer. After the free transfer from West Brom and unsettled period at Peterborough, he was pleased to have established himself as a professional footballer; he would go on to miss only four of Rochdale's matches all season. He was disappointed that the early season results were poor but was satisfied with his own game; he was doing his bit. He was liked by the fans and even had his own song, 'Viva Bobby Downes'.

* * *

Although relatively well staffed in the 1970s, local newspapers were still selective about jobs considered worthy of sending out a reporter to cover. *The Rochdale Observer* heard about strange goings-on at a house in Fieldhead Avenue, Bamford. Rather than having curtains or blinds at the windows, the occupant had put up posters of semi-nude men and women. A reporter was dispatched, spiral-bound notebook in coat pocket. The front door remained unanswered but a neighbour gave an intriguing insight: 'This young man's latest escapade is one of the many pranks we've had to put up with,' she said. 'One day, he asked if he could take me to a hotel in Manchester, saying that he was having an all-night party and didn't wish to keep me awake. It is nothing for him to prune his rose trees at 3am or vacuum his carpet in the early hours of the morning.' A few months later, reporters would call again at the house.

8

A Poor Urban Environment

ROOTS HALL, the home of Southend United, was much the same as Plymouth Argyle's Home Park – a geographical outpost that visiting footballers dreaded. Both grounds were next to the sea, too, so a microclimate of driving wind and rain often added to the toil. On this occasion, Walter Joyce was happy to make the 500-mile round trip, pleased to be away from Spotland and out of sight of supporters whose moans and groans were unsettling the players, making them 'narrow' their game so that most passes were square or backwards and no one was willing to run with the ball or risk that 'killer' pass.

He usually kept his pre-match talks brief because he recognised that close to kick-off the players were too nervous, too agitated to take much in. He clenched his fists, wished them the best, implored them to express themselves, and that was usually it. But he'd spent the journey down in deep thought and had something to say. He made them get up from the benches at the perimeter of the dressing room and draw closer: 'Look, lads – do you know what this lot [Southend] will be thinking? They'll consider us a fucking pushover. We're bottom of the league. We've been all day on a bus, 17 piss stops and an egg butty at a grotty service station. We'll have bugger all fans here, so they'll imagine we'll want to hide, go in on ourselves and spend most of the match dreaming about getting back on the bloody bus and heading home. Well, we're not having it, are we? Put a few sighters in [hard tackles made early in the match], let them know you're up for it and they'll not know what's fucking going on. Get out there and show them.'

They did show them. They won 2-1, their first league victory of the season, after eight matches. Unfortunately, Fred Ratcliffe missed most of the first half. He was among a party of directors, associates and pressmen who had travelled to the match by train. 'We all got off in London,' said Stan Townsend. 'The cry went out, "Where's Fred?" We couldn't find him and presumed he'd got off and gone ahead of the main party. When we got to the ground, he wasn't in the boardroom and still wasn't there when the match started. Everyone was asking, "Has anyone here seen Fred?" It turned out that he'd been stuck on the train and could only get off when he pulled the cord. He was absolutely steaming when he finally arrived at the ground.'

Afterwards, as the players clambered on the coach, made light on their feet by the helium of winning, they patted each other on the back, congratulating one another, talking excitedly. A win, at last. Easy. Back to the routine, then: the losing, the drawing *and* the winning, rather than merely losing and drawing. In their well-earned, well-deserved singing and shouting joy they had no idea of the singularity of what they had done, how the date of Saturday, 29 September would stand tall in their calendar of a season. For now, it was the click of ring pulls sprung from beer cans and everyone singing 'Up the Dale, Up the Dale'.

Stan Townsend, writing in the *Rochdale Observer*, noted that none of the home fixtures had attracted more than 3,000 fans and this 'probably meant cash must be in very short supply at Spotland'. Unusually for a comment of such resonance, it featured almost as an afterthought. Fans who had made their way to the bottom of the page, past the short reports on the reserves and youth matches and the winners of the weekly draw, must have wondered: what is going on? It was almost as though Ratcliffe had leaned over from the directors' box and had a word with Townsend. He was making supporters aware, in his own idiosyncratic way, that in addition to the team's poor form (the Southend win excepted), the club was still, as ever, stalked by financial worries.

* * *

A Rochdale couple on a luxury coach trip found themselves at the epicentre of an international conflict that would eventually claim more than 15,000 lives and have repercussions throughout the world. Mr and Mrs Thorneycroft were among a group of tourists heading to the Israeli city of Tiberias on the western shore of the Sea of Galilee. On 6 October 1973 – the Jewish holy day of Yom Kippur – an Arab coalition force drawn chiefly from Egypt and Syria entered disputed territory in the Sinai Peninsula and Golan Heights, which the Israelis had occupied since 1967. The coach party became snagged among tanks and jeeps loaded with artillery in a convoy of Israeli soldiers heading to the fighting. 'There we were, 40-odd tourists going to war in a posh coach,' said Jack Thorneycroft. 'It was a situation made for one of those old-time British comedy films.'

The comedic element evaporated when the Thorneycrofts of Cliftonville Avenue, Thornham reached Tiberias. Sirens rang out continuously and, from their hotel balcony, they could hear fighter jets zooming by and guns fired. Still, they were determined to enjoy their holiday. 'It felt a bit odd, going out swimming with the fighters hurtling across the sky and the guns booming, but we soon got used to it,' he said. The conflict provoked global tension as the two nuclear superpowers, the United States and Soviet Union, viewed it as a theatre of war, whereby they provided finance and military supplies to each side. The Soviets backed the Arabs; the Americans, the Israelis.

A public meeting to address 'the Middle East Situation' was held at the headquarters of the Christadelphians in Yorkshire Street, Rochdale. As believers in millenarianism – the notion that society will be transformed and 'all things will be changed' – they were understandably stirred. Posters were affixed to walls around town reading: 'The present Israeli/Arab conflict heralds the reappearing of Jesus Christ to establish God's Kingdom.'

* * *

Despite Fred Ratcliffe's augury about finances, Walter Joyce was on a promise that he could spend a portion of the income from the sale of Malcolm Darling on finding a replacement. He'd hoped for about half of it, £7,000, but was rebuffed: 'If I give you that much, we won't be able to pay the tax bill and if we don't do that, we're all buggered,' Ratcliffe told him.

Joyce returned to Manchester City for another player similar to Keith Hanvey – a former schoolboy prodigy who had been on the fringes of the first team. Mike Brennan had frequently scored 90 to 100 goals per season for Salford Grammar School and had an impressive record for Whitehill Boys, the junior club from Levenshulme, affiliated to Manchester City. He'd signed for City in July 1968 and scored 14 goals in his first four matches with the A and B teams. In March 1971, aged 18, he found himself warming up on the touchline at the Baseball Ground, Derby County's former ground, about to make his debut as a substitute for the first team. Brian Clough, Derby's manager, attracted his attention. 'Have you seen who's out there waiting for you?' he asked. The centre-backs Brennan was about to face were Roy McFarland and Dave Mackay, two players renowned for their strength and aggression. Brennan smiled. 'I'm not sure you'll be smiling in a few minutes, laddie,' said Clough. 'There's a lot of mud out there – you'll do well to keep out of their way.'

Although he made four first-team appearances for Manchester City, Brennan realised it was unlikely he'd be able to dislodge players such as Colin Bell, Francis Lee and Mike Summerbee. 'It wasn't like today when you've got agents galore angling to find you a club,' said Brennan. 'I'd been on loan at Stockport but no one had made any overtures towards signing me. I was desperate to play first-team football and thought it was something I deserved.'

Walter Joyce travelled to Heald Green, Stockport, where Brennan was living at the time, and they quickly agreed a deal; the weekly wage would be between £30 and £40 per week, depending on bonuses. City received a transfer fee of £4,000. 'Walter was great to talk to and a nice fella. I could tell straight away that he was committed to management and had been a good pro in his time,' he said.

Brennan was able to resume his friendship with former City team-mate, Keith Hanvey. 'I used to catch two buses to get to Keith's house, only to find him sitting at the breakfast table with his porridge and honey courtesy of his doting mum. He'd be in his pyjamas and dressing gown and I used to think: how could someone be so laid-back like that and yet on the pitch he was this big, strong centre-half,' he said.

The facilities at Spotland were, of course, considerably inferior to those at Maine Road. Bob Stokoe, a previous Rochdale manager, insisted on signing players at their homes, so that they would see Spotland *after* they had already committed themselves to the club. 'We'd train at Fred Ratcliffe's place at Sparth Bottoms,' said Brennan. 'If it was heavy rain, you could almost disappear down some of the holes. We also used to go to a local park or on the council's pitches at Firgrove. We'd take pegs and set up makeshift goals. Spotland itself was in a pretty dilapidated state. There was a hole in the roof and we'd sometimes find leaves in the bath. We used to say it did us good, having a herbal bath. There was a rat that we'd see occasionally in the dressing rooms. We called him Ronnie. I remember Rod Jones, the goalie, saying the bath was in such a bad state and the water so mucky that even Ronnie would get out of it and clear off.'

Another player, Graham Smith, recalls the bath being particularly small and players undressing quickly to ensure they secured a place in it. 'It used to take ages to warm up the water. Someone would have to turn on the heater at about 10am to be ready for us getting in after the match at 5pm. It can't have been very hygienic, all of us squashed up in there, full of muck. It was the same at most places, though. I think there was a shower over the bath but very few clubs had rows of showers. I played a reserve game once at Villa Park and they had individual baths for each player – it felt like the height of sophistication,' said Smith.

Two days after signing for Rochdale, Mike Brennan was with the squad undertaking another long journey to the south coast, this time to play Bournemouth on a Wednesday evening.

* * *

Over several weeks in the autumn of 1973, the local media gorged on a story that coalesced the words 'nude' and 'headmaster's daughter', framed within an international setting. Mary Randle, aged 19, a student from Norden, was arrested and jailed for two months in Neapolis, Crete for allegedly swimming nude in the sea with Timothy Cosgrave, another student, aged 21, from Derby. Her father, Frank Randle, *deputy* head at St Wilfrid's RC School, Rochdale, reported that the Foreign Office was trying to 'obtain her release'. Cyril Smith made a plea to the Greek Minister of Justice, appealing for clemency. 'It was perhaps a foolish thing for her to do, but I feel that a prison sentence was extremely harsh. I know Mary personally. She's a grand girl,' he said.

Mr Randle said his daughter was due to start a sociology degree at Exeter University. She told the court in Crete that she hadn't intended to offend and was unaware she'd broken the law; she merely wanted an all-over suntan. The matter escalated when reports reached Greek officials that there were claims Mary and Timothy had been kicked and slapped by a police officer and kept in a cell without mattresses, where cockroaches 'crawled across the floor'. 'Everything which has been written is totally false,' said Nicholas Canellopoulos, general director of the corrective department of the Greek Justice Ministry. He said the prison where they were detained was 'new, clean and kept strictly to all international regulations'. 'They will spend two months there, whatever happens,' he added. The 'Nude-swim girl' was made to serve her sentence before returning to the family home in Edenfield Road, Norden.

* * *

On the coach to Bournemouth and in the dressing room, Joyce repeated continually, 'More of the same.' He was referring to how they had played against Southend. He issued his final entreaty: 'Plenty of graft, lads. Cover the runs. Win those second balls. Play your own game in possession. Don't be afraid to shoot. Leo [Skeete] – come short when you have to but play on the shoulder of their last man to stretch them and create space where you can. Mike [Brennan] – if it's tight inside, don't be afraid to move to the flanks and keep looking for those knock-downs from the big man [Skeete].'

Skeete, at 6ft 2in, had fast feet for a tall, strong player. Born in Liverpool, he'd played for Burscough in the Cheshire County League and Ellesmere Port Town in the Northern Premier League, for whom he scored 26 goals in the 1971/72 season. He was one of few black players in the Football League and his afro and thick moustache saw him stand out even more. In newspapers he was referred to as 'dusky' and 'well-proportioned'. Among the Rochdale players, he was considered 'typically Scouse' – chirpy and brash. 'Leo had a chip on both shoulders and felt the world owed him a living,' said a team-mate. 'He was a decent player but not as good as he thought he was. He drove

Walter mad by not working hard enough. The ball had to be played right to his feet or he'd have a moan.' Others praised his 'big heart' and willingness to 'show' for the ball, however much pressure he was under. 'He was like a lot of lads from non-league, full of effort but unorthodox. You didn't know what he was going to do next, which was more often a quality, rather than a weakness,' said another player.

Two weeks earlier, Rochdale had done well to draw with Bournemouth at Spotland but, even with a defensive reinforcement – Steve Arnold playing as a sweeper – they were unable to repel the home team: Bournemouth 2, Rochdale 0. The defeat had been expected and the mood remained reasonably high, principally because Rochdale, after the victory at Southend, were no longer winless. Beforehand, it had been mentioned repeatedly in the local media and 'blob pars' (very short pieces) running in the national press. The next 'monkey on their back' according to the *Football Pink* (a sports newspaper published by the *Manchester Evening News*) was the lack of a home win.

Three days after losing at Bournemouth, they drew 1-1 at Spotland against Huddersfield Town. The monkey was still present; it would remain for some time.

* * *

Rochdale was named as one of the worst towns in the country in October 1973. The report, commissioned by the government, summarised it as 'a poor urban environment' and listed six main factors: pollution, overcrowding, shortage of basic amenities, a surfeit of derelict land, road noise and a dearth of open spaces. In greater detail, it revealed that rivers 'were the most polluted in the country' – the River Roch and most of its tributaries were found to be 'grossly polluted'. Even with improvements to sewage works 'it may be the 1990s before anything like a clean river system is seen'. Between one-fifth and one-half of the local population were subject to noise levels above the permitted maximum. Rochdale's 6.54 acres of open space per 1,000 people was significantly below the recommended 9.5 acres. Most of the town was listed as a 'black area', with a high frequency of smog and large amounts of air pollution. The total cost to clear land and buildings classed as derelict was estimated at £32m.

Mr James Anthony Haddaway was so desperate to move from Rochdale, or the Belfield estate at least, that he devised a plan – he threatened to sell his seven children if he wasn't rehoused. He didn't reveal how this would be possible in a country where selling children was illegal and the question wasn't asked by journalists and camera crews descending on his four-bedroomed home in Beal Crescent. He lived there with his wife, Thelma, and children, aged 3 to 16, where a shortage of space meant he and Thelma slept downstairs on a bed-settee. He was shown smoking a cigarette, wearing a vest without a shirt, despondent amid his brood. 'I'm really thinking about doing it,' he said. 'If it came to the point where it was me against the local authority, I'm afraid I would do it. Once I say a thing, I do it. Nobody loves children more than I do and I don't want to have to do it.' He said the family had suffered abuse during the two years they had lived in Belfield since moving from Oldham. Their eldest son had been beaten up and the family's pet rabbit had been cut open and its body nailed to the back door of the house.

The council acknowledged the poor state of housing on the estate and sent in contractors to carry out modernisation. They were on site a few days before downing tools; they claimed to be 'loaded with fleas'. A site meeting was called with Derek Broadbent, the borough architect. 'There can be no doubt that there is a great deal of unrest among contractors who have to go into these houses. As well as being infested with fleas, some of them are generally filthy,' he said. Mr H.E. Peaper, chief public health inspector, confirmed that the workmen had become flea-infested. 'Now, as a standard procedure, every house will be treated before it is handed over to contractors,' he said.

'House-proud housewives' (headline in the *Rochdale Observer*) were irate to learn Belfield had been branded as a 'filthy' estate. Christine Rowland, of Albert Royds Street, said, 'When people ask you where you live and you say Belfield, they think you must be dirty. This makes us all seem the same. I have an auntie living in Australia. What will she think when she sees this in the paper?' Christine Saukura, of Belfield Mill Lane, said she was 'ashamed of being from Belfield', while Anne Hampton, also of Belfield Mill Lane, complained that her husband's workmates in Oldham had been talking of the 'Belfield Fleas'. 'It's not what they say to your face, it's the snide remarks they make,' she said. Another resident, Mrs Jean Bannon, said she'd scrubbed the paintwork before the contractors had moved in, so they wouldn't think her house was dirty.

* * *

The opening few weeks of a football season often proffered unexpected, erratic results. Teams that would later become promotion contenders lost to those relegated at the end of the season. Others started 'like a house on fire', convincingly winning their opening few matches, only to fall away to mid-table. As teams either 'knitted' or didn't, form and results became more predictable. By the beginning of official British wintertime – Sunday, 28 October in 1973 – it was generally agreed teams had settled into a pattern of results that reflected their competency, and their league position was a reliable approximation of where they would finish at the season's end.

Rochdale's handful of creditable performances – the win at Southend United, the comeback against Bournemouth and a draw against a strong Huddersfield Town – suggested that the rest of the season wasn't necessarily set for disappointment. Three other clubs had made worse starts than Rochdale – Shrewsbury

Town, Southend United and Aldershot. When players, coaching staff and fans saw the team standing four places from bottom of the table, they felt no pressing reason to fret. After all, two consecutive wins and they were practically mid-table.

Over a five-week period, from mid-October to mid-November, everything changed. Rochdale lost seven times in eight matches, conceding 24 goals and falling to the bottom of the table. They were knocked out of both the League Cup and Lancashire Senior Cup. The abject run began with a 4-0 defeat against Bolton Wanderers at Spotland in the League Cup. Rochdale barely crossed the halfway line and earned their solitary corner seconds before the final whistle. Before the match, the coach carrying the Bolton squad had been pelted with stones as it travelled through Rochdale. The driver gave chase and caught a 13-year-old boy from Freehold. He denied the offence at Rochdale Juvenile Court but was found guilty of causing £84 of damage.

Reg Jenkins had attended the match after returning to Rochdale to complete the sale of his house. He was now playing for his hometown club, Millbrook FC, in the Plymouth and District League; he'd scored 14 goals in the first three fixtures of the season, including eight in one match. 'Brought your boots with you, Reggie?' fans shouted when he was spied in the Main Stand. 'You're just what this team needs,' yelled another. Fred Ratcliffe grimaced.

The day after the Bolton defeat, Walter Joyce insisted that the squad meet up at Spotland for light training and a scrutiny of their performance. He told them that he could, *just about*, deal with losing but not in that manner: they hadn't done the basics – ran themselves into the ground, covered for one another. They had hid, he said, melted away when it mattered most. Oldham Athletic were next up and they were 'flying', with only one defeat in the first ten league matches of the season. 'I want a win there,' Joyce told them. 'It's another local derby and a chance for you to show the fans that you've got some backbone and can bounce back from a hiding.'

* * *

A national strike by tanker drivers in November 1973 led to a shortage of petrol, which instigated a rash of panic buying. Most petrol stations introduced a limit of £1 of fuel per car. The government issued ration books to post offices, available to motorists on presenting their vehicle's logbook and tax disc. A black market for fuel led to thieves in a lorry crashing through the gates at Wilkinson's Transport Ltd, Canal Wharf, Rochdale. They drew 55 gallons of diesel from the pumps, worth £22.55. Two 45-gallon drums of diesel oil worth £15 were stolen from a building site in Arm Road, Littleborough.

Firemen (presumably there were no female 'firefighters' at the time) announced a work-to-rule in a bid to have the working week reduced from 56 to 48 hours. Mr Schofield, Rochdale's chief fire officer, promised the public that firemen would attend emergencies and the work-to rule was 'confined to administration'. Rochdale's 26 ambulancemen ('paramedic' wasn't in common usage) also staged a work-to-rule protest as part of the national strike by the National Union of Public Employees; Keith Joseph, secretary of state for social services, had rejected a petition for a wage increase. The ambulancemen apologised for being unable to take home discharged patients or drive people to appointments at the clinic or outpatient department. They suggested patients called on friends or family, or took a taxi.

Lorry drivers and loading staff at Wilkinson's Transport found themselves locked out when they returned one lunchtime. Management had taken this retaliatory action in response to a request by the 200 members of staff for a wage rise and reduction of the working week to 45 hours. Peter Keefe of the Transport and General Workers' Union said talks had reached deadlock.

Union representatives were called to Ensor Mill, Queensway but were told it was too late to save most of the jobs. Carrington Viyella employed 350 at the mill, producing yarn for the carpet industry. Mr Battersby, managing director, said closure was due to 'developments in technology coupled with the obsolete condition of machinery at Ensor'. Production was transferred to Lily Mill in Shaw, Oldham. After a three-hour meeting, the company agreed that a small number of staff would be transferred to Shaw.

* * *

Rochdale lost 3-1 against Oldham Athletic at Boundary Park and, two days later, lost 4-0 again to Bolton Wanderers, this time in the Lancashire Senior Cup. In the league they lost 3-0 at Charlton, 3-1 at home to Plymouth Argyle, 3-1 at Port Vale, 3-1 at home to Watford and 3-0 at Wrexham.

Supporters vented their frustration with perverse humour. Keith Hanvey was carried from the pitch with a badly cut ankle against Plymouth and a fan shouted, 'Cut his leg off.' Walter Joyce was understandably indignant: 'Some people just seem to want to ridicule the players. If that's what they shout at a player who has been doing quite well [Hanvey], what do they shout at the lad who is having a stinker?' Hanvey's injury was treated by Peter Blakey, Manchester City's physio who, as a favour to his friend, Walter Joyce – as players they had both been part of Burnley's youth system – often visited Spotland to help players return to fitness.

At least Stan Townsend was able to share in a moment of light relief after travelling on the team bus to Charlton. 'As we got off, one of the players said, "Come on Townsend, make yourself useful." I helped them unload the kitbags from the coach. As we were doing this, a young lad approached and asked for our autographs. There's some kid now grown up in Charlton who still has my autograph and thinks I'm one of the players!'

Directors often travelled on the team coach, sitting on seats at the front. 'We'd sometimes stop off and have a beer somewhere or scampi and chips. One of the directors would always pick up the bill or present us with an envelope with a few quid in it,' said a former player. 'They were all very nice men. We had a laugh with them now and again but always called them Mr whatever, rather than use their first names.' Before and after games, Fred Ratcliffe called in the dressing room. Players took this in good spirit and believed he did it out of a sense of duty rather than in the hope of asserting any influence or as a show of vainglory.

The sole point gained over this period was secured in a 1-1 draw with Grimsby Town at Spotland. After the defeat against Wrexham on 17 November, Rochdale fell to the foot of the table and were already five points adrift of safety from relegation. The shocking run had eliminated any ambiguity about the team and their situation – they were poor and in the mire.

* * *

The most talked about dispute in Rochdale was at local coach company Yelloway. Staff and management were at loggerheads over pay and conditions. The brightly coloured Yelloway coaches featuring a rising-sun logo were symbolic of holidays or weekend trips, either east (Filey) or west (Blackpool); they also supplied coaches to Rochdale AFC. Against the backdrop of short days, long nights and the multitude of strikes and closures, a summer getaway was greatly anticipated.

Brothers Robert and Ernest Holt of Hyde Park Farm, Newbold had formed the company in the early 1900s. At first they delivered parcels by pony and cart but later bought steam and motor lorries. These were converted to charabancs and outings were organised to Hollingworth Lake or the White House pub, high above Littleborough, where people could picnic and take in the panoramic view of Rochdale. Gracie Fields, then aged 13, had been a passenger on one of Yelloway's first long-distance trips, when she travelled to Torquay in 1911 with 25 others and a pet dog. The local printing firm, Edwards and Brynings, had hired the charabanc for the staff's annual trip to see the Torquay Regatta; Fields was a good friend of the daughter of one of the firm's directors. While on holiday, she won a talent competition on Paignton seafront and received a prize of a pair of roller skates.

The 30 Yelloway drivers had staged a walkout after calling for a five-day working week. They also sought a pay rise of £4 on top of their weekly wage of £21.15, for a 40-hour week. Mr Graham Shaw, shop steward, said, 'We are victimised because we work for a private company and are the poorest paid long-distance coach drivers in the country. We want a bit of the cake.' After a few days of bickering, Hubert Allen, managing director, said both sides had come to a 'satisfactory understanding'. The drivers returned to work. Summer holidays were back in the diary.

* * *

Fred Ratcliffe resented the presumption of 'rightful place' – that people, families and football clubs should accept their lot and recognise a limit on their ambition. His ingenuity and resolve had seen him rise from relative poverty to become one of the richest men in town. He'd been undersized as a boy and a man, in a town where people were sharp with a jibe, ready to put you in your place; this hadn't disheartened him either.

The other Fred at Spotland, O'Donoghue, had often wondered how Ratcliffe had known he was discontent while scouting for Arsenal. 'I can't think who would have told him,' he said to his wife, Cathy, again and again. 'It doesn't add up.' Within a few weeks, he'd solved the conundrum. He'd been in close quarters and seen how Ratcliffe worked, how he happily faded away in company, letting others hold court. At times, it had felt as if the chairman wasn't there, such was his anonymity. 'It's all an act,' said O'Donoghue. 'He doesn't miss a trick. He's a little Jodrell Bank, on the quiet.'

O'Donoghue often chatted with Angus McLean and the conversation invariably turned to Ratcliffe; he had much more magnetism than most of the players. 'I think it's because he's so little,' said McLean who, at 6ft 2in, was almost a foot taller than the chairman. 'What do you mean?' asked O'Donoghue. 'He's obviously aware of his size and I think he uses it to deliberately place himself on the edge of a group. He's always in that massive fur overcoat as well, as if he's trying to disappear into it. The thing is, he really *listens* but, because he's down there, not giving much away, no one notices that he's clocked everything. Fred's having the last laugh, though. You don't need anyone fussing over you when you're about 100 times richer than everyone else in the room,' said McLean.

Across boardrooms, Carlisle United to Plymouth Argyle, Ratcliffe was accustomed to his football club being patronised by toffee-nosed directors; it spurred him on. He was proud that Rochdale stood toe to toe with clubs the stature of Bristol Rovers, Charlton Athletic and Blackburn Rovers in the Third Division. He and the club were one: determined, tenacious, refuting any designation of 'rightful place'. All the same, in his less emphatic moments, when he looked at the falling-down state of Spotland and noted, once more, the paltriness of the 'crowd', he thought – although he never told anyone this – that the club spending five seasons in the Third Division had been a remarkable achievement. He imagined most fans felt the same and, considering this elevated status, would show more tolerance to a new manager and a team made up of young players. He'd been surprised by the fans' visceral response to the poor run of form, especially after the home defeat to Plymouth Argyle, when they were at the perimeter fence booing the players from the field, screaming abuse at Walter Joyce.

Stan Townsend had caught this rancorous mood. He wrote (beneath the headline, 'Dale Face Drop in this Bleak Form'):

> This is the poorest display Rochdale have offered spectators for a long, long time. They were diabolical. There was no aggression, no initiative, no momentum and certainly no challenge. Their passing verged on the pathetic and what ball was won in the tackle was foolishly thrown away by slap-happy distribution.

Few contemporary reporters would be so unequivocal and, if they were, would probably find themselves excommunicated by the club. 'I was lucky,' said Townsend. 'They accepted me for what I was. I always wrote the truth and the players knew I would never write anything I wouldn't say to them in person, if asked.'

The backroom staff was in agreement with Townsend after the Plymouth defeat. In his after-match interview, Walter Joyce also used the word 'pathetic'. His assistant, Dennis Butler, did likewise. 'Things aren't happening out there and, what is worse, the players are not trying to make them happen,' said Butler. 'They are not responding to a situation and the set-piece marking is pathetic. We have worked things out and discussed them with the players but when they get out there everything seems to be thrown to the wind. I don't understand it.'

Years later, Butler would recognise the futility of his frustration. 'The players weren't good enough. The teams we played against were much better; it was as simple as that. It was depressing because we just couldn't get results. There was no magic wand we could wave to put things right. One or two players *could* play and went on to do okay with other clubs but one or two doesn't make a team,' he said.

In his match report for the defeat at Port Vale, another *Rochdale Observer* sports journalist, David Sugden, was scathing:

This was yet another in a succession of abject performances turned in by 12 men, who, on Saturday at least, appeared to be masquerading as a football team. I would be only too pleased to single out one facet of Rochdale's play which looked to be a pointer to a better future, but there was nothing other than a mundane diet of kick and rush stuff.

Sugden played football himself, turning out regularly for Spotland Methodists FC, where he was known as Noddy Sugden because he was reportedly able to head a ball further than others could kick it.

When all the swearing and shouting was over after the Plymouth match and the players had dressed and left Spotland, Fred Ratcliffe beckoned Angus McLean to his table in the directors' lounge. 'How many were on today, Gus?' McLean had expected the query. He pulled out a piece of paper from the inside pocket of his jacket. '1,432, Fred.' Fred Ratcliffe sighed. 'That's the lowest we've ever had in this division,' added McLean. The next day, Ratcliffe called the board together. Stan Townsend asked whether he could term it as a 'crisis' meeting. Ratcliffe agreed that he could; it would send a message to fans that the directors cared enough to respond to their frustration and disappointment.

After the meeting, Ratcliffe announced, 'We'll make some signings.'

* * *

City and town centres were being revamped through the late 1960s and into the 1970s. The slow, connatural development of shops, offices and civic buildings along particular streets, each constructed chiefly from locally sourced materials, became viewed as outdated and it was assumed people would prefer larger, weatherproof structures with a greater variety of retailers, similar to the United States – this 'Americanisation' of Britain had become a strong compulsion.

The Birmingham Bull Ring Centre, the country's first indoor city-centre shopping precinct, opened in May 1964, housing 140 retail units. Planners were beguiled by its success and look – the heavy use of concrete and plastic, set to angular and functional designs. Similar schemes were advanced across the country, including Rochdale.

The plan to restructure Rochdale town centre was first mooted in 1966. Lengthy discussions took place between councillors and there were two public inquiries before Laing Development was instructed to design and build a £3m shopping centre. At the time, Laing ('making infrastructure happen') was the favoured company for public bodies and was responsible for the Bull Ring along with hospitals, cathedrals, the M1 motorway, London's Westway trunk road and even nuclear power stations. 'I think it will change the face of Rochdale for the better as far as the shopping public is concerned. It will be a great benefit and boon,' said Councillor Derrick Walker, chairman of the policy committee.

* * *

Fred Ratcliffe, with his majority shareholding, was able to make arbitrary, unilateral statements such as 'we'll make more signings' but he preferred to have the endorsement of the board. Cynics said the other directors were 'yes men' or 'nodding dogs' but they were each strong characters and, although hand-picked by Ratcliffe, could be recalcitrant and contrary at times. 'Rochdale had such a lot of small businesses, especially in manufacturing, and they tried to help each other out. My dad treated everyone the same and never looked down on anybody,' said Judith Hilton, Ratcliffe's daughter.

His main confidant was Joe Stoney, a solicitor and club vice-chairman. Their families often went on holiday together and mixed at each other's houses or at Rochdale Golf Club. When he qualified at the age of 21, Stoney was thought to be the youngest practising solicitor in the country. He served on a wealth of civic and sporting bodies and had been a Liberal councillor for Norden and Bamford.

Board meetings were held at the Crimble, a country hall standing in three acres of countryside between Bamford and Heywood, a place dubbed 'a Mecca of middle-class aspirers' and 'home of the Bamford in-crowd'. Fred Ratcliffe had bought it in 1960 with Norman Ledson, a prominent Mason, Conservative party member and mayor of Rochdale from 1961–62; such alliances of dignitaries were typical in the town. Rochdale's directors would gather amid the art deco furnishings in the dining room, beneath two enormous crystal chandeliers, commandeered from a cruise ship. An acquaintance of Ratcliffe's said, 'He was often in the Crimble until 3am. He loved talking to people at the bar until the early hours.' One of Ratcliffe's favourite sayings was 'when there are not enough hours in the day, you pinch some from the night'. Joe Stoney was his regular drinking companion, knocking back pink gins, while Ratcliffe preferred Black Label whisky drawn from his own personal optic.

Later, board meetings were switched from 8.30pm at the Crimble to 5.30pm at the football club. This change of policy was a considerable concession by Ratcliffe; he liked to sleep in the early evening before heading out into the night. 'It meant we had more chance of getting on with business and talking sense,' said a former director. 'They were nearly always pissed by the time we started at the Crimble.'

Leonard Hilton, aged 39 in 1973, another director, was most commonly referred to as 'the Pie Man'. He first visited Spotland in the 1930s as an 11-year-old, when he sold cigarettes from a tray to supporters. The bakery he owned with his wife, Alice, supplied pies on matchdays – the usual order was between 80 and 100 dozen per match. He joined the board after writing a letter to the *Rochdale Observer* about the stupidity of hurling toilet rolls on to the pitch while a match was in progress; this was a frequent occurrence in the 1960s and 1970s. Ratcliffe deduced that anyone willing to write such a letter clearly had the club's best interests at heart and should be invited on to the board, especially if he ran a local business.

Hilton often arrived late at matches because he spent most Saturdays on horseback as a member of the Holcombe Hunt in Bury. He led an active life, surfing in Newquay, waterskiing on Lake Windermere and Alpine skiing in Austria. He'd been a PE instructor in the RAF and an attendant at Castleton Baths before helping Alice run the business, where his speciality was making wedding cakes. 'They were short of directors at the time,' said Andrew Hilton, Leonard's son. 'Money was tight and the club rundown, as a lot of others were at that time. They were on the lookout for gullible people to join them and I think my dad was flattered when asked.'

Many Rochdale fans joked that the quality of the pies compensated for the dreadful football. Hilton also supplied the food for the press, dignitaries and, wisely, the referee and linesmen. 'It was always really good,' said Stan Townsend. 'Managers and scouts used to come from all over – I'm sure it was mainly for the half-time buffet. There were all kinds of sandwiches, chicken legs and those lovely Hilton pies. Lawrie McMenemy [manager of Grimsby Town and later Southampton] was always there. He could hold court for about 20 minutes without anyone having to say anything. He was about 6ft 4in and stood head and shoulders over Freddie [Ratcliffe] but they were really good pals.'

Leonard Hilton used to joke with friends that Rochdale ended up with the 'sweepings up' – players that other clubs felt were of no real value. During a match against Newport County in 1969, both he and another director, Rod Brierley, had been impressed by their striker, Tony Buck. They put it to Ratcliffe that the club should eschew its policy of signing free transfer players, but were told funds weren't available. They inquired about Buck and learned that his wages were being paid by Newport's chairman, out of his own pocket. He was keen for this arrangement to end and agreed to sell Buck to Rochdale for £5,000 – a fee that was covered personally by Hilton and Brierley. 'My dad kept a lot of this away from my mother,' said Andrew Hilton. 'I don't think she'd really wanted him to join the board but she sort of tolerated it. He didn't have the disposable income of some of the other directors who had long-established businesses.'

* * *

The grand scheme to transform Rochdale town centre would take four years to complete, the public was informed. It would include a multistorey car park for 1,000 vehicles and extensions to the department stores owned by the Rochdale Equitable Pioneers Society and Woolworths. Three pubs would be demolished – the Red Lion, the Coach and Horses and the Old Clock Face Hotel, the site of the birthplace of the poet Edwin Waugh, and a regular rendezvous for folk singers. The Red Lion had been run in the 1960s by Wilf Fleming, who claimed to be 'the smallest landlord in England'. He was 4ft 10in and had to stand on a specially made platform to reach the beer taps. Little Wilf, as he was known, was proud to run a peaceable drinking house. If faced with a truculent customer, he'd say, 'Please conduct yourself properly or I will have you out. Don't let these spectacles fool you.' These pubs had been serving drinks for more than a century and were the base for community groups. The Red Lion hosted meetings of the Rochdale Rotary Club, the Central Lancashire Cricket League and the Royal Antediluvian Order of Buffaloes.

Compulsory purchase orders were also placed on shops, while the market was to be relocated in the shopping precinct.

Dougie Freedman ran a bric-a-brac stall with his wife, Flo. He agreed that the market needed modernising but objected, in prescient terms, to the restructure of the town centre, which would see the new centre linked to the bus station via an overhead walkway. 'These precincts destroy a town's individuality,' he said. 'Rochdale's shopping centre will end up looking like Oldham's, Preston's or a town 100 miles away. They're taking down old buildings to put up concrete Lego jungles.' Christine Morris ran a shop due for demolition called the Needlework Box, which had stood in Toad Lane for more than 50 years. She said: 'They're trying to get rid of all the little shops. A lot of the old market stallholders have gone because they don't want to be bothered with the upheaval. Yet the big shops won't stock the things we do.'

The building in Toad Lane that had housed the original Rochdale Pioneers was to remain, but the rest of this portion of land was due to be restructured. The town was about to metaphorically turn its back on an area rich in history – the Saint Mary in the Baum Church, designed by the famous Gothic Revivalist architect Sir John Ninian Comper, was a few yards from Toad Lane. The new layout would see these eminent buildings sandwiched between two busy roads, in the shadow of the back wall and car park of the shopping centre, and accessible on foot from the market only via a gloomy subway. Several declared that it reminded them of another piece of unfathomable planning from earlier years. Rochdale Town Hall, widely regarded as one of the finest in the country, had been left standing as an island, set adrift from the rest of the centre and surrounded by a municipal car park.

RAP issued a rallying call:

Rochdale is going to end up a regimented, geometric, symmetrical, concrete, planner's dream. Let it rather be the people's vision. Rochdale is a spiralling, imaginative, awe-inspiring, artistic, Mecca of the north-west. Let us have a town centre of which we can be proud, with which we can identify and in which we can belong. Now, before it's too late.

It *was* too late. The bulldozers arrived in November 1973. Councillor Walker revealed that it would reach break-even after 20 years and the shopping centre site would revert back to local authority ownership in the year 2076.

* * *

The other board members were considerably less wealthy than Fred Ratcliffe and struggled to make regular 'directors' loans'. These were tranches of money put into club funds, ostensibly to be paid back at a later date but, in practice, rarely reimbursed. Leonard Hilton left the board for eight months in 1973 but soon returned. 'It's a shame but it got to the stage where I was dreading going to board meetings. The financial strain had become too great. Your pocket is only a certain depth,' he said at the time.

Every Thursday, Angus McLean phoned Lloyds Bank to check whether there were enough funds in the club's account to cover players' wages. If not, he'd hunt down directors and ask them to make a payment from their personal accounts; sometimes this would exceed £2,000. The club was usually run to its maximum £60,000 overdraft and McLean later told a newspaper that part of his job was to tell 'fairy stories' to creditors about why they hadn't received their money.

Goodwill at various banks was regularly exhausted and another would be sourced to secure loans. Directors were often asked to act as a guarantor for these and, with the club in such debt, this understandably caused great stress. Fans sometimes added to the anxiety. 'You get a lot of earache when you're on the board of a football club,' said Hilton. 'In running the pie business, I'd go round to the markets where the fellas would give me stick from six in the morning when I first turned up,' he said.

Hilton suffered with stomach ulcers that required surgery. 'He didn't cope with it very well,' said his son, Andrew. 'He was being asked to take money out of the business and hand it over to the club, wrapped in a brown paper parcel. It was a constant demand on his finances. My mum died in 1972 and it meant he had to run the bakery. We had some great away trips watching Rochdale and Dad liked meeting people and helping the club find new players, but a lot of the fun was taken out of it with morale being so low.'

Geoffrey Roderick Brierley (known as Rod Brierley), aged 37 in 1973, was the youngest on the original board and is still alive, although he suffered a stroke in 2021. He lives with his wife Gillian in a detached house with a wide veranda overlooking Lake Windermere. Brierley took over the family's wallpaper and paint business, which had been set up in Rochdale in 1875. Along with his brother, Cedric, seven years the elder, he built up the business until it had 75 staff and 25 vans delivering paint and paper to decorators throughout north-west England.

As a boy, Brierley had been taken to Spotland by his father. He was one of the 24,231 – Rochdale's record home attendance – packed into the ground in December 1949 for an FA Cup tie against Notts County. The main attraction had been the appearance of Tommy Lawton for Notts County, an ex-England captain and, at the time, the country's most expensive signing. Brierley was close to Ratcliffe; their families went to Spain on holidays together. 'He was alright, Fred. Straightforward. He was quite hard. You know, like a lot of people who make money, business people,' said Brierley.

Edward 'Teddy' Lord, another director, was the proprietor of an industrial decorating business in which Ratcliffe held shares. He grumbled sometimes that the focus was too often on Ratcliffe, to the exclusion of the others. 'Teddy used to train greyhounds and he ran them in the evenings, so he was never at a board meeting before 10pm,' said Trevor Butterworth. 'As soon as he came in the Oak Room at the Crimble, Fred would ask him what he wanted to drink. I remember one time he was given a short and he swished it around the glass. Fred asked him what he was up to and Ted said he was looking to see if there were any goldfish in it, it was that murky.'

The most recent addition to the board in 1973 was Ken Leary, an estate agent from Middleton who had branched out into the hospitality business. Several of his venues were part of a fad of the early 1970s, whereby traditional pubs were renamed and themed. The Wrecker, formerly the Lion and Lamb, in Blackley, north Manchester, had its interior redesigned to emulate a wrecked sailing ship, with the mast in the centre of the room and large portholes along the side. A film was projected on to the wall showing palm trees and clouds scudding by. The lights were dimmed intermittently and the sound of a thunderstorm played through speakers. The main attraction was an alligator kept inside a tank covered with wire mesh. Unfortunately, it often choked on discarded cigarette butts and empty crisp packets. Leary also had a stake in the Brown Cow disco pub in Slattocks, Middleton and the Richmond Club in Heywood (later known as the Candy Peel). He'd been invited on to Rochdale's board to bring his expertise to running the social club.

* * *

The dispute between the government and miners' unions continued throughout 1973. Many in Edward Heath's cabinet were irked by Lord Wilberforce's pay recommendation, feeling it was too generous and would precipitate a rash of pay claims at a time when inflation was running at nearly 10 per cent. In the autumn of 1973, the NUM claimed its members were receiving an average of 2.3 per cent less than the promised 27 per cent.

A national ballot was held and the vote to strike was lost by 143,006 to 82,631. The government saw this as a victory for common sense: did it really matter if pay was a few per cent short of such a substantial hike?

The NUM, with support from the TUC, held its position. Members withdrew overtime working. The government underestimated the impact but it was soon evident. Output was halved within days. Without enough coal to fire power stations, the electricity produced for the National Grid was appreciably reduced. The government hurriedly brought in the Fuel and Electricity (Control) Act, which, to save power, limited the permitted temperature in business premises. A three-day working week was introduced on 13 December 1973. Television broadcasts were to shut down at 10.30pm each evening, although this would be suspended for the Christmas and New Year period.

The major employers in Rochdale, among them TBA, Fothergill & Harvey Ltd, the John Bright Group (operating five mills in the town) and Farrel Bridge Ltd, each told the press that they were discussing how best to respond to the crisis. The three-day week was a measure of their probity. Did they accept that the situation was temporary and forced upon their staff, and carry on with full pay? Or did they adjust payments according to the fall in productivity? Courtaulds Ltd, which also had five mills in the town, agreed to pay three-quarters of the usual daily rate on the two days the mills were closed. TBA later said it would lead to a reduction in profit and laid off 28 workers.

Most shops in the town tried to cut their power use by 50 per cent to reflect the national availability. The newly opened Tesco store was unable to dim its lights, so kept on just enough for staff and customers to navigate the aisles. Street lighting across Rochdale was turned off from 11pm until 7am. The heating was switched off intermittently at Rochdale's 12 'homes for the elderly'; blankets were donated to help keep approximately 300 residents warm. Councillors decided not to put up lights on the 35ft Christmas tree in the town centre supplied by the Forestry Commission at Dunsop Bridge, Clitheroe. Silver trimmings would be added to the tree to give it at least a little sparkle. Lanterns wouldn't be put up in the Town Hall Gardens for the first time in living memory. A spokesman for the borough engineers department conceded 'it's going to be a miserable Christmas'.

* * *

The promise of imminent new signings cheered the Rochdale supporters. Fans scanned the back pages of the *Manchester Evening News* waiting to read of these new additions, when they came across an unexpected headline: 'Dale Release Senior Trio'. A few days before the announcement, Walter Joyce had called in his coaching staff; this happened often in the midst of the poor run. 'I think we're going about this half-arsed,' he told them. 'Either we do the job properly or not at all.' His coaching team knew he was talking about the older pros. 'They're not buying into it,' said Joyce. 'You can see it on their faces and how they're playing. They're still bloody dreaming about Dick Conner. I bet half of them are on the phone to him most afternoons, angling to get a move to Darlington. Let's get shut.'

Colin Blant, Len Kinsella and Dick Renwick, three players with more than 700 league appearances between them, were put on the transfer list; none of them would play for Rochdale again. Blant and Renwick did indeed sign for Darlington. 'The youngsters we have at the club are potentially far better than Blant, Kinsella and Renwick, and I have decided we must build for the future,' Joyce told the press.

Rochdale supporter Andrew Harrison was disappointed to learn that Blant had been released. 'He was an icon to a lot of fans and it was a shock to hear that he was leaving. All the momentum of the promotion season [1968/69] was lost. The bubble had burst and you felt as if Dale were destined to go back to the Fourth Division,' he said.

Many years later, in the 1990s, Harrison became a coach at Rochdale AFC's Centre of Excellence, where Colin Blant also worked on a part-time basis. Blant was still upset by how he'd been treated by Joyce, nearly two decades earlier; not in itself an unusual mindset for an ex-footballer. 'He had a few choice words to say about him,' said Harrison. 'But generally he is a lovely man, Colin – very honest.'

At the time, Harrison had attended a seminar and befriended the progressive sports coach Bill Beswick, whose book, *Focused for Soccer*, published a year or so later, offered a psychological approach to coaching. 'I became a bit of a devotee,' said Harrison. 'Before, I was a shouting, bollocking, blustering coach, barking orders from the touchline. After my sessions with Bill, I was more player-centred, encouraging and positive. But Blanty would have none of it – he called me "Mishra" [the name given to a Hindu class of teachers and priests] and took the piss out of me for being into all this pink and fluffy stuff. He said footballers needed a bollocking and that would sort them out.'

As the senior trio left the club, three young players from the squad were told to prepare themselves for regular first-team appearances: Eamonn Kavanagh, aged 19, midfielder, an ex-Manchester City apprentice; Barry Bradbury, 21, a defender from Castleton, Rochdale; and Gary Cooper, the striker who had been an apprentice at Bolton Wanderers. Also returning to the squad was the experienced Graham Smith; a thigh strain had kept him out for almost two months. Jim Burt was told he would not be kept on after his trial because 'he was not as good as the players we already have at the club' – Joyce. Kavanagh would go on to play only three matches and, again, the press was told why in categorical terms: 'While he has looked promising in the reserves, he has had his chance in the first team and not made an impact. We have younger players at the club for the same position who look to have far more potential,' said Joyce.

* * *

Queues at petrol stations became a familiar sight in Rochdale. The strike by tanker drivers was naught compared to the disruption caused by OPEC (Organisation of Petroleum Exporting Countries) placing an embargo on exporting fuel to Britain. OPEC comprised mainly Arab countries – Iraq, Saudi Arabia, Iran and Kuwait – and was retaliating for Britain's support of the Israelis in the conflict at Golan Heights. The price of oil increased threefold, causing a devastating effect on the economy. Cyril Smith held a crystalline view: 'We must resist sheer blackmail – and this is what the Arabs appear to be practising,' he said.

More than 90 workers were made redundant at Dunlop Ltd. Meanwhile, Alderglen found itself the subject of national news coverage over a 'modern slavery' row. Sidney Rubin, managing director, felt he'd exhausted the local employment pool and had sought workers from overseas to manufacture nylon garments at the firm's Spotland Bridge Mills. He recruited from Italy and Malta but, when Alderglen expanded into Harp Mill in Queensway, Rochdale, he turned to the Philippines. He placed an advert in the *Taliba*, a newspaper of the Tagalog, an ethnic group comprising a quarter of the population of the Philippines. The lure was a wage of £20 per week and the chance to 'live in the hometown of Gracie Fields'. Rubin had banked on the girls (no men took up the offer) being aware of Fields; she'd been the highest-paid film star in the world in 1937 and her songs and films were popular worldwide. By the end of 1972, 126 Filipinos had moved to Rochdale.

Councillors accused Alderglen of using its Filipino workers as 'bond slaves' because they each had £1 a week taken from their wages to cover the rent on shared accommodation. They were housed in lodgings bought or rented by the company in Ipswich Street, Rooley Moor Road, Mellor Street, Beaufort Street and Spotland Road. Mr R. Rabe, the Philippines vice-consul, visited a house in Spotland Road. He said, 'The girls are generally satisfied and are getting on well with the local community.'

Mr Rubin offered to fund any worker's return to the Philippines; only four took up the offer. A letter signed by 73 of the girls was sent to the Philippines embassy. It read:

> Calling us bond slaves is an insult not only to us but also to our British friends who have been our co-workers and have been so kind to us, to the people of Rochdale and also the trade union officials. We are happy. In fact if we were not happy we would not encourage our friends and relations to come and join us here. In this country we all enjoy a higher standard of living than the one we had in the Philippines. We regularly send money home to our parents and family to enable them to have a better life.

Priscilla Amio, aged 23, of Clement Royds Street, Spotland, was particularly pleased to be in Rochdale. She was chosen as Miss Alderglen of 1973. She beat 19 other entrants at Kirkholt Community Centre and received a trophy from Alderman Cyril Smith. The girls showed locals how to do Filipino national dancing.

9

A Dire Capitulation
and Complete Collapse

ROCHDALE WERE drawn at home to South Shields in the first round of the FA Cup. In the build-up, the media referred to South Shields, of the Northern Premier League, as a 'strong side'. The previous week they had beaten Morecambe 7-1 and were said to be 'marching up the league'; they were seventh at the time. Understandably, there were references to 'struggling' Rochdale and a reminder that the season before they had been knocked out of the cup by non-league Bangor City, while this season they had conceded more goals than any other team in the Football League and hadn't won in the last nine matches.

Letters had started to appear in the *Rochdale Observer* criticising the board for being 'miserly' and replacing Dick Conner with a managerial novice, Walter Joyce. The correspondence from L.M. Butterworth of Brown Edge, Stoke, was typical: 'I, myself, up to a couple of weeks ago, would often make the journey to see the Dale, even during midweek. But now the interest has gone and I'm sorry to admit it, but, in common with others, I no longer really care.'

As they took the field at gale-blown Spotland, the Rochdale players, despite their professional status, felt to be underdogs against South Shields, such was the expectation of defeat. Before the 2.30pm kick-off – to save power by not using floodlights – fans were gladdened to see that the tea bar (aka: pie hut) was open at the corner of the Willbutts Lane and Sandy Lane End of the ground. The Fighting Fund, a group of mainly older fans who voluntarily ran and manned the tea bars/pie huts, had promised since the start of the season that it would reopen 'by the end of October'. The same arrangement stood as it had on previous seasons – Jack Ashworth, chairman of the fund, had told the club he was unwilling to hand over cash from sales on a piecemeal basis. Directors often badgered them for help with particular bills but Ashworth insisted profits were passed on to the club on an annual basis.

Warmed up with pies, peas and Bovril, fans saw Rochdale pass the ball well and win 2-0 with relative ease, the goals coming in the first half, from Arthur Marsh and Lee Brogden. 'Nice one, Oddjob,' shouted fans. Marsh was known as Oddjob due to his similarity to the character played by Harold Sakata in the James Bond film, *Goldfinger*. Walter Joyce hadn't enjoyed the week leading up to the match and how his team had been portrayed. After the victory, he was polite with the press but what he really wanted to say was: we're a professional football club, show us some respect.

Almost unnoticed amid the 'cup fever' was the postponement of a home fixture against Cambridge United scheduled for Monday, 12 November; heavy overnight rain had left the pitch waterlogged. The news barely registered at the time but when the match was finally staged it became one of the most infamous ever played in the Football League.

* * *

Churches were frequent targets for vandals. Stained-glass windows were smashed at Milnrow Parish Church and the masonry chipped away on the outside of the building. A member of its congregation said the graveyard was being used as a 'rubbish dump', with bedsteads and bicycle parts often thrown over the wall. 'It is costing the church hundreds of pounds,' said Councillor R. Taylor. 'It is shocking and disgusting and we're sick and tired of the situation.'

Thieves stole the model train used to give children rides at Springfield Park. The engine had been donated by Roy Bairstow of Norden, who had made it himself over a four-year period, painting it in the dark green livery of British Rail with 'Great Northern Express' written on the side. A few days after the theft, the engine turned up at the Steam Age Model Shop in Chelsea, London. The shopkeeper told police he'd paid £250 for it and gave a good description of the three men who had sold it. The engine was reunited with Mr Bairstow. He promised to give it a 'major overhaul' before it returned to the park.

Miss M. Grindrod of Whitworth was tending a family grave at Christ Church, Healey when she saw two boys kneeling while clutching heather and a bunch of flowers. She asked what they were doing. 'We don't know whose graves they are, but we thought we'd put some on a few,' said one of them. Miss Greenwood wrote to the *Rochdale Observer*, saying, 'One reads and hears so much of vandalism these days that I feel a gesture like this from two little boys should be made headline news.'

* * *

During the 1970s, football matches were often peripheral to the territorial battles fought on the terraces. Home supporters had a designated 'end' (place of gathering) from where they would chant encouragement to their team and taunt visiting supporters. Away fans would congregate as close as possible and, if able to breach lines held by 'gatemen' (they had yet to be termed 'stewards'), they would steam in and attempt to 'take' the end by chasing away the home support. Much of it was posturing, essentially a series of charges and counter-charges. Occasionally, though, if each side stood their ground, the violence was hostile and sickening. Any supporter isolated from their 'crew' was set upon by the pack and sometimes kicked unconscious.

Rival 'hooligans' generally held to a code of fighting solely among themselves; they could identify their counterparts from other clubs in manner and attire. This covenant wasn't always upheld and sometimes fans were picked on randomly. At its worst, if the few police officers on duty were overwhelmed – and they often were – a football ground could resemble a war zone. On any given Saturday, for example, within a single section of terracing, a small gang might be regrouping ready to return to the fray; dazed and bloodied supporters would be tending wounds with handkerchiefs; police would be shouting down walkie-talkies for reinforcements, while St John Ambulance staff were racing to a prostrate fan lying on the concrete. A few yards away, a football match was taking place, if anyone still had the stomach for it.

Rochdale's 'kop' was behind the goals in the Sandy Lane End. Songs would be sung eulogising this speck of sacred land – 'I was born in the Sandy Lane' to the tune of 'Wand'rin' Star' and then the foreboding rhythmical war cry of 'no one takes the Sandy'. If rival fans were spotted amassing close by, they were warned: 'You're gonna get your fuckin' heads kicked in' or 'you're going home in a Rochdale ambulance'. Most hooliganism occurred when visiting clubs brought with them significant numbers of fans. Derby matches were fraught with constant flashpoints occurring throughout the match.

The home match against Huddersfield Town had been particularly charged, with police making several arrests. A 21-year-old from Freehold, Rochdale admitted using threatening behaviour when he later appeared before Rochdale Magistrates' Court. A policeman said he'd seen him holding on to a stand-support to steady himself while he kicked two Huddersfield fans as they lay on the ground. An 18-year-old from Belfield had shouted obscenities and was told to refrain by PC Rodney Howarth; the youth incited the crowd to attack the officer. In court, he denied using threatening behaviour and said PC Howarth had hit him on the back of the head. He was found guilty and fined £25. A 20-year-old Huddersfield youth was found guilty of a similar offence after police said he'd led a charge of about 100 fans from one end of the ground to the other, shouting 'come on, let's get them'. In the Bolton match played at Spotland, one of their fans, a 21-year-old, admitted kicking a Rochdale supporter while he was on the ground. He told the magistrates, 'I just lost my temper.' Mrs W.H. Moir, chair of the bench, said, 'This is the type of behaviour we have got to stop. We take it very seriously and we are determined to stamp it out.'

The *Rochdale Observer* took to the streets to conduct a 'vox pop' on the subject of football hooliganism. 'Corporal punishment should be brought back. Many of the young people today are callous and they should be birched,' said John Holt of Ashfield Valley. Stephen Nuttall, a pensioner from Manchester, agreed: 'It's ridiculous the way they go around smashing windows and things. The birch would be a deterrent and I think it would stop hooliganism.' Mrs Alice Naton, also of Ashfield Valley, said there should be a minimum age for people allowed into football grounds if unaccompanied by their parents. As a football 'insider', Angus McLean was asked his opinion. He responded: 'Football gets the blame for this violence but they are smashing things before the match even starts.'

* * *

Milnrow was one of the few districts in Rochdale to have lights on its civic Christmas tree in 1973. They didn't last long. Vandals smashed bulbs and pulled down wiring. Staff from Milnrow Parks Department repaired the damage. Two days later, it was attacked again but this time bulbs and decorations were stolen. The annual carol service went ahead with light provided by hand-held torches. The Rev. James Henderson, vicar of Newhey, said, 'The devil always finds work for idle hands to do.'

Vandalism remained rife with barely a day or two passing without an attack on civic or personal property. Attacks to buildings belonging to Rochdale Corporation were costing between £8,000 and £10,000 per year. 'What they gain out of this, I just don't know. It must be a sick type of individual,' said Mr R. Gossick, head of the council's parks department. He was speaking after discovering a 'trail of destruction' at the bowling green area in Falinge Park. Benches had been dragged on to the green and uprooted toilet signs jabbed into the ground. The contents of litter bins were strewn everywhere. Flowers had been trampled down. 'It really makes me sick. I was so disgusted to think of the effort my chaps put in to get these greens ready,' he said.

* * *

The victory against South Shields lifted the squad. Walter Joyce noticed that they trained with more intensity through the week; there were even one or two smiles. 'The difference a win makes, hey?' said Dennis Butler. 'Too right,' responded Joyce. 'So what if it was only against South Shields?' 'Right now, Butts, I'm not bothered whether we've beat Real Madrid or dribbled our way past a load of bloody dustbins – a win is a win.'

The coaching staff had been a little concerned about Joyce; they knew how much he cared, how much he put in. He was, for the times, young to be a manager, at 36. Many others were in their 50s, paternal figures in a suit and tie who delegated the everyday graft to their staff. They might take a look at training now and again, assessing the mood of the camp and general fitness, but otherwise they were seen mainly on matchdays, fastening the team sheet to the wall. Joyce wanted to be everywhere, always. He was still in the transitional stage between player and manager, eager to stay fit and strong. He felt this would harvest more respect from the players, knowing that he was still within touching distance of being a sportsman, rather than a mere administrator. He enjoyed the machismo of the dressing room, standing square to the players, shoulders back. His body language was saying that he was still one of them, as good as ready to dig out his boots and go toe to toe with the opposition.

Joyce had an unusual ruse to test whether a player was being vigilant: he'd punch him randomly in the stomach. His further justification for doing this was that it was a way of checking the strength of a player's abdominal muscles. He did it once to a reserve player, Pat Phillips. 'I wouldn't do that again,' Phillips told him. 'Why not?' asked Joyce. 'Because I'll give it you back.' 'Will you?' 'I will – and I'm half your age and twice as strong.'

* * *

Councillors agreed to introduce dog patrols to deter vandals after an injury to Frank Milne, a 69-year-old part-time ranger at Denehurst Park. He'd asked a gang of about 18 youths to move on to the playing fields from the sun house in the ornamental gardens, where they were kicking a football. A 14-year-old boy shouted an obscenity at him and a 15-year-old kicked him about the body. The ranger lost his footing and broke his shoulder in the fall. The case against the 14-year-old was discharged but the 15-year-old was put on probation for two years and fined £15.

Three youths appeared at Rochdale Juvenile Court for placing sleepers on the railway line as it passed through Smithy Bridge. The driver, Tom Jeffs, said the train was travelling at 25mph when it hit the objects, causing it to bounce and come to a standstill 200 feet along the track. One of the youths told the police, 'We lay down in the grass at the side of the line to see what would happen. We were going to watch the wood splinter.' They were each fined £50 and told by the presiding magistrate,

W.S. Edwards, that if they came before the court again 'they would be for it'.

A 22-year-old man from Spotland broke four windows in two separate incidents at a chip shop in Rooley Moor Road. He said he did it because the owner refused to serve him and would shout out to him 'naughty boy' when he walked past. The man was put on probation for a year and told to pay £20 restitution. In Dearnley, Littleborough, a life-size statue of an angel was pushed over by vandals, causing £300 of damage to its wings. The statue, made from Italian white marble, had stood outside the monument business of the Kilpatrick family for 15 years.

Staff at a Rochdale shoe factory lost a day's work when vandals ran riot after breaking into the premises. Fire extinguishers were set off and paint splashed on the walls and floor at Fairfield Shoe and Slipper Company in Belfield Road. Conveyor belts were slashed. Mr Norman Shepherd, managing director, said, 'It was an appalling shambles. The production losses will be well over £1,000.' Thirty of the 200-strong workforce volunteered to go into work on a Sunday to clean up the mess and repair damaged machinery. 'They did a tremendous job,' said Mr Shepherd.

Rochdale Hornets suffered a similar attack at their Athletic Grounds. Vandals wrecked the scoreboard, broke a large window and tried to set fire to an office at the back of the Main Stand. Fred Kershaw, club secretary, was incandescent: 'This is senseless destruction by people who can only be described as savages and animals. They have no respect for other people's property and it is costing us money we can ill afford.'

* * *

Fans were hopeful of a good performance against Blackburn Rovers at Spotland, especially after learning that Ken Furphy, their manager, had left the club to join Sheffield United; Richard Dinnis was made acting manager. Rochdale attacked from the kick-off and, in the 28th minute, Lee Brogden thumped the ball into the roof of the net. The referee, Robert Raby, signalled that it was a goal but changed his mind. The ball had bounced back from the netting and, under pressure from Blackburn players, he was persuaded it had struck the goalpost. Next, he was ambushed by Rochdale players, beseeching him to reconsider the decision. They argued too forcefully. Keith Bebbington was sent off and Leo Skeete booked. Raby agreed to consult a linesman, who confirmed that the ball had crossed the line and the goal should stand. Bebbington was waved back on to the pitch and both he and Skeete were told the dismissal and booking would be rescinded. The furore had lasted four minutes and the dénouement left the Blackburn Rovers fans – who comprised the majority of a crowd of 3,721 – seething.

Police ran on to the pitch at half-time to protect Raby. He was spat at and subjected to a torrent of abuse as he made his way to the dressing rooms. Fans picked up handfuls of cinder from around the pitch and threw it at the departing Rochdale players. About 80 Rovers fans in the Main Stand left their seats to yell at Raby and tried to clamber through the directors' box to get at him. They began pushing and shoving Leonard Hilton, a director, until a police sergeant took hold of the ringleader and led him from the box. 'To react like that to a game of football is incredible,' said Ken Leary, another Rochdale director. 'One can see why wars start. These were people with hate in their hearts. The referee suffered terrible abuse.'

Blackburn, driven on by a partisan crowd and a misplaced sense of injustice, attacked repeatedly in the second half. Steve Arnold moved to tackle Tony Field on the byline but, as he did, the winger fell to the ground. The referee awarded a penalty. Field scored and then added a winner ten minutes before full time. 'After that cock-up in the first half, he made sure Rovers won so that he could get out of here alive,' Joyce told his coaching staff afterwards.

The comment may have appeared melodramatic but perhaps not so in the context of the times. There was no stewarding. Instead, there were 'gatemen', usually senior citizens in warehousemen coats, who literally opened and closed gates to certain sections of the ground. Fans weren't segregated but marshalled on an ad hoc basis. Police were understaffed in and around football grounds. Although they each had a truncheon, they didn't wear protective clothing and had no specialised training in crowd control. The grounds were in a dilapidated state and it was easy to fashion weapons from the crumbling concrete or rotted wood, whether torn from the perimeter fence or stands. There was no CCTV and fans found it easy to evade capture, quickly lost among the crowd. Hooliganism thrived because a football ground was, for many years, a locale where mob rule could hold sway.

David Gartside, a Rochdale fan, recalled 'all hell breaking loose' on several occasions at Spotland. A 'really nasty atmosphere' had prevailed in a league match against Luton Town in April 1970, with continual fighting around the ground, while in a League Cup match with Crystal Palace in August 1970, scores of 'really menacing' skinheads chased Rochdale fans through the streets. 'Football grounds were pretty scary places in the 1970s,' he said. 'I was punched in the back of the head at Crewe. Another time, I was in the Sandy Lane with my grandad against Hull when he was hit. He was 80 at the time and luckily it was a glancing blow. I hit the lad who'd done it really hard and knocked him off his feet. There was always trouble when we played Port Vale, Burnley, Swansea, Hull, Barnsley, Oldham and Grimsby. I call these *fighting* towns – places with a history of working-class struggles.'

Volunteers from the Fighting Fund also subscribed to this theory. 'They wouldn't just steal from the hut, they'd be running at it trying to wreck things, pushing over the tea urns and threatening staff with physical violence,' said Andrew Hilton, son of director Leonard Hilton. 'You're not allowed to say this anymore but the Fighting Fund lads used to say it was because they were all inbred!'

The aftermath of the Blackburn match was particularly grim. An 18-year-old Rovers fan was slashed across the face with a razor; 26 stitches were inserted in the wound. A couple living in Willbutts Lane received cuts from flying glass when stones were thrown through their window. 'There was a mob of about 100 outside. My wife was hit in the eye by a fragment of glass. I had my hand cut. Believe me, it was frightening,' said Brian Fielding. Two houses were damaged in Spotland Road. Toilets were smashed up at a petrol station in Mellor Street. Shops in the town centre were robbed and damaged by youths. 'Rovers' was sprayed on the outside wall of The Galleon pub in Drake Street, where fans had been drinking.

* * *

Superintendent Harold Dickson of the Rochdale Police sub-division gave a familiar response to why more vandals weren't apprehended: a shortage of manpower. 'Bearing in mind the number of police officers we have – which is a nationwide problem – we haven't enough men to put in panda cars and on the beat,' he told members of Rochdale Rotary Club. If he prioritised vandalism, he said, it meant fewer officers could attend emergency calls. He reported that behaviour had worsened noticeably in Rochdale. The sub-division had 1,510 criminal cases presented to the courts in 1969, while in 1972 it was 4,384.

Interestingly, acts of vandalism would remain at a similar level until the 2000s when numbers began to fall. Optimists saw this as evidence of an improvement in the conduct of youths. Their view was challenged by others who pointed out that more youths had been on the streets in the 1970s, before the introduction of extensive home entertainment – computers, satellite TV, iPads, etc. Also, an industry had grown up to resist vandalism, from shutters on doors and windows, to CCTV. Evidence showed vandalism had become so commonplace that people no longer reported it to the police. Finally, some suggested that social media was the new hang-out for vandals, a place where they could pass the time acting irresponsibly and antagonistically.

* * *

Angus McLean was dispatched to London Road, the home of Grantham, to compile a report on Rochdale's forthcoming opponents in the second round of the FA Cup. He saw them beat Kettering Town 2-0 in the Southern Premier League and summarised that they were 'a very fair side with a good work-rate'. Grantham hadn't lost at home all season and were on a ten-match unbeaten run. They were the antithesis of Rochdale, with a great deal of stability in their set-up. Terry Bly had been player and manager for ten years and the squad had barely changed over the previous three or four seasons.

Walter Joyce had been warned about 'the hollow' – a slope at one end of the pitch, which was extremely difficult to defend. He chose a defensive-minded team, expecting to come under intensive pressure. Dennis Benskin scored for Grantham but Lee Brogden equalised in the 75th minute. Grantham bombarded the Rochdale goal but in the final minute, on a rare breakaway, Leo Skeete was put through but his shot hit the post. The miss was to prove costly. Rochdale – according to David Sugden of the *Rochdale Observer* – had been 'out-played, outrun and generally looked second-class'.

David Gartside was one of a small number of Rochdale fans who had made the trip to Grantham for the 1.45pm kick-off. They each paid 40p to sit in a stand with a capacity of nearly 400. 'It was a shitty journey. It took hours. The game was played on a horrible pitch,' he said. 'It was the FA Cup so it felt different than a league game. It's the hope that kills you and the belief that you're going to improve. In each match, there were periods when we played okay but the end result was always the same – we'd lose.'

Three days later, the replay was set for Spotland. Snow had fallen over the weekend. Michael Lowe, the referee, travelled from his home in Leeds early on Tuesday morning to check the pitch. He pressed down to see if the turf would take a stud and shouted to Angus McLean to throw him a football. He kicked it a few times, stopped and turned while running and then announced: game on. 'Got to say, fellas, we wouldn't stand a chance if we were talking about an evening kick-off, when the ground sets solid,' he said.

The power shortage meant that the match kicked off at 1.45pm; a proposal to suspend the league and another to extend the season until June had both been rejected by the Football League. The draw for the third round had already been made; the winners would face Middlesbrough at home.

Rochdale started well. Alan Taylor scored in the first minute and Keith Hanvey added another after eight minutes. At half-time they were 3-1 ahead, the other goal scored by Bobby Downes. 'More of the same, lads,' implored Walter Joyce in his half-time team talk. 'Keep up the work rate. Get the ball moving and you'll be back in here in 45 minutes with a cup tie against Middlesbrough to look forward to – and that'll make Mr Ratcliffe a very happy man. You might even find a few extra bob in your pay packet this week. Come on, let's finish the job.'

Jack Charlton, Middlesbrough's manager, was in the Main Stand. He'd have noted Rochdale's professionalism, at least until half-time. They had passed the ball well and shown superior fitness to Grantham, whose players had other jobs and trained two evenings a week. Stan Townsend introduced himself to Charlton and asked whether he'd been impressed by the

Rochdale players and might be putting a bid in for any of them. Charlton, wearing a voluminous sheepskin coat, smiled broadly and summoned his famous Geordie wit to put Townsend in his place. 'Fuck off,' he told him.

Rochdale didn't 'finish the job'. They made an utter mess of the job. The score at full time was 3-3. In extra time, with the light fading fast, Grantham scored two more goals to finish 5-3 winners. Many of the 1,266 fans who had taken the day off work clapped Grantham from the pitch; they had shown much more endeavour and heart. The chilly wind made it difficult to shout and boo and, besides, many supporters had come to accept ignominious defeats to non-league clubs as a feature of being a Rochdale fan. They fastened their coats, banged the snow from their shoes and headed to the exits. Under their breath, they muttered their hurt and dissatisfaction, the cold setting their teeth to a chattering rhythm: shit, shit, shit.

The defeat had a crushing effect on many Rochdale fans. Steve Murray, a psychology student at Middlesex Polytechnic, was home for Christmas and had attended the match with his brother, John, and father, also called John. 'It was a dire capitulation and complete collapse. The mood among the crowd was pretty foul at the end. I didn't start watching Dale again until around 1978 and my dad, who had supported them since he was a lad when they first entered the Football League, lived on for another 34 years but never set foot in Spotland again. He thought the club was on the verge of closing and the ground would be sold for housing,' he said.

Graham Smith can remember nothing of the match, only that Rochdale, as a team of professionals, should have won. 'We knew that they'd raise their game but we should have raised ours. Lads at non-league clubs are always out to prove they are better than pros. It was up to us to go out there and do the job, not to believe we'd won before we even kicked off,' he said.

* * *

Cyril Smith seemed to be everywhere. He'd realised early in his adult life that his gargantuan size marked him out as a cartoon set loose; as *RAP* had gleefully acknowledged. Newspaper photographers fell over their camera bags finding new ways to frame the peculiarity of his body shape. They lay on their backs, asking him to stick out his belly while taking shots from shoe level. No problem, lads. He twanged his braces for them, put on kiss-me-quick hats. They put him in roller skates. They had him sitting with his feet up across a pair of deckchairs on Brighton beach. He looked on, scratching his head, while two pouting models squeezed into one of his outsize shirts.

Trips into Rochdale town centre for his weekly shop became civic walkabouts. Hello love, are you well? Bit nippy out today. Can't beat a bit of tripe, can you? And if he was questioned on political matters, he had a retort at the ready: I'll sort it, don't worry. He was loved: a local boy made good who still spoke and acted like them. He could do indignant or dismissive with aplomb. He's just playing silly buggers, he'd say of Ted Heath or Harold Wilson or anyone else seeing the world differently than him. He had a face that brilliantly serviced his moods – the thundering scowl of an unpaid rent collector or a cheeky, boyish smile that set his dimples dancing. He was more than three times the size of many of his constituents and his personality was, as even his detractors agreed, three times that of most people.

* * *

The defeat by Grantham was a scar on Rochdale Association Football Club that everyone associated with it knew would take years to fade. Walter Joyce put it in splendid perspective: 'I have never felt as bad about anything in my life as I did about what happened on Tuesday. I feel ashamed and humiliated, to put it mildly. It was pathetic. The public of this town should not be paying to watch a team play like that. The players were heartless and spineless.'

Fred Ratcliffe was next in line to condemn the players: 'Our lads seemed to give up once they allowed Grantham to get level, and I was disappointed, as were most supporters, the manager and the other directors. The FA Cup gave people an interest in the club. They have now lost interest in everything and what crowd will be at our next home match is anyone's guess.' He expressed his continued support of the manager: 'There will be no recriminations against Walter Joyce. He is setting up a pattern in the club and, as a board, we back him all the way.' Ratcliffe revealed that Middlesbrough, expecting Rochdale to win, had placed a provisional order of 7,500 tickets for the third-round tie.

Keith Hanvey has never forgotten the cup defeat to Grantham. 'It left me devastated. It was the game that brought home to me what the team was all about. You need two or three strong individuals at any club, lads who are like captains. But we didn't have anyone. We needed coaching and cajoling but we had no leader figure.' He felt the team was riven by factions – the older pros were 'out for themselves' while the 'scousers', most of whom travelled to and from training together, had formed a clique. Other players felt 'team-mates' had been ordered to purposefully undermine them, 'taking the piss' so that their form suffered and they would lose their place in the team. 'It might seem a small thing but there was no initiation ceremony when I joined the club,' said Hanvey. 'At City, everyone had to endure the "blue goldfish" where they'd flush your head down the toilet. They also blackened my balls with Kiwi shoe polish – it took ages to get off. They did this, picking on your weakest point, so that afterwards you weren't scared of anything. Nothing like this happened at Rochdale, which was why the team spirit wasn't very good.'

At nearby Oldham Athletic, from where Joyce had recruited several players, of course, the initiation was to tell young players it was part of their job to 'wipe the muck off the floodlights'. They were given a wet sponge and, after taking a few steps up the ladder fastened to a pylon, they were shouted down, amid much laughter.

Mike Brennan also detected malcontent among the senior players. 'I was only a kid, so I didn't see it as my place to challenge them,' he said. 'A couple of guys in particular were from the school of hard knocks and they were very, very tough. They didn't give an inch. I think they had an attitude of going out there and giving it their best but, deep down, believing we were never going to turn a corner. They probably looked at young lads playing upfront like Alan Taylor, Leo Skeete and myself and thought, "We're not going to win too often with these fellas."'

Harold Holburt had spent time working with Alan Taylor and found him 'headstrong' and 'a little bit cocky'. 'You need that in football,' said Holburt. 'But I wasn't sure I always got through to Alan. I told him once that he should chase down the centre-backs as they came out with the ball because, at first, he was just leaving them to it, letting them build attacks from the back.'

Several players were surprised at Taylor's later success, playing in the First Division and Europe with West Ham United and Norwich City. They had considered him 'one of them' and not noticeably of greater ability, although at Rochdale he was often played out of position in midfield. In the Grantham match, the same as the rest of the team, he was, in football speak, judged to have 'disappeared'.

* * *

Fred Ratcliffe had heard Cyril Smith's name mentioned at social gatherings. Even from afar, he'd marked him out as a straight-talker, a social gadder who, much as he'd done, had decided on a version of himself he wanted to present to the world, take it or leave it.

In the late 1950s Smith had been invited by Ratcliffe to raise funds for the club, with a cut for himself. Smith, a wrestling fan, began staging bouts at the social club. They were popular and soon afterwards the pair went into business together, opening Rochdale's first bingo hall. The venture was a success and they became closer when Smith started work as a production controller at Ratcliffe's spring works. Some believed Smith was earmarked for a senior position but others were sceptical and assumed Smith, who had been mayor of Rochdale in 1966, was being courted for brokerage at the council – Ratcliffe had done similar before, employing another former mayor, Norman Ledson, and leader of the Rochdale Conservative party, Tommy Rose. While spring-making was Ratcliffe's core business, he also held shares in painting contractors, Arthur Lord and Sons (Rochdale) Ltd, and a garage, Summer Street Motors Ltd; a sympathetic ear at the council was a boon for any business.

Within three years of starting at Ratcliffe's, Smith had left to set up his own spring-making business. Along with five others, he bought a former joiner's shop in Flannel Street, on the edge of Rochdale town centre. They paid £4,000 for a second-hand lathe, furnace, oil bath and grinding wheel and set to work making springs. Ratcliffe broke off all ties with Smith. Rumours spread that Smith had purloined a substantial order or contacts book from Ratcliffe's and then undercut his former employer. On hearing Ratcliffe refer to Smith as 'bad news', several took it to mean that he was also aware of allegations of paedophilia.

* * *

At a time before radio phone-ins and internet message boards, the letter was the only recourse for football fans, sent to either the chairman, manager or local newspaper. In the week of the Grantham defeat, a mock 'In Memoriam' appeared in the *Rochdale Observer*:

In loving memory of Rochdale AFC, which died of shame on Tuesday, 18 December 1973. A memorial service, which will be conducted by the Archdeacon of Grantham, will be held at Willbutts Lane late in the month. The choir will sing the anthem 'Rejoice in the Lord always'. The Bishop of Bangor will preach the sermon and the vicar of Altrincham will give the blessing. [Bangor City, in 1972, and Altrincham, in 1965, both non-league clubs, had also previously knocked Rochdale out of the FA Cup.]

Another correspondent, 'MW', wrote:

A supporter at Spotland for over 40 years, I came away from the Grantham match appalled. I have never seen so much apathy, lack of skill and brains on a football field. I have nothing but sympathy for the new manager having to cope with such a situation. One or two of the team really tried, but the majority…? To misquote Churchill, 'Never on a football field have so many done so little for so much.'

'Irate Supporter' asked:

How much more rubbish do we have to suffer at Spotland? As a regular Rochdale fan I have been continually disgusted by the standard of football played by the team of late. The cup defeat was the final blow. We are certainties for relegation with the worst defensive record in the four divisions. What is going to be done about it?

The answer, a familiar one in football, was to undertake more 'hard work'. The players were given the impression by Walter

Joyce that any faults in their game or attitude could be addressed through hard work; more and more running. 'All that running felt like a punishment at times,' said Mike Brennan. 'If we lost away at places like Colchester or Peterborough, he'd have us in for training the next day. We would barely have had any sleep after getting off the coach in the early hours.' Graham Smith also recalled this emphasis on running. 'When I think back to the training at Rochdale, I always remember the running. We went round and round those fields at Firgrove and sometimes we'd be on the running track at Springfield Park. Football was like that then, with managers believing that if you could outrun your opponents, nine times out of ten, you'd win the match,' he said.

Many players in the 1970s complained that football clubs were akin to military academies. There was a clearly delineated hierarchy, strict rules, emphasis on teamwork and a punishing regime of fitness. Most of the coaches and senior players had done National Service, so it was perhaps inevitable they would replicate a faux-military dominion; it didn't suit modest or hesitant personalities. 'Lads had to have a certain mentality,' said Holburt. 'They might love football but the pitches were heavy, the balls were heavy and the conditions were often terrible. Only a certain number could hack it; the rest fell by the wayside.'

Mike Brennan was dropped after the Grantham match and found himself 'frozen out'. Along with one or two others, he was banished from the main squad and made to train in a smaller, separate group. 'We were thrown a ball and just got on with it, having a kickaround on some cinders at the Pearl Street End of the ground. It happens at a lot of clubs and I'm not sure what managers hope to achieve by it. As an older player, I would have said something and tried to understand what I'd done to justify that kind of treatment but, as a young lad, unsure of my ability, I accepted it. It became a bit of a laugh at the end and we used to refer to where we played as "Wembley",' he said.

* * *

Cyril Smith was in his pomp and fully expected to be re-elected as MP for Rochdale as news spread of the possibility of a General Election being called by Edward Heath. Smith was the self-professed Emperor of Rochdale (or maharajah, as some would have it) with an ever-rising national profile. He'd employed masterful strategy to see himself elected as a Liberal MP in the by-election held in 1972, overturning a Labour majority by more than 5,000 votes. He'd recognised his appeal as a 'man of the people' and succumbed to the caricature of the blunt, down-to-earth northerner. He grafted – knocking on doors, opening fetes and diligently carrying out humdrum constituency work.

He was among the first politicians to solicit backing from the immigrant community. An estimated 130,000 Pakistanis were living in the UK in 1972, 9,000 of them in Rochdale. He'd first made overtures when he was mayor, calling a 'Welcome to Rochdale' meeting at the town hall in 1966. As he often did, he made sure the *Rochdale Observer* – the paper became known in some quarters as the *Cyril Smith Gazette* – was in attendance, to photograph him shaking hands with Rahman Malik, the secretary of the Pakistani Welfare Association (PWA) – 'serving the community since 1960'. A few months later, in January 1967, Smith had attended a special service at the Golden Mosque in Spotland to celebrate the end of Ramadan. 'We should all remember we meet as members of a vast Commonwealth and therefore as brothers sharing the wealth of each other's countries,' he told them.

* * *

Walter Joyce went looking for 'fighters' and returned with two midfielders from Chester City – Jim Grummett and Stan Horne. 'After what happened against Grantham we obviously need fighters and these two players will give us that,' he said.

Much of Stan Horne's hunger for the game stemmed from a misdiagnosis that almost cost him a career in football. He'd played just six times for Aston Villa when, in the summer of 1963, the club's medical staff told him he had an unusually high blood pressure. He was advised to stop playing and left Villa at the age of 19. On his own volition, he visited Professor Sir George Pickering, a renowned expert in hypertension (high blood pressure) at the John Radcliffe Hospital in Oxford, close to Clanfield, the village where Horne had been brought up. 'He did all sorts of tests on me but couldn't find anything wrong,' said Horne. 'He put it down to "white coat syndrome" brought on by my nerves about being in hospital. I asked him if he thought I should play football and he said, "I don't see why not."'

Horne wrote a letter to Joe Mercer, who had been appointed manager of Manchester City after being sacked by Aston Villa. He included a photocopy of the medical report, passing him fit to play football. 'Joe was a lovely man. I could never say anything bad about him. He was my mentor and my guiding light,' he said. Horne was invited to Maine Road in September 1965 on a month's trial and after two weeks he was picked for the first team in a 3-1 win against Leicester City in the League Cup.

He was the first black player to turn out for Manchester City. He'd first encountered racism in football while at Aston Villa. 'I was playing for the reserves in a match against the first team and it was the first time I had any grief,' he said. 'One of the first-team players called me a black bastard. Afterwards, the club made him send me a letter of apology. During matches, if you went to take a throw-in or corner, you'd hear abuse from the crowd. It could be nasty at times but I got used to shrugging it off. It used to spur me on. I'd make sure the next tackle was all that bit harder.'

Rochdale, the same as all clubs at the time, had a level of institutionalised racism. Visiting black players were booed and subject to monkey chants. The acceptance of this behaviour was broad and considered part of the theatre of football. In fact, many fans presumed they were helping their team by distressing visiting players, making them lose concentration and play less well. In the 1970s, Rochdale had a negligible black minority and, in the most recent census, has only 0.3 per cent, compared to the national average of 2.3 per cent. For many, the arrival at Spotland of a black player in a football kit was their first encounter, albeit at a distance, with someone who wasn't white or Asian. Under different societal mores, hundreds saw fit to bait and jeer them, without public censure or moral contrition.

As a football club, Rochdale had been a pioneer on matters of race, with occasional missteps. Tony Collins was the first black manager in England when he took charge of the team from 1960 to 1967; he was sometimes referred to as 'Midnight'. In the late 1960s, a club director had complained to police after he heard a fan yell to a black player, 'Get back up that tree.' In August 1974, against Shrewsbury Town, the club fielded three black players (Tony Whelan, Leo Skeete and Stan Horne) in its starting line-up, thought to be the first time at an English lower-league club. Whelan, incidentally, a signing from Manchester City, was nicknamed Urko, after the gorilla chief of security in the television series and film, *Planet of the Apes*.

Although there was crude 'humour' within the dressing room and on the training ground, with little out of bounds, malicious racism among players was rare. 'Black lads were treated like everyone else,' said Keith Hanvey. 'I was always known as a big-nosed, ginger-haired bastard; that's the way it was. We called one of the black lads I played with "Coonie" but nothing was meant by it.'

Horne had played regularly for City but suffered a badly torn Achilles tendon that kept him out of the game for almost a year. Sidney Rose, City's director and a vascular surgeon, carried out the operation to repair it. On his return to full training, Horne was told by Mercer that first-team opportunities would be limited because of the emergence of Mike Doyle in his position. Horne signed for Fulham after an ill-fated first trip to Craven Cottage. On his way there, the train broke down for three hours and the taxi to the ground also spluttered to a halt. He spent four years at Fulham where he was often captain, before signing for Chester City in the summer of 1973. 'I wasn't enjoying my football at Chester and when I met Walter [Joyce] I liked him straight away,' he said. 'He was a solid Lancashire lad, with no fannying about. He liked the way I played and that I didn't mind getting stuck in. All I knew beforehand about Rochdale was that it was a mill town up north, quite close to Manchester. There was no training ground at Rochdale but that wasn't unusual – Fulham didn't have one either. I just wanted to be happy playing football again.'

* * *

Mohammad Pasha, a teacher and another leader of the PWA in Rochdale, was befriended by Cyril Smith. Pasha invited Smith to a meeting where the MP promised to do all he could to integrate and uphold the rights of Asians living in the town. At the same time, Smith contacted Khandaker Abdul Musabbir, chairman of the Bangladesh Association Community Project, a smaller ethnic grouping in the town. Musabbir, then aged 24, had arrived in Rochdale in 1963 from Sylhet, a sub-tropical region in the north of Bangladesh. He'd worked at a mill in Littleborough before entering the restaurant trade, later owning the Star of Bengal, one of Rochdale's most popular restaurants. Musabbir was pleased to find an ally among the indigenous community, and such a powerful one.

* * *

Both Stan Horne and Jimmy Grummett made their debuts in the match against Southend United at Spotland, four days after the cup defeat and on the last Saturday before Christmas. The atmosphere in the ground was eerie. Supporters were silent, as if too angry and frustrated to even muster a cheer or clap of encouragement. When Chris Guthrie scored for the visitors, a sound was heard at last: a round of boos and a few yells in Joyce's direction to 'sort it out'. Lee Brogden equalised close to half-time. The match ended a 1-1 draw. David Sugden wrote that the two debutants had made 'steady rather than spectacular debuts'.

Only 1,073 fans had made their way to Spotland for the match against Southend. Afterwards, sipping his whisky, Ratcliffe told fellow directors that he was pleased they had at least exceeded 1,000 – anything below (which seldom occurred in the professional game) was a humiliation. 'Considering what an arseholes we made of it against Grantham, we've done okay getting that many out in the middle of winter with all these bloody strikes and power cuts,' he said. He then made a statement he'd later regret. 'I think this is as low as we can get right now,' he said.

In the car park after the game, Mike Poole distributed the turkeys he'd promised to supply to team-mates; his family ran a farm and landscaping business in Morley, near Leeds. They had been in the boot of his car. The day was so cold, they had remained frozen.

* * *

Cyril Smith played a key role in expanding the Jalalia Jaame from a terraced house in Dudley Street to a purpose-built mosque in Wardleworth, an area where most Bengalis had settled. While he focused on local issues – helping with deportation cases, holding surgeries in Asian districts, etc. – he also spoke out on wider concerns. He argued in Parliament that Pakistan should have nuclear weapons ('Every country has a right to defend itself') and headed a march in February 1973 through Rochdale with 300 Pakistanis calling for the release of the country's prisoners-of-war serving time in India. Many Asians in the town referred to him as 'Mr Cyril'. 'I would stress that we are not asking for these people to be released and then sent to Britain. We are asking for them to be released and then sent to Pakistan,' he said.

The quote was typical of Smith's diplomacy; it served to appease the settled Rochdale community and appeal to incomers from the Indian sub-continent. Smith had recognised that to retain the Rochdale seat, he had to ensure his background and personality would charm traditional Labour voters and make them switch allegiance. The text in his election leaflet was typically expedient: 'I am of proud working-class background; my mother (of whom I am proud) is a cleaner. All my life I have worked for the working class. Much of the work I have done for charity has been to help poor people and poor children. I have never been a snob – I know what poverty is. I saw it last Christmas when I organised and helped to deliver toys for over 1,000 Rochdale children, many of them on housing estates.'

10

New Year, Old Rochdale

ANY SEMBLANCE of team spirit was quashed by an episode that would further darken the season. Money was stolen from the dressing room and, naturally, players began to speculate on the culprit or *culprits*. Dozens had access to the dressing room, including trialists, youth players, reserves, first-teamers and the admin and coaching staff. Outside of matchdays, there was no security in the inner sanctum of Spotland and keys in doors were seldom turned to a locked position. There didn't feel to be any need – it was an unwritten absolute that footballers didn't steal from one another. They were a team, all united, and anyone breaking this code was beneath contempt.

Walter Joyce was hoping it would be a one-off, a single and solitary incident, very much regretted now that the guilty party had seen the consequences, player set against player. Had it really been worth it for a few quid? Joyce gathered the players around him, young and senior. He knew that some of the lads were 'rum' or 'latch key' and had to be allowed some concession, a little lenience, at least until football became their surrogate 'family' and they learned the value of honesty and integrity; football usually had that effect.

'Look, whoever did it shouldn't have done it and I don't want it to happen again; do you hear me?' said Joyce. 'As a group of people, as a football club, we've got to put it down to someone temporarily losing their bloody marbles and move on, forget it. After this chat, if anyone wants to quietly have a word with me, admitting what they've done and offering to pay back the money, I promise this: nothing more will be said. That's so long as nothing like this happens again because, make no mistake, if it does, the guilty person will be bombed out of this football club pronto – their feet won't touch the floor.'

Rochdale's final two matches of 1973 were away at Chesterfield on Boxing Day and Tranmere Rovers three days later. They lost 1-0 at Chesterfield with a new forward pairing of Gary Cooper and Alan Taylor. David Sugden wrote that Cooper was 'still a little bewildered by the pace of first-team football', while Taylor was 'over enthusiastic, resulting in wasted opportunities'. Cooper, incidentally, rejoiced under the nickname 'The Sheriff' and was often greeted with 'hi, noon' when he arrived at training; both were abstruse references to the film star of the same name. Rochdale defended well at Tranmere and hit upon a strategy to reduce the chances of conceding a goal – they continually kicked the ball out of the ground. They did this six times in quick succession. On the final occasion, Tranmere's staff had to return to the kit room after running out of match balls. Bobby Downes scored from the penalty spot. The match ended a 1-1 draw.

Any Rochdale fans seeking respite from the dismal football had a limited selection of live entertainment over the Christmas period. Reginald Dixon, famous for his 40 years as a resident organist at the Tower Ballroom, Blackpool, performed at the Champness Hall. The Slaithwaite Brass Band was at Rochdale College, while Acker Bilk and his Paramount Jazz Band followed the Ian Campbell Folk Group on to the stage at Whitworth Civic Hall. Blasting out from pub jukeboxes across town was the Slade number-one hit, 'Merry Xmas Everybody'. The song, with its raucous delivery and defiant sentiment, felt to be a riposte to the despondency of the times – 'Look to the future now, it's only just begun.'

On New Year's Eve 1973, Rochdale were at the foot of the table after winning once in 21 league matches. They were eight points away from safety from relegation. As the players did their best to enjoy the evening, dispersed to various points across the north-west, they were each pondering on when there might be an upturn in form. Another thought was also criss-crossing their minds, bothering them, annoying them – the identity of the thief who had rifled through their pockets.

* * *

On securing the block support of Asians, Cyril Smith adopted a similarly enlightened policy to another neglected demographic – women. He invited members of the Young Wives and Rochdale Widows, among others, to join him on 'The Smith Liner', a specially chartered train on a return journey from Rochdale to London. More than 500 clambered aboard to travel to Euston Station, where they were met by the press, of course, before boarding 14 coaches for a sightseeing tour, finishing with a trip to the House of Commons.

During the return journey, in response to cries of 'give us a song, Cyril', he borrowed a guitar from the Bishop Henshaw School Folk Group and performed a version of 'She's a Lassie from Lancashire'. The song was Smith's party piece. He'd sung it a few months earlier on a Saturday night television variety show hosted by Jimmy Savile.

As a thank you for organising the trip, the Young Wives serenaded their MP with a chorus of 'Nice One Cyril'. The *Rochdale Observer* covered it in meticulous detail, genuflecting to Smith with a full page devoted to the event: 'This was no political platform, no signal of self-aggrandisement, just Cyril showing how much he cared for his townsfolk – and how they responded.'

Others had started to take a more cynical view of Cyril Smith. They saw self-interest and opportunism in his various alliances and a growing minority was discomfited by what they saw as 'cosying up' to Asians, prioritising their needs ahead of Rochdale's established white community. Also, further rumours were beginning to circulate about Smith's sexual predilection for 'little boys'.

* * *

New Year, old Rochdale. Ice had set hard across the Spotland pitch on New Year's Day 1974. The areas in the shadow of the stands were especially slippy. Walsall, the visitors, showed more intelligence by seeking out the softer sections and passing the ball quickly rather than attempting to run with it. David Sugden, another reporter stapled to the truth, wrote that Rochdale were 'clueless in the knack of goalscoring'. The only goal came when Keith Hanvey lost his footing and deflected the ball past Mike Poole: Rochdale 0, Walsall 1. The players were called in for extra afternoon training sessions before the match away at York City. They lost 2-1.

On Saturday, 12 January 1974, five months into the season, after 11 matches comprising 16 hours and 30 minutes of football, Rochdale finally won a league match at Spotland. David Sugden summed up the muted response to the 3-2 victory against Shrewsbury Town, reporting that the cheer at the final whistle was ironic rather than euphoric. 'Rochdale played badly but won,' he wrote. 'It would be foolish to look at this game for a pointer to Rochdale's Third Division future because, without doubt, Shrewsbury were the worst side seen at Spotland this season and themselves look to have a mammoth task on avoiding the drop.' While delighted with the win, Fred Ratcliffe was crestfallen on hearing the attendance. Only 957 had braved the chill to make their way to Spotland – the club's lowest ever post-war crowd.

Attendances had fallen at all levels of professional football. The downturn caused by strikes, with ensuing political and economic instability, had greatly reduced disposable income. The Rochdale board had held a few meetings specifically to discuss the matter. One or two directors felt the changing demographic of the town was a principal factor. The terraced houses in Deeplish, Brimrod and Newbold (and Spotland itself) had been the homes of long-standing Rochdale residents, where there was generational support for the football club. Many from the indigenous population had started to move out of these districts – the phenomenon was termed 'white flight'– to the leafier outskirts, such as Littleborough or Milnrow, while others had left the town altogether.

Families mainly from the Indian sub-continent had moved into this cheaper housing stock when they came to work in the town. 'We won't get the Pakis [the term 'Pakis' wasn't pejorative at this time] coming up here,' said one director. 'Why not?' asked another. 'They're probably scared of getting a good hiding, for one – all this stuff you read in the papers about football thugs. And it's not just that. They're all into their cricket and going to the mosque. They're not fussed about football.' 'I'm not sure about that. I often see them kicking a ball about on bits of grass. I asked one of the lads once why he didn't come to Spotland and do you know what he said? "What's Spotland?" I pointed to the floodlights and told him to keep walking until he got there.'

In a bid to attract more fans, the Football League allowed a tranche of fixtures to be played on Sundays. Rochdale's away match at Brighton and Hove Albion was one of 12 selected on Sunday, 20 January 1974. The Sunday Observance Act of 1780 prohibited 'the use of any building or room for public entertainment or debate on a Sunday if it invoked an admission charge'. So, clubs waived the conventional entrance fee but insisted fans bought a copy of the match programme instead, which sold at a much higher price than usual – the cost of a match ticket. Nine of the 12 clubs taking part in the Sunday football experiment reported their highest attendances of the season. The increase wasn't sustained and its initial success was widely felt to have been due to the novelty element.

Brighton raced into a two-goal lead at the Goldstone Ground but Rochdale stunned the large crowd of 18,885 with a goal by Leo Skeete. The visitors attacked strongly in the second half but Brighton held out for the win. Brian Clough, their manager, conceded that Rochdale had 'played well'. After the match, the Rochdale squad was spared the immediate long journey home by a kind gesture from Bill Lawton, a friend of Walter Joyce. The pair knew each other from playing football and cricket in the Oldham area. Lawton owned the Clarges Hotel in Brighton with his wife, the famous actress, Dora Bryan. The Rochdale party was granted free accommodation on the second of their two-night stay. The couple were perhaps too generous with such offers. They were later declared bankrupt and forced to sell most of the building, although they retained a first-floor flat with a sea view for many years.

* * *

Many Rochdalians didn't share Cyril Smith's enthusiasm about the influx of Asians and how the appearance of the town was changing. They saw domes and minarets appear on the skyline as mosques were built. Shops opened with their wares in baskets on the pavement – chickpeas, aubergines, rice and spices. They passed people dressed differently, men and women in the shalwar kameez, the national dress of Pakistan: a long shirt or tunic and trousers wide at the waist falling to a narrow cuff. When they cooked food, their biryani and tikka, the aroma wafted and lingered across backyards and alleyways. These immigrants were clannish, and extended families clustered to certain streets in particular areas – Deeplish, Wardleworth, Heybrook, Hamer, etc. Many of the white, working-class population that remained in these districts said they felt to be strangers on home ground, their neighbourhoods looking and smelling and *feeling* different. They said that they felt 'swamped' or 'taken over'. Their dissatisfaction was generally racism in a passive form, a grumble and a moan, rather than malevolence.

* * *

A week later, Rochdale were back by the sea on the other side of the country, when they travelled to Blundell Park, home of Grimsby Town. The pitch was a mere two feet above sea level, the lowest in England. The wind picked up out in the North Sea and swept across Cleethorpes beach to pound Blundell Park. Every visiting manager gave the same speech to his players, and Walter Joyce was no different. 'Get a feel for the conditions before you start knocking 30-yard passes. It's freezing out there and blowing a gale. Treat the wind as another challenge, something to get the better of. Run about, keep warm. Be braver than them. Whatever is thrown at you, bloody well own it,' he said.

They played with the wind at their backs and at half-time were level 1-1. In the second half, as the gale rocked them to their heels, they capitulated and lost 5-1. David Sugden was typically forthright: 'It was utter and complete second half chaos, created by an apparent disinterest in fighting to stay in the game, serving to impress one thing: football does not owe Rochdale a place in Division Three and if they are to stay up, it will have to be because of more wholehearted performances than this.'

Stan Horne was adapting to playing at a lower level and, initially at least, had been impressed with his team-mates. He was now beginning to have doubts. 'Walter was trying to build a team with young players and the standard seemed pretty good,' he said. 'But if you go down the leagues, as I'd done, you're often two or three moves ahead of the other players thinking-wise and can struggle if they can't read your game.' Horne was 29 with more than a decade of football experience. He felt players of a similar pedigree were needed at Rochdale. 'I had a fall-out with Walter when I went to the papers criticising the team selection,' he said. 'I thought he was playing too many young lads and, when we were constantly getting battered, it was causing them to lose enthusiasm. We got to the point where, if we couldn't actually win a match, we'd aim at least to do better than we had done the week before.'

* * *

As the Asian population swelled, racism increased proportionally and became sinister and formalised. The British Campaign to Stop Immigration (BCSI) opened a branch in Rochdale and found itself at loggerheads with the Rochdale and District Community Relations Council (RADCRC) – the fact these bodies existed was testimony to the entrenched nature of the problem. Alderman William Quinn, chairman of RADCRC, said, 'We must redouble our efforts to re-educate our townspeople and have them jettison their prejudices about coloured people.'

Jim Merrick, secretary of the BCSI (Rochdale branch), said Black Power leaders had been telling people for whom they should vote. He complained that 'vast numbers' of refugees were coming into England, mainly from Uganda, when 'a million Englishmen were without jobs'. Alderman Quinn accused Merrick of being a racist and he responded: 'I find it a compliment to be called racist. In fact, we are planning the publication of a quarterly magazine to be called *Racialism*. I feel pride in my racialism and I expect Indians and Pakistanis do also.' Alderman Quinn closed the meeting at Rochdale Art Gallery on a stirring note: 'There is absolutely no difference in the mechanism of a black and white man and anyone who thinks that the whites are a superhuman race ought to see a psychiatrist.'

* * *

Graham Smith, at 27, was one of few senior pros regularly chosen by Walter Joyce to play in the first team. Unlike Horne, he didn't publicly question Joyce's selection policy. One or two team-mates referred to him as a 'steady Eddie' but this was because he'd purposefully decided to shut out the gossip and politics of football and focus squarely on his own game: playing well, keeping fit, staying in the team.

He'd joined Rochdale in the summer of 1966 from Leeds United and, seven seasons later, was the club's longest-serving player. He was born in Pudsey, West Yorkshire and had signed to Leeds as a groundstaff boy in 1964. The closest he came to a first-team appearance was when he travelled with the squad to play at Northampton Town in December 1965. When they arrived at the County Ground, the pitch was waterlogged and the game postponed. He was released by Leeds manager, Don Revie, and he tipped off his friend, Rochdale manager, Tony Collins, who offered Smith a contract. He received a signing-on fee of £500, which he used to buy a Triumph Herald. 'I liked it straight away at Rochdale; it felt to be a homely club,' he said. 'Unfortunately for me – being a full-back – Alf Ramsey had just won the World Cup with England, where he'd done away with wingers. This meant full-backs were expected to overlap, which meant I was pegging it up and down the pitch all the game.'

The same as most of the promotion team of 1968/69, he'd moved to live in the town. At first he was in digs with fellow Rochdale player, Laurie Calloway, at the Deeplish home of Florrie Rhodes, a lady who cleaned at the club. Bobby Downes was another in digs. He stayed with Mrs King in her terraced house in Rupert Street, about half a mile from the ground. He remembers being told to 'put the sausage in the door' every time he entered the house – she was asking him to put the draught excluder against the bottom of the front door.

Smith later moved with his wife, Jean, into Tentercroft, one of the high-rise flats on the College Bank estate (better known as 'the Seven Sisters') in Rochdale town centre. They had been built in the mid-1960s to a high standard in the hope of attracting professionals to the town. The football club had an arrangement with the council whereby players were able to pay reduced rent.

After three years in the flats, Smith moved to Higher Bank Road, Littleborough, close to Hollingworth Lake. 'I often used to run round the lake,' he said. 'And I really felt to be part of the town. We mixed with the supporters. Now and again, a few would tell you that you'd played a load of rubbish but it was never malicious.'

Unlike the players of 1973/1974, the promotion squad had socialised after training and matches, visiting local working men's clubs and pubs; the Bowling Green on Spotland Road was a favourite. 'There was none of that dashing off in your car as soon as training had finished. We all mixed well and our wives knew one another, too. I think having that kind of camaraderie made a real difference, but over a few seasons it started to fade away,' said Smith.

He sometimes delivered sports kit on behalf of Trevor Butterworth, dropping supplies at local schools. 'He was a lovely bloke, Graham, and happy to work for me on the odd afternoon,' said Butterworth. 'He just got on with it and didn't think it was beneath him. I used to think it was good for business, having footballers associated with the shop.'

* * *

The *Rochdale Observer* carried a quarter-page advert for the BCSI, featuring a photograph of Mike Sellors and the slogan 'Stop Immigration'. Remarkably, it also included a residential address and phone number. Sellors, chairman of the BCSI (Rochdale branch), came from Bradford and had stood in the Deeplish/Brimrod ward in 1972, securing almost 500 votes – 15 per cent of the total cast.

Soon afterwards, the BCSI and other anti-immigration groups merged with the far-right political party, the National Front (NF), which had formed in 1966. In Rochdale, the NF's principal activity was distributing the magazine *Spearhead*, and handing out leaflets. Sellors claimed that the Rochdale branch had a membership of 'about 20', although others estimated it to be under ten. While out campaigning on the streets, Peter McGrath, the NF's election agent, was challenged by a member of the Rochdale Anti-Fascist Committee. They had a discussion about McGrath's Irish ancestry and he admitted that, under the NF's standpoint on repatriation, if the party ever got into power, he'd have to leave England.

A 'severe racial problem' was reported in 1973 by teachers at Greenhill Upper School, attended by many Asian teenagers. A teacher writing anonymously in *RAP* said:

> All through the school, the harsh Urdu and Punjabi language rings out as they shout to one another. Nothing but jabber, jabber, jabber. Teachers' lives are threatened. Everything is swept under the carpet and it is high time it was suctioned out with a great big Hoover. They talk of our wonderful race relations but the Pakistanis and English hate each other's guts. We have a severe racial problem.

In response, the school organised for indigenous pupils to visit the homes of Pakistanis, 'to equip children for life in a multiracial and multicultural world'.

In another attempt to integrate cultures, the family of two-year-old Sunjal Kapila invited 200 of their co-workers at Mutual Mills, Heywood to a mundan ceremony held at the St John Ambulance headquarters in Redcross Street, Rochdale. During the Hindu ritual, Sunjal's hair was shaved off by local barber, Edmund Grindrod, before turmeric and sandalwood paste was applied to sooth the skin. After tucking in to a buffet dinner, attendees were informed that the removed hair would be sent to Sunjal's grandparents in the Punjab, northern India, to be blessed and scattered in the Ganges.

* * *

Walter Joyce was aware that he was being optimistic in expecting the players to overlook the theft from the dressing room, to forget it and move on. He knew of human nature, especially in the claustrophobic environment of a football club: the gossip, the accusations and aspersions. His coaches, Harold Holburt and Dennis Butler, told him that some of the lads said they were sure who had done it and planned to 'string up the bastard'. Joyce understood their feelings. A dressing room was a near-holy place, where, often literally in blood, you affirmed a brotherhood: us vs them, us vs the world. Years later, in the rear-view mirror of life, whether you failed or succeeded, you were supposed to remember these men at the next peg as your forever-friends. You'd run for each other, tackled for each other, covered for each other, across mud and through the pissing rain, at horrible outposts on freezing nights with ignorant fans on your back, yelling and bellyaching. You'd done all that for a few quid and a pat on the back but, most of all, for *each other*. For fuck's sake, you didn't rob off one another, weaselling about in the dressing room, dip-dipping while everyone else was out there kicking against the wind.

* * *

Racist attacks became commonplace. Three youths appeared before Manchester Crown Court after indulging in what they referred to as 'Paki-bashing'. The victim was walking in Tweedale Street, Deeplish when he was baited before being punched and kicked. The judge, Desmond Bailey, sent them for borstal training and said, 'You are three cowardly young bullies, as this offence indicates.' Five youths appeared before magistrates after a 'whites versus Pakistanis' fight on Ashfield Valley estate. A Pakistani youth said he was walking with his mother on the Rochdale Canal towpath, carrying a radio, when approached by a group of white youths. A row broke out and others joined in. 'One of the Pakistanis was on the floor being kicked and there was a running battle going on,' a resident told the police. Mr N.R. Woolfenden, presiding magistrate, said, 'We are simply not having it, coloured or white. You have got to live in peace.'

In the workplace, the social and cultural differences soon became apparent and sometimes led to tension. Immigrant workers, most of whom supported large extended families, were viewed as too compliant, eager for more overtime or willing to work unsocial hours. Many did double shifts, rumoured to be napping in between in cotton skips. 'I keep telling them that it's dangerous, a fire hazard, but as soon as I tip one of them out, there's another bedding down somewhere,' a foreman told the *Rochdale Observer.*

Some of the immigrants had been driven out of their places of origin. The installation of the Mangla Dam in Mirpur, Azad Kashmir in 1960 left over 100,000 people homeless, many of whom settled in the north of England. More than 500,000 died in Bangladesh in the Bhola cyclone of 1970 and thousands lost their homes. Families became bonded by these shared experiences and, along with their speaking a different language and strict adherence to Islam (more than 90 per cent of immigrants from south Asia were Muslims), they were often viewed as 'cliquey' by fellow workers. An unnamed shop steward working at David Bridge & Co., the engineering firm based in Castleton, Rochdale, revealed the level of institutionalised racism when he told the *Manchester Evening News*, 'We don't mind training our own people but not Pakistanis. Once you let them in, they take the place over.'

* * *

Rochdale's turn to play a Sunday match at home came with the visit of York City, early in February. Before, Walter Joyce was fretful that the trial might not succeed because Rochdale Hornets were at home on the same day, to Halifax in the first round of the Rugby League Challenge Cup; Hornets were on an 11-match unbeaten run. Bury and Blackburn Rovers also had home fixtures.

He needn't have worried. The 'gate' was more than double the previous home match, with 2,205 turning up to see Rochdale go 2-0 down within 18 minutes, and lose 3-1. David Sugden was on top form. He wrote: 'Rochdale spent the first 20 minutes ambling around as if frightened to incur the wrath of the Lord's Day Observance Society.' The hope had been that the extra supporters, many of them perhaps visiting Spotland for the first time, would enjoy the experience and wish to return two days later (should they be free on a weekday afternoon; it was another 2pm kick-off) to see Rochdale take on Cambridge United. This hope wasn't realised, far from it.

* * *

Two soldiers from Rochdale, David Kirby and Peter Steriker, both aged 19, were among others and their families returning to barracks at Catterick in north Yorkshire after a weekend break. The coach had passed through the section of the M62 within the Rochdale border and was between junctions 26 and 27 on the outskirts of Leeds, when a bomb exploded in the early hours of Monday, 4 February 1974. 'Some people were talking and others were dozing,' said Fusilier Kirby. 'I was chatting to Nigel [Nigel Boden, another fusilier] and complaining that the seats weren't comfy enough to get some sleep. Then it happened. There was a terrific bang. For a split second I thought the tyres had burst. Everything went black and the coach seemed to come apart. The back end collapsed and we were left sitting in the section that was still intact. We just sat there dazed and shocked. Suddenly it dawned on us what had happened but there was no panic.'

Kirby and Boden jumped clear of the debris and ran across fields to a farm and rang the emergency services. They returned to help the injured and dying. The blast was so powerful that bodies and severed limbs were found 250 yards away. 'A few people were trapped in the wreckage and we couldn't get them out. There were also a lot of people lying in the road at the back of the coach. It was a terrible sight,' said Kirby.

Nine soldiers and three civilians were killed in the bombing and 38 injured. The 25-pound bomb had been hidden inside a suitcase in the luggage compartment. Routinely, soldiers travelled by train but, because of strike action by railway workers, coaches had been laid on. The vehicle had been travelling at 60mph and the driver, Roland Handley, aged 39, steered it to a halt on the hard shoulder despite being cut by flying glass. He was later praised for his skill and bravery. Earlier in the evening, he'd asked the coach party to 'hutch up a bit' when a soldier and his family arrived late, asking for a lift. Tommy Judge, aged 17, had been lying across two seats and gave them up for the Haughton family, moving nearer to the front of the coach; this decision saved his life. Corporal Cliff Haughton, aged 23, and his wife, Linda, 23, sat together on these seats at the back, with their sons Lee, five, and Robert, two, on their laps. They were all killed.

The Rochdale pair of David Kirby and Peter Steriker were members of the 2nd Battalion of the Royal Fusiliers. They had been friends from childhood, both attending Redbrook School, and had served together in the Anderstown area of Belfast. A week later, Roland Handley completed the same journey, carrying soldiers to the barracks in Catterick. He said it was the only way to deal with such a horror: life went on.

Although the Provisional IRA didn't claim responsibility for the bombing, it was believed that its members or sympathisers had staged it. There were hopes that the atrocity might form the nadir of such acts of terrorism, especially since children and civilians had been killed or injured and several of the victims were of Irish Catholic descent. Later in 1974, there were similar indiscriminate bombings in Guildford, Birmingham and Bristol.

The next day, a handful of the Yorkshire-based Rochdale players travelling to the home match against Cambridge United had to pass the scene of the M62 massacre (as it became known). The coach was still in situ as forensic experts combed it for evidence.

* * *

Tuesday, 5 February 1974, the day after the motorway coach bombing, is considered one of the bleakest in modern British history. The country was in deep recession. The government was in disarray. Inflation was running at nearly 10 per cent. The three-day working week was in place. Miners had announced another national strike. Petrol was running out. And bombs were being detonated across England. Supporters of Rochdale thought it fitting that the worst day in the club's history should fall on such a wretched day.

After many rumours, Edward Heath finally called for a General Election, to be held on Thursday, 28 February. He promised to base the Conservative party campaign around the slogan 'Who governs Britain?' He believed the public was exhausted by strikes and exasperated by the power wielded by unions.

The league match against Cambridge United had been scheduled to take place in November but heavy rain had led to a postponement. A low crowd was expected for this rearranged fixture, kicking off at 2pm on an overcast afternoon of a working day. By 'low', Fred Ratcliffe et al. had anticipated a figure close to but probably not exceeding 1,000. They assumed Rochdale had a nucleus of perhaps 700 to 800 supporters who would literally turn up to watch the grass grow, such was their commitment to the routine of attendance. Two days earlier, the performance against York City had been poor but, if just over a third of the fans returned for the Cambridge match, dishonour could be averted.

They didn't return. The official attendance was 588 but this was almost certainly falsified to save revealing the depth of disillusionment the town held for its football team. The more likely figure was 450. Either way, it was the lowest ever post-war attendance for a Football League match and remains so, almost 50 years later.

As kick-off approached, it had been noted in the press box that the 'crowd' was particularly sparse. Stan Townsend, his colleague from the *Rochdale Observer*, Alan Tweedale, and local freelance, Jack Hammill, hit upon an idea. 'We decided to do a headcount,' said Townsend. 'I did one end, Jack the other and Alan did everyone in the middle. We counted up 340 and put that out on PA [Press Association]. Freddie Ratcliffe burst a blood vessel and said it wasn't making Rochdale look very good. He rang Jack afterwards and said, "Don't you ever put the attendance in again like that – we'll tell you what it is."' Jack Hammill had fallen out with Ratcliffe on an earlier occasion. 'I never really got on with Fred, it was always an uneasy truce,' he said. 'That might have been something to do with what I said once during a meeting. Fred had asked if everyone could take a new face with them to the next home match. I said it was okay for him, as he'd always been two-faced – and it got back to him.'

Chris Dunphy, who later joined the board at Rochdale and was chairman for 12 years, believes the attendance against Cambridge was even lower than counted by the three journalists. 'I remember the day well as I had recently set up my own heating business and felt guilty for taking a half day off work. There were all sorts of numbers put out, but I'm pretty sure 150 was closer to the real figure,' he said.

There was conjecture among Rochdale fans that Ratcliffe hadn't attended the Cambridge match, nor any of the others played on weekday afternoons. Instead, he was in his office at the spring works. He'd told everyone it was his duty to set an example to the workforce and 'muck in' at such a volatile time. 'That might have been the case but he was also aware of how good it would look, the PR of it, him missing his beloved Rochdale to keep the spring works afloat during an economic crisis,' said a relative of a former director. 'He put money into the club and liked to be seen as "Mr Rochdale" but I don't think he put in quite as much as some might think.'

The players would remember the day for the rest of their lives. 'It was harrowing,' said Keith Hanvey. 'It was such a small crowd; it was embarrassing to play in the game. We could hear almost everything people were saying.' Very few photographs were taken on the day but a handful exist that have been used extensively in reference books. 'There's one of me that pops up a lot,' said Stan Horne. 'I'm almost on the floor with my arse over the ball between my legs. I played all those years to a reasonable level but I'm remembered most for that bloody picture. They were awful times. It felt as if there were more of us on the pitch than in the stands.'

Mike Brennan had an inkling of the low turnout when, a few days before, he'd accompanied team-mate, Dave Carrick, to a bookmakers near the ground. The pair were best friends and other players joked that if you kicked one of them in training, they both limped. 'Dave wanted to put a bet on this particular horse and we were behind these two old fellas in the queue,' said Brennan. 'One of them asked the other if he was going to Spotland and his mate said, "I'd rather have toothache than watch that lot".' Brennan has vivid memories of the Cambridge match: 'It was an eerie experience. Playing at that time of day on a Tuesday was odd to start with and there was so much going on in the country with the power cuts and everything. It was drab, one of those still, overcast days when the weather can't make up its mind what to do,' he said.

Andrew Harrison, a Rochdale fan, played truant from Greenhill School where he was in his last year of education. 'There was a scattering of people in the ground, the majority of them in the Main Stand,' he said. 'It was a weird atmosphere and a weird game. I was near the tea hut in the Willbutts Lane and then moved to Pearl Street to stand on the cinders. We knew we were going down after the Cambridge game. Apathy had really set in. I wish Walter Joyce had done something else in his life, like gardening, rather than trying to be a football manager.' Bill Leivers, the Cambridge United manager, said the atmosphere had been 'absolutely shocking'. Before the match, Rochdale were hopeful of a victory – Cambridge had lost ten and drawn two of their previous 12 away matches. Cambridge won 2-0.

The usual number of match programmes had been printed but many remained unsold. These were tipped into a couple of braziers on the club car park and burned, along with other scrap paper, making the programme extremely rare. The paltry attendance and Rochdale's position at the foot of the table (ten points adrift of safety from relegation) drew media interest for a week or so after the match. Granada TV sent a film crew from its regional news programme, *On the Spot*, to interview Joyce and Ratcliffe. The *Rochdale Observer* referred to the club's treatment as 'a public mauling'. Another crew, this time from the BBC, turned up and Len Hilton told them straight: 'We're doomed. We have made a lot of mistakes as a board. All I can add is that I don't blame the public for withdrawing their support. They are punishing us now by staying away. I will admit that we are just not good enough to stay in Division Three.'

Fred Ratcliffe said he was a 'self-confessed super-optimist' and refused to accept the club was certain to be relegated, especially with 18 matches still to play. Walter Joyce concurred: 'I believe things can happen. It is difficult to believe that here, but they could, even now. It has sickened me losing every week and I have been really low. But you have to say to yourself, "Am I doing the right thing?" and I believe I am. Even though we are in a poor position, I would say there are more assets here now than in the last four years.'

Once more (he often mentioned this to journalists), Walter Joyce referenced Jimmy McIlroy. He admired McIlroy and viewed him as a mentor. They had been team-mates at Burnley and, when McIlroy was manager of Oldham Athletic, he'd signed him as a player. McIlroy, according to Joyce, had 'banked on youth' but it took three years for Oldham to start winning matches regularly, by which time McIlroy had resigned due to the pressures of the role. Joyce was disappointed that it wasn't widely acknowledged that McIlroy had largely built the Oldham team, which was currently near the top of the Third Division.

In a bid to show that better days lay ahead at Rochdale, Joyce repeatedly focused on the success of the reserves, a squad comprising mainly young players: they were often top of the Lancashire League. While this might have been testament to a fresh crop of talent ready to service the first team, it wasn't necessarily the natural progression. Most young players struggled to bridge the divide between reserves and first-team football, either because they lacked the physical and mental resolve or sheer ability. Rochdale fans were pleased to learn that the reserves were doing well but it offered no salve to the misery of enduring the performances of the first team. They had been watching Rochdale for many years and had been made cynical. They knew where most of these lads would end up (whatever Joyce might tell them) – playing for Bacup Borough or Whitworth Valley at best but, more likely, driving vans or working in warehouses. 'We played against Oldham's youth team – the one that delivered so many players to the first team – and we hammered them 6-0,' said Dennis Butler. 'The fact that we won so easily didn't matter. You could see they were lads with ability and that, when they filled out and got stronger, they were going to make good, solid pros. I don't think you could look at our young lads and say that about them.'

Although Rochdale AFC often felt to be a principality, it was still subject to the vagaries that affected the rest of the town. In the worst week of its life, with the light literally and metaphorically fading on the club, there was one last torment. Thieves broke into the laundry room beneath the Main Stand and made off with eight shirts and socks worth a total of £28. 'We can't afford this sort of thing,' said Angus McLean.

* * *

'It's in the bag,' said Alan Taylor, Cyril Smith's election agent. 'We've won already!' 'What do you mean, lad?' asked Smith. The campaign team had already downed a few pints in nearby pubs, the Navigation Inn and the Woolpack, before making their way to the Liberal party headquarters at 144 Drake Street. They had just heard the news and were giddy; this was going to be easier than expected. In the by-election of 1972, Smith had secured a 5,000 majority but, in a working-class town such as Rochdale, with its predisposition to support Labour, the team knew it had to be wary of its main rival. 'You'll never guess who the daft buggers have put up against you,' said Taylor.

They had imagined Labour would put up a strong candidate in a bid to reclaim a seat that it had held for most of the previous 50 years. The canvassers sitting at tables in the club wearing 'Vote Cyril' rosettes with photocopied sheets in plastic bags at their feet had all agreed on the profile of an adversary who would run them closest. He (or she) would be local and have a largely non-union profile to appeal to the moderate working man (or woman) who felt the unions, the miners specifically, had become too confrontational.

Alan Taylor and his team were in a mood of triumphalism because the man put up against Smith was Lawrence Cunliffe.

He was 45, lived in Farnworth, near Bolton, and was a mining engineer and member of the NUM. In fact, he was the same candidate Smith had defeated in the by-election of October 1972 when Cunliffe received 5,000 fewer votes than Labour had received in the General Election of 1970. 'They've already thrown in the towel,' shouted someone from the bar, waving a pint pot. 'Now then,' said Smith. 'Let's not put the bunting up just yet. We've got to see this home and dry.'

* * *

The Cambridge defeat hung as smog over Spotland. Players complained that they felt 'leggy' and several went down with colds. Walter Joyce told them it was to be expected. 'You've been through it,' he told them. 'All the losing is bad enough but then playing in front of practically no one – it's bound to feel like a punch in the guts. Listen, remember this, how bloody awful you feel right now, and make sure it doesn't happen again. Learn from it. Grow as footballers and men.'

Joyce refused to focus on particular matches in isolation. He believed that if you picked the best available players, employed appropriate tactics and everyone was aggressive in the tackle, ran hard and expressed themselves wherever possible, success would follow. His back-up staff felt much the same but, after the Cambridge debacle, they each held a hushed delight in anticipation of the next match. In short, Southport were (nearly) as bad as Rochdale. They had only five more points and, the same as Rochdale, had won twice in the league all season. The news emanating from their home ground of Haig Avenue was also pleasing the Rochdale contingent. They were suffering an injury crisis, with eight players doubtful for the match and two more suspended after picking up disciplinary points. Their plea to the Football League to have the fixture postponed had been rebuffed. 'They'll have to play their kids. We might even win this one!' joked Frank Campbell.

On the morning of the match, Walter Joyce had finished his breakfast and was sipping a mug of tea while reading a newspaper opened out on the kitchen table. The phone rang. It was Angus McLean. 'Bad news, Walter. The match is off.' On their second appeal, Southport had managed to persuade the Football League that the match shouldn't go ahead. 'How's that happened? I thought they'd told them to bugger off,' said Joyce. 'I bet Bally [Southport's manager, Alan Ball Sr] nipped over to Lytham [Lytham St Annes, former headquarters of the Football League] with a bloody big bottle of brandy for Hardacre [Alan Hardacre, secretary of the Football League]!' answered McLean.

Walter Joyce told everyone that teams should be proficient enough so that 'turning a corner' or 'kicking on' wasn't necessary but, on this occasion, this was exactly how he'd viewed a positive outcome of the Southport match. He didn't believe in 'bad luck' either; you made your own luck in life. He muttered it anyway without thinking – will anything ever go right for us?

* * *

The Conservative candidate in the General Election was Lillian Green, a 'sharp-witted young woman with a gift of political repartee the equal of any of her opponents' (election leaflet). She lived in Darwen and worked on her family's greengrocer's stall at Blackburn market, where she started work each morning at 6am. She was stridently against the actions of the NUM and other 'militant' unions: 'What would anyone say to a democracy that gives way to blackmail?' she asked.

Mike Sellors, the NF candidate, laid out his party's main policies – withdrawal from the Common Market; introduction of the death penalty for terrorists; making the IRA an illegal organisation; and the 'gradual repatriation of coloured immigrants and their dependents who have arrived in the UK since 1948'. Sellors, a chartered accountant, said, 'Immigrants are the main cause of overcrowding in our schools. They create slums and then expect to be given a council house.'

Liberal party activists toured the town putting up posters. Next to the photo of Cyril Smith was the slogan 'Rochdale's Son is Second to None. You're Safe with Cyril.' 'I will be talking about prices and incomes, about industrial affairs, about housing, about social services and about "the system",' he said. The experienced Labour MP, Stanley Orme, who represented Salford West, issued a broadside: 'Cyril Smith has made about as much impact on the House of Commons as a wet blanket.'

11

They're Like Bloody Ghouls

THE DIRECTORS and coaching staff agreed that the worst impact of the theft from the dressing room would be a deepening of existing divisions in the squad. But this is what happened. The first team blamed the reserves. The older players blamed the younger ones. The Mancs blamed the Scousers. The Yorkies blamed the Mancs. The Scousers blamed the Yorkies. And the circle went round for weeks, everyone keeping a watchful eye on their bags and tipping up watches, necklaces, loose change and notes to Frank Campbell for safekeeping; this was no way to run a football club.

Theories were being shared as to the identity of the thief. A group of players had been meeting and muttering for weeks and were sure they knew the culprit. They formed a delegation and marched to Joyce's office. They named a name. 'Right,' said Joyce. 'I'll look into it and get back to you. I did ask you to leave it be, but since you've clearly not been able to, we need to sort this out once and for all.'

That afternoon, Joyce asked the accused player to stay on after training. 'So no one has any idea what's going on, get in your car as if you're driving home, have a spin round Rochdale and arrive here half an hour later when everyone's gone,' he told him. Back at the ground, the player denied that he'd carried out the theft. He said he could prove it, too. 'Go and get Peter's book,' he said. He was referring to the book kept by Peter Blakey, the physio, in which he wrote who he'd seen on a particular day and jotted down any treatment updates. Joyce found the book and saw the player's name (and only his) in there and next to it 'three hours' – Blakey charged the club for his services by the hour. 'That means, Gaffer, I was with him all that morning, having my leg sorted, while the ressies [reserves] and first team were out training. That proves I didn't nick nothing. Have a word with Pete, if you like. He'll back me up.'

Joyce said he fully expected that the player's story would be corroborated. As he was leaving, the player stopped by the door. 'I might as well have done it,' he said. 'Why's that?' asked Joyce. 'Well, if they all think I'm a thief anyway, they obviously don't trust me, do they? Would you want to be with a load of people who saw you that way? We're supposed to be team-mates.' He closed the door behind him and Joyce leaned forward towards the desk, supporting his head with the palm of his hands. He shouldn't have done what he'd just done, he realised. He'd made the matter worse. He'd been cowed by a kangaroo court composed of the more assertive, voluble players. Aitch (Harold Holburt) had counselled him, how he shouldn't allow them to have a disproportionate influence. He could hear Holburt's words in his head: 'Just because they act all sure about something, doesn't mean they're right. Most people are out for themselves in football, one way or another.'

Joyce tapped a fist on his brow as if trying to knock the thoughts out of his mind; he had a football match to focus on. If Southport had been considered a relatively easy fixture, the forthcoming match was its antithesis: Oldham Athletic. Oldham were chasing promotion and stood in fifth position in the table. The match had particular resonance for Joyce because Oldham were a team he felt to have partly built. Three of his former youth players were now first-team regulars – Chris Ogden (21), Keith

Hicks (19) and Ian Robins (21). They had been blended into the team alongside experienced pros such as Andy Lochhead (31) and were playing forceful, effective football that Joyce wanted to emulate at Rochdale. 'Walter brought me through and played a large part in developing me as a player. He was firm – you didn't mess with him,' said Keith Hicks.

A rare occasion when they did 'mess with him' invoked repercussions. 'At Christmas time, we went to a pub in Oldham and when we came out all the players pelted Walter with snowballs. He told us we would pay for it and at the next training session we had to be sick before he allowed us to stop running. Some of the lads were putting their fingers down their throat, they were so desperate to stop,' said Hicks.

Hicks had met up with Joyce one time on a social basis. A couple of weeks after his 17th birthday, in August 1971, he and team-mate, goalkeeper Ian Taylor, were invited to accompany Joyce to Anfield. The match was between Manchester United and Arsenal; United had been ordered to play their first two 'home' matches away from Old Trafford after outbreaks of hooliganism during the previous season. 'We called at Walter's house and, looking through the window to the back garden, we could see he had installed a track and his lad [Warren, aged six at the time] was running round as if he was doing a proper training session. Both me and Ian thought it was a bit much,' he said. After the match, which United won 3-1, Joyce dropped them off at Shaw Street train station in St Helens, unaware that they had missed the last train back to Manchester. 'We set off running down the East Lancs. A group of lads chased us and wouldn't give up. This must have gone on for a few miles before we finally hitched a lift,' said Hicks.

Harold Holburt was another occasional visitor to the Joyce homestead, which he remembered being 'an old farmhouse or it might have formerly been a pub'. He recalled that the land, stretching about 60 yards at the back of the house, was fashioned into a small football pitch. 'I went up there once with my son, Glen [briefly affiliated to Rochdale AFC], and Walter insisted we had a lads vs dads game on this pitch. Even then, I could tell that he wanted to win and couldn't just see it as a kick-about,' he said.

Roger Denton, a 20-year-old full-back, was taken on loan from Bradford City and played against Oldham. Rochdale lost 3-1. The adjective appearing most often in match reports afterwards was 'plucky' rather than the more usual 'pathetic'.

* * *

On the day before the General Election, the *Rochdale Observer* ran an editorial, which intrinsically called upon the townspeople to vote Liberal. It read:

> For nearly half a century, two political parties in Britain have assumed a divine right to make the government of the country a private fight between themselves. People want to see whether a third contender will give them better value for money. We have long argued that British politics desperately needs a third force.

The writer, presumably briefed by the proprietors, added: 'We face a graver national crisis today than we have known since Hitler set about trying to destroy us.'

Cyril Smith trounced Labour, adding another 4,000 votes to his majority. Lawrence Cunliffe, the Labour candidate, claimed it was because Smith had the 'block' Asian vote – an estimated 95 per cent of whom had voted Liberal. 'It seems to me that the people of Rochdale have voted for a local personality. They have ignored the policies which people should consider when voting in a General Election,' he said. The *Rochdale Observer* further lent its gleeful support: 'Alderman Smith has become a national figure, projecting his political image so successfully that he looks like making the Rochdale seat his own for as long as he wants it.'

* * *

Walter Joyce made the same request of the ringleader of the accusers as he had of the accused – to drive around Rochdale for half an hour and then call back at Spotland. Joyce explained that the player in question had an alibi and there was written evidence to show he was somewhere else at the time of the theft. 'Was he with Pete [Blakey] the whole time?' asked the player. 'Pete says he was, yes,' replied Joyce. 'So he didn't have a piss or wander off to get a brew in all that time? It would only take a minute or two to do his pilfering.' 'Come on, be realistic,' said Joyce. 'We still think he's done it.' 'Well, without any evidence, there's not a lot anyone can do.' 'We've thought about that.' 'Have you? What have you thought?' 'A few of the lads want to mark up a couple of pound notes and see where they end up, if you know what I mean.' 'You're not doing that.' The player shuffled awkwardly in his seat. He lowered his voice: 'Your shout, Boss.'

Joyce had heard enough, seen enough, had enough. 'Yes, it *is* my bloody shout and I'm done with all this. I've already given it more time than it deserves; we all have. Let's get back to what we're supposed to be doing – playing bloody football and trying to win matches. Instead of hating on this lad, whoever it is, maybe we should be feeling sorry for him. Have you thought about that? There's something not right about stealing from your mates. Anyone doing it needs help, not a bloody hiding. Tell the lads to leave it now and if I hear that any player is having accusations made about him or taking any shit whatsoever, I'll come down on whoever is doing it like a ton of bricks.'

Joyce's diktat settled down the players and the atmosphere improved in training. Another loan player was added to the squad when Ian Buckley, a 20-year-old defender, joined from

Oldham Athletic. He went into the team to play Huddersfield Town at their Leeds Road ground. Rochdale played well and were level 0-0 at half-time. The second half was a disaster. Rochdale conceded five goals for the third time in the season, without reply. David Sugden wrote: 'Rochdale were trampled underfoot by a more determined, more dedicated and obviously more skilful Huddersfield Town side.' Walter Joyce missed the match. He was suffering from stomach ache, influenza *and* tonsillitis. 'Born to lose,' he joked to staff when he finally returned to work, still sneezing and complaining of a throat that 'felt like sandpaper'.

* * *

The charge that the *Rochdale Observer* gave disproportionate coverage to Cyril Smith was made with greater frequency after the General Election. He appeared, usually in several different 'news' pieces, in almost every issue, both the Wednesday and Saturday editions. Years after the election victory, he revealed an insight into his relationship with the newspaper. In August 2007, the paper celebrated its 150th anniversary and Smith was asked to pen a eulogy. He referred to its former long-term owners, the Scotts, as 'a great family' and praised the 'superb editorial columns', before adding: 'We have much to thank it for. When I was MP, the *Observer* gave me great support in my work, by publishing a weekly MP's newsletter on my activities written by me. It was, and is, a campaigning paper.'

* * *

The Football League and Hereford United appeared to be in cahoots to bring more scorn upon Rochdale. The scheduled match between them had earlier been postponed because of Hereford's FA Cup run, which included ties against West Ham United and Bristol City. The match was reorganised for the afternoon of Tuesday, 26 February. Rochdale were fearful of a repeat of the Cambridge humiliation, so Angus McLean spent hours on the phone trying to rearrange the fixture for a time when supporters would find it easier to attend. The alternative times and dates were rejected by Hereford, and league officials insisted the match went ahead as planned. Fred Ratcliffe called an emergency board meeting. 'We're not having that lot [the media] down here taking the piss out of us again,' he said. 'They're like bloody ghouls. Angus tells me he's already had about half a dozen press lads on the phone trying to cadge tickets.' A generator was hired to power the floodlights and the match went ahead in the evening. Ratcliffe said he'd 'stump up most of the money' but asked each director to make a token contribution. The match finished 1-1 and was played in front of 1,195 spectators.

Dave Seddon, a 22-year-old PE teacher from nearby Whitworth High School, had been called into the first team to play against Hereford. He'd been affiliated to the club for almost a decade, playing almost 300 times for the youth and reserves teams while also turning out regularly for the amateur club, Bagslate Youth Club FC. 'Walter told me on the morning of the match that I was playing. I don't remember being given any instruction at all, just to go out there and try and enjoy myself,' he said.

Ian Goodwin, a Rochdale supporter, grew up in Bamford and often played football with Seddon, who was three years his senior. 'He was so much better than the rest of us,' he said. 'It made me realise how good you had to be to make it, when a lad such as Dave had so much trouble breaking into the first team.' Seddon was selected to play at left-back, a position he'd never played before; he was routinely a sweeper or midfielder. 'I'm not sure how Walter didn't know that I had no left foot to speak of – I'd played enough games for the club at various levels. To give myself a better chance of playing well, I should have said I wanted to play in my normal position. I wish I'd have stood up for myself really but back then you did as you were told,' he said.

He'd been on the periphery of the first team for a year or so and had earlier received an induction to the dressing room by Reg Jenkins. 'I loved Reg to bits, both as a player and a person, but he gave it to me straight this particular day. It was a pre-season friendly and he thought I was playing within myself. And I *was* – I was like a rabbit caught in the headlights. He got me up against the wall and said he was going to chin me. He was huge, one of his legs was about as big as me, and I was a gibbering wreck. He said to me, "You are costing me money [presumably a win bonus] and if you don't start playing, I'm going to smack you one." I was terrified at the time but it was great advice.'

Jenkins, as a senior pro, had been known for these impromptu offers of guidance; his counsel was missed among the current squad. 'I had just broken into the first team when Reg pulled me to one side,' said David Cross, who had left Spotland to join Norwich City in 1971. 'He said to me, "Look, this is your first season – play your football and don't ever chase money because it will come to you if you're good enough." He was right. It was fantastic advice. In all my years in football, I never knocked on a manager's door asking for money. If you were playing well and scoring goals, it was reflected in your wage packet.'

Cross, from Heywood, had undergone an experience similar to Seddon. He'd played for the club at various levels as a right-winger from the age of 14 but, on his debut with the first team – a pre-season friendly at Spotland against East Fife in July 1969 – he was told he was playing centre-forward but given no direction whatsoever by the manager, Dick Conner, or coaching staff. He turned to team-mate Bobby Downes, who had lodged with the Cross family after joining the club from Peterborough. 'He told me to keep on the move, running off at angles and making myself available at all times to receive a pass. When it came, I was to control the ball, protect it and then lay it off and get into the box ready to score a goal. I basically followed this advice for the next 20 years in football and it did me more than okay,' he said.

Downes had himself received scant coaching at his three clubs – West Bromwich Albion, Peterborough United and Rochdale. 'It was all running and running, which you were left to do while the coaches sat on their arses talking about you. A lot of them were lazy bastards back then, on an easy number,' he said. He received his first personal coaching – almost a decade into his career – when he joined Watford, and Graham Taylor had taken over as manager. 'Graham was literally the first person to give me any advice about how to play, what my role was and how I was to go about it. He gave me the aim of scoring ten goals a season and creating 30 more for others,' he said.

At Rochdale, the communication was so poor, especially during Dick Conner's regime, that the coaches were sometimes unable to remember players' surnames. 'Everyone was given a nickname, usually according to their size,' said Downes. 'I was always "Little Bobby", for example, and Bill Atkins was "Big Bill".'

* * *

As foretold by the *Rochdale Observer*, Cyril Smith did hold the parliamentary seat in Rochdale for 'as long as he wants it'. He decided not to stand in the General Election of April 1992, after the death of his mother, Eva, and his failing health. He died in September 2010, aged 82. Two years later, the Crown Prosecution Service admitted that he should have faced paedophilia charges during his lifetime. Steve Heywood, assistant chief constable of Greater Manchester Police, said there was 'overwhelming evidence' that Smith had sexually and physically abused young boys.

More than 30 years earlier, *RAP* had run a cover story ('Strange Case of Smith the Man') and two-page spread containing stark details of Smith's predatory sexual behaviour at Cambridge House, a boys' hostel in Rochdale. The piece read:

> During the 1960s Cyril Smith was using his position to get lads aged 15–18 to undress in front of him in order that he could then get them to bend over his knee while he spanked their bare bottoms or let him hold their testicles in a bizarre 'medical inspection'.

Although the *Rochdale Observer*, the same as all the local and national media, carried numerous stories condemning Smith posthumously, it didn't investigate or acknowledge the revelations made by *RAP* in May 1979. In fact, *Private Eye* and the *New Statesman* were the only publications to do so.

A few years before his death, TBA workers discovered why Smith had been curiously reluctant to pursue grievances on their behalf and his underplaying of the dangers of asbestos. It emerged that he held 1,300 shares in TBA and was so nested with its hierarchy that he corresponded with Sydney Marks, head of personnel, asking him 'what do you want me to say?' before parliamentary debates involving asbestos and TBA. Smith defended his position in a television interview: 'There were people that worked there who knew they were in danger of it [serious illness] but nobody made them work there. They could have left.' In the General Election of December 2019, Tony Lloyd, the Labour candidate, won the Rochdale seat with 24,475 votes. The Liberal Democrat candidate, Andy Kelly, received 3,312 votes.

* * *

Walter Joyce agreed that the victory against Shrewsbury Town seemed 'light years ago' (it was actually six weeks) but a new fighting spirit felt to have fallen over the squad after the hammering at Huddersfield. 'If they all graft and stick to the plan, we can at least make ourselves hard to beat,' said Joyce.

Chesterfield were in third place and expected to gain an easy victory at Spotland. They won 2-1 but Rochdale's performance was said by Dave Sugden to be 'encouraging'. He singled out Mike Brennan for special praise after he'd scored for the second time in two matches: 'He did no amount of unselfish running during the game, winning balls in the air and generally looking a far better prospect than when he first arrived.' Brennan had taken a few months adjusting to lower-league football but didn't feel his team-mates were significantly inferior to those he'd been among at Manchester City. 'It's a fine margin. They are not that much better at the higher levels of the game,' he said. 'It's difficult to put into words but they are more *seasoned* somehow, so they are more comfortable on the ball and appear to have more time.'

He believed players needed a good number of consecutive matches to settle into top-level football and to accept that they belonged there; they also needed encouragement to foster their self-belief and confidence. 'When you break into the first team, those first games are so important. If you're coming on as a sub now and again or you're in the team and then out for a few weeks, you can't really grow into your game, so the manager and fans don't see you at your best,' he said.

His first few matches at Manchester City had been inauspicious and afterwards he sensed that he was 'branded' – perceived in a way that was almost impossible to recant. He'd made his full league debut in March 1973, when he was selected in place of the injured Francis Lee against Wolverhampton Wanderers at Molineux. Despite the City team containing Colin Bell, Mike Doyle, Rodney Marsh et al., they were 5-0 down at half-time and eventually lost 5-1. Two weeks later, he came on at half-time against Coventry City when City lost 2-1. In all, during the period Brennan was on the fringes of the first team, they lost six out of seven matches. 'I remember cutting in from the left against Coventry and flashing a shot past the post. Someone said to me afterwards that if I'd have scored, it would have secured me a few more games and everything would have been different. You need that run of games to establish yourself, especially when you've got outstanding footballers playing in your position,' he said.

* * *

Many felt the owners and senior editorial staff of the *Rochdale Observer* might have been 'in on it' and purposely ignoring Smith's transgressions. Such accusations had to be placed in the context of the times. Smith, over several decades, was *loved* by most in the town. He was adept at playing roles. To some, he was boyish and to others, paternal; it meant he had appeal across generations. He *appeared* to be caring and charitable, putting the first £10 in the kitty and then conducting the raffle, whether to raise money for Birch Hill Hospital or a pensioners' trip to Anglesey. Smith was at all the socials, first to arrive and last to leave. He was also admired for 'coming from nowt' and staying true to himself: the cobbled-street kid who could outsmart posh, public-school politicians. And him a fat lad, too. Nothing going for him really, but he was hard-working and intrepid and didn't let it deter him. If Smith was on the front page, the *Rochdale Observer* sold more copies. He tipped them off about stories too, picking them up as he caroused around town, cracking jokes and shaking hands. His charisma was matched only by his mastery of deception.

* * *

Rochdale put in an estimable performance against another team at the top of the division. They were expected to lose heavily at Bristol Rovers but took the lead through Keith Bebbington and held on for a 1-1 draw. 'For the first half hour, no one could have told which team was top of the division and which was at the bottom,' said Don Megson, the Bristol Rovers manager.

During the match, Dave Seddon was injured in a challenge with Bristol's Bruce Bannister. A member of Rovers' staff drove Seddon to Bristol Royal Infirmary, where a stress fracture was diagnosed. He was kept in overnight for observation. 'When I got up the next morning, the lads had obviously all gone back on the coach and I realised I was on my own. There were no mobile phones in those days, so I couldn't get in touch with anyone unless I found a phone box. I made it to the train station but there were no trains. In the end, I got home by taking a series of buses; it took me ages,' he said.

Such a haphazard approach typified the club, as it did most others in the 1970s. Seddon has no memory of signing a contract to play in this run of fixtures and is almost certain he played while uninsured. This level of laxity also stretched to the administration of the team. 'I trained twice a week with the reserves and it was mainly running round the pitch or up and down the hill at the Pearl Street End of the ground. Tom [Nichol] used to slip me ten bob now and again for playing; I'm sure it was out of his own pocket. You only found out if you were playing or not when the team sheet went up on the wall,' he said.

The avuncular Nichol was typical of the unsung backroom personnel at football clubs. Quietly spoken, he did much to forge the club's friendly image. He'd first joined Rochdale in 1953. His own playing career had ended prematurely when he suffered a knee injury while playing in a trial match for Northampton Town. Walter Joyce had persuaded him to leave his job as a dyer at Lancashire Tanning works in Littleborough and work full-time at the club. Nichol's mustard-coloured Datsun Cherry was often seen parked on side streets near amateur football pitches across the north as he sought out players for Rochdale. 'Tom was great,' said Seddon. 'In fact, most of those around the club were nice people. Frank Campbell was a decent bloke – he never blasted anyone. Maybe the club missed a bit of that edge, on and off the field.'

David Cross had been one of Tom Nichol's 'discoveries'. Cross was spotted playing for Hollang FC (an amalgam of Hollins and Langley, two estates in Middleton) and his school team, Heywood Grammar. 'We weren't allowed on to the pitch and so spent a lot of time running up and down the terraces,' said Cross. 'There was a small area in front of the Willbutts Lane stand where we'd play four-a-side games. I remember being shocked at how quick the football was but, at each stage, as I went through the various teams, I worked really hard and adapted. I knew I wasn't the most gifted player, so I made up for it with hard work.' Cross was sold to Norwich City for £40,000 in 1971, aged 21, and later played for Coventry City, West Ham United and Manchester City among others, averaging more than a goal every three matches in a career spanning 600 appearances. 'I was always grateful that Rochdale gave me a chance to learn how to become a professional footballer but, after I left, the same as all footballers, I was totally focused on whatever club I was playing for and wasn't really aware of what was happening at Spotland,' he said.

* * *

Although viewed as heinous today, many people were aware of Smith's proclivity for young boys at the time but imagined it to be small-scale – some touching and spanking maybe, on almost a consensual, playful basis. Society was much less inclusive in the 1970s, with little compassion shown to the lower classes, especially the feral kids who, it could appear (through reading the newspapers), were either stealing from garden sheds, dousing them in petrol or otherwise mounting racist attacks or fighting at football grounds. Smith was sorting them out, the town's self-appointed minister of justice, with his own bounty of punishments. Did it really matter, they thought, if he got a frisson of sexual pleasure from his role, when you weighed it against all the good he did for Rochdale?

The indifference to *RAP*'s revelations also owed much to an attitude Smith, and others, propagated. Although he issued a 'pre-writ document' (known these days as a 'letter before action' or 'letter of claim'), he didn't take the matter further. He was saying to the world that he was a man of such unimpeachable morals that these malevolent Lilliputians and their grubby 'leftie' magazine were unworthy even of acknowledgement. *RAP* (specifically the editors David Bartlett and John Walker) had shown great bravery in publishing the piece, risking their life savings and homes if legal proceedings had ensued. They knew, however, much as Smith did, that truth was an absolute defence of libel. And the truth was that Smith was a devious and black-hearted man who had preyed on young boys on an institutionalised basis.

* * *

Rochdale had wanted to play Southport in the midst of their injury crisis to give them the best possible opportunity to record a third league win of the season. Although the Football League had granted Southport a postponement, the rearranged match appeared similarly propitious. Southport were instructed to field a team against Rochdale on Sunday, 10 March 1974 after drawing 1-1 with Chesterfield the previous afternoon. 'They'll be absolutely knackered,' said Dennis Butler. Walter Joyce responded, 'They might be absolutely fuming about being told to play two matches in two days and mad keen to take it out on someone – us.' 'I never thought of that,' said Butler. The match finished 0-0 and David Sugden shaped his pen into a poison arrow once more, referring to the performance as 'comical' and stating, 'How a side could play so badly from start to finish and still come out on level terms was little short of a miracle. Maybe Rochdale should try for more Sunday matches and keep praying for this sort of luck.'

Three days later, Rochdale played at Aldershot and lost 4-0 with 'an atrocious display of negative football' – *Rochdale Observer*. Hopes were raised for a victory, when, in the next match, Charlton Athletic had their goalkeeper, John Dunn, sent off. Dunn had berated the referee, Colin Seel, after three of his team-mates were left injured in the penalty area following a Rochdale corner. 'It would only have been a simple caution,' said Mr Seel after the match. 'But he went on and on. We don't want to hear that kind of language.' Peter Reeves, a midfielder, donned the goalkeeper's jersey. The match was played before 850 fans at Spotland and finished 1-1.

David Gartside, supporter, had missed the Cambridge match because he was unable to take the afternoon off school, but he attended all the other home fixtures. 'Once the losing became a habit, the crowds dwindled. The place looked awful when there was hardly anyone in it. You noticed things, like the water leaking through the roof. The whole club began to look ready to die,' he said.

Rochdale suffered another 4-0 defeat, this time at Watford. David Sugden openly ridiculed the team: 'It's difficult to decide which the greater hardship was on Saturday – watching Rochdale or the eight-hour slog up and down the M1, one of the most monotonous roads in the country.' Rochdale played Bristol Rovers again, this time at Spotland, and lost 1-0 to the league leaders. Mike Poole, the goalkeeper, was outstanding, managing to keep the visitors to a single goal, scored by the prolific Bruce Bannister.

David Gartside remembered leaving Spotland after the match feeling relatively cheerful. 'I suppose I'm the eternal optimist,' he said. 'Everyone expected us to lose by about four goals but, because we'd only lost by one, I thought that from then on we'd get better, whatever division we were in. I'd been hurting all season from how ineffective we'd been. I was impressionable and couldn't understand how they could do this to me. I remember a distinct dawn of realisation, about halfway through the season: that we were crap.'

* * *

The General Election of February 1974 had provided a brief diversion but the discord that had bedevilled the country was ongoing. Petrol remained in short supply, with queues, often several hundred yards long, stretching across forecourts and along main roads. Police were sometimes called out in Rochdale as tempers frayed. Motorists started banging on the doors and windows at Oakenrod Service Station in Bury Road when staff decided to shut at 8pm despite scores of cars waiting outside. Carcraft Motorist Service Station at Entwistle Road stayed open until 10.30pm to serve motorists, several of whom had waited for two or three hours. Mr Frank McKee, manager, said many people were 'stocking up' on petrol, which meant there wasn't enough to go round.

The three-day week was having an impact on the local economy. 'It's heartbreaking,' said Mr Wilkinson of Boys & Co. Ltd sheet metal workers. 'It makes you weep to see our machines stopped for two days of the week when our order books are full.'

12

April Fool's Day, 1974

TWO NEW players were added to the first-team squad. Don Tobin, aged 18, was promoted from the reserves and David Carrick, aged 26, joined from Preston North End. Carrick had previously played for Witton Albion, where he was considered by Walter Joyce to be 'the best player in the Cheshire League'.

Tobin had spent his youth playing for Huyton Boys FC, a club that, in the early 1970s, was considered one of England's most outstanding schoolboy teams. They were coached by two men steeped in football. Alan Bleasdale, later well known as a television screenwriter, had spent two years as an apprentice at Liverpool, while Eddie Kilshaw had been a professional at Bury and Sheffield Wednesday. Both were working as teachers at St Columba's Secondary Modern, Huyton when the team they had assembled won the English Schools Football Trophy in 1971. Tobin played alongside the future England international, Peter Reid, and George Telfer who spent nearly a decade at Everton. Tobin had also signed for Everton as an apprentice. 'I thought I was doing really well but for some reason I seemed to fall out of the picture. It happens in football,' he said. 'Walter Joyce invited me to Rochdale and I saw it as an opportunity to improve as a footballer. That was my goal and Walter provided a great environment for me. He let me play and express myself and I loved it.'

Football scouts had flocked to Huyton. The understated and principled approach of Joyce and Harold Holburt, both working for Oldham Athletic at the time, had seen them forge relationships with the boys and their parents. Peter Reid trained at Boundary Park but had already pledged to join Bolton Wanderers and went on to make his debut at the age of 17. The most dynamic player at Huyton, most agreed, was striker Pat Phillips. He joined Oldham Athletic on a non-contract basis. 'One day, I was putting in these crosses to Pat and he was taking them on either his chest or knee, and then smashing every single one of them into the back of the net,' said Holburt. 'Jim Fryatt [Oldham's experienced striker] was passing on the way to the dressing room and stopped in his tracks. "Who's he – he's bloody brilliant," he shouted over to me.' Phillips, as several young players did, swapped Oldham for Rochdale, to work again with Campbell, Holburt and Joyce, but he failed to make the progression from the reserves to the first team. 'I had a long career in and around football clubs and I'd say Phillips not making it was the biggest surprise. He had bags of natural talent,' said Holburt.

A few weeks before the end of the season, Walter Joyce received a transatlantic phone call from Ken Bracewell, player-coach of Denver Dynamos. They had been friends for many years after starting their playing careers at Burnley, although Bracewell hadn't made the first team. Denver had been admitted to the Central Division of the North American Soccer League (NASL) and Bracewell was recruiting players from England, specifically the north-west, from where he originated and had most contacts. Ian Wood and Andy Lochhead, both from Oldham Athletic, had already agreed to join and his shopping list included several Rochdale players. Initially, at least, Joyce was prepared to release only Jim Grummett to spend his summer in the United States. Joyce believed it would benefit both Rochdale and the player: 'We think it will do him good because he is a lad who puts on weight quickly. This will help keep him fit.'

* * *

The loss of production in the various mills caused by the three-day week was estimated at being between 30 and 50 per cent. F. Friedland and Co. announced 40 redundancies from its curtain-making department at Eclipse Mill; it blamed a shortage of raw materials. The town's only brewery, the Rochdale and Manor Brewery in Molesworth Street, announced its closure after more than 100 years of brewing. Mr Jordan, chairman of Fothergill & Harvey Ltd, took a pay cut of 10 per cent to show solidarity with the workforce; he earned £289 per week, while shop-floor staff had an average weekly wage of £25. TBA had special dispensation from the three-day week by claiming its machinery had to run continuously to save it seizing up and bringing the plant to a halt.

The good people of Norden and Bamford were keen to show their benevolence at such a time and formed a branch of the League of Pity. The organisation – a section of the NSPCC that encouraged children to raise money for other children – issued a leaflet asking that people 'show sympathy for their underprivileged counterparts'.

* * *

A free kick taken quickly by Stan Horne caught the Port Vale defence by surprise and flew into the net. Rochdale hadn't won for 14 matches and the 982 fans at Spotland were hopeful of witnessing their third league win of the season. The match turned scrappy and a ball kicked towards Rochdale's goal fell to the head of Bob Mountford, the Port Vale striker (and ten months later a Rochdale signing): 1-1.

Afterwards, those Rochdale fans with a bent for mathematics were busy working out whether the club had been relegated.

Rochdale had seven matches remaining and were 14 points behind Tranmere Rovers, the only team they could 'catch' to avoid relegation. Under modern protocol, Rochdale's goal difference of minus 52, compared to Tranmere's minus 6, would have meant avoiding relegation was near-impossible. Back then, when teams shared the same points tally, goal average came into play. As Rochdale had scored 30 and Tranmere 31, *all* Rochdale had to do was win their remaining matches while Tranmere, and others, lost all theirs.

Relegation was confirmed for Rochdale two days later – on April Fool's Day, 1974 – without them having to take part in a football match. Almost 50 miles away from Spotland, in Birkenhead, Tranmere Rovers beat Port Vale 3-0, which meant their points tally could no longer be equalled. There was no need anymore for scribbling down numbers or praying for divine intervention – Rochdale were down. 'I'm sick we have got relegated and there can be nobody more disappointed than I am,' said Walter Joyce. 'When I came here I never thought anything like this would happen.'

Don Tobin occasionally travelled to Spotland with Joyce and saw how the poor form had affected him. 'This was a man who was a competitor in anything he did, whether table tennis, cricket or football. He never gave up and his work ethic was unbelievable. He was up at 7am and was still at it beyond nine o'clock at night,' he said. Harold Holburt had seen evidence of this combative streak many times, sometimes in humorous circumstances. 'We used to play cricket matches against Rochdale Cricket Club and even then he was desperate to win. I was bowling one time and they sent in this little lad to bat. He was only about 11. I shortened my run so the ball wouldn't come at him too fast and Walter shouted over, asking what I was doing. Anyway, this lad battered me all around the ground and Walter was shaking his head, telling me I should have bowled at full pelt and it was my fault we were going to lose the game,' he said.

Walter Joyce defended, once more, his decision to release experienced players such as Dick Renwick, Colin Blant and Bill Atkins. 'I think a lot of the players I inherited were past it. To manage my way, what we have done here has had to be done. I sympathise with the public having had to watch some of our displays. The only thing I would ask the fans is to be patient with our young players because I think they have a great say in either building or shattering a player's confidence,' he said. Harold Holburt felt that, through it all, Joyce had never 'lost the dressing room'. 'Most of the players were on his side. They could see that he took everything to heart and was always determined to carry on, looking forward to the next game. He was maybe a bit over the top in training, working them too hard and the older players couldn't hack it,' he said.

The season had a month to run and fans still had a reason to make that journey to Spotland – to see if the team could win at least one more match.

* * *

The ills and chills of the times seemingly had no effect on Melvin Grubberman (probably not his real name), a doppelganger for Antony Sher playing Howard Kirk in *The History Man* – sideburns, Zapata moustache, polo neck, oleaginous grin. The 34-year-old had turned his house at 9 Fieldhead Avenue, Bamford into a 'Temple of Love'. The residence was easily discerned from others (as the *Rochdale Observer* had earlier noted) by its pictures of nudes and semi-nudes (women *and* men) stuck to the windows.

He claimed the property should be exempt from rates because of its 'religious' status. Four years earlier, he'd formed his own religion after a dream he had while on a business trip to the Middle East. In it, he saw huge vultures circle overhead and received from them a 'love technique' that had led to him having, he claimed, more than 200 women visit him on a regular basis. 'I believe in freedom of life and I am against the Establishment and society. The men are afraid I will take their wives and girlfriends from them. They are jealous of me and have no respect for a house of worship,' he said.

* * *

The pattern of the season continued for the last seven matches, although Rochdale at least managed to avoid heavy defeats. They lost 2-1 at Hereford United, where Don Tobin made his full debut and 'seldom wasted a pass' – *Manchester Evening News*. He'd travelled with the squad but hadn't expected to play. 'We were in this crappy hotel and it was about four o'clock in the afternoon,' he said. 'We'd had something to eat – steak probably, we often had it before a match – and Walter shouted me over and said, "You're starting tonight." He left it late to purposely avoid me getting nervous throughout the day. His man-management was on a different level. He really cared about us and it made you want to play for him. I've taken a lot from Walter and, in coaching, added it to my own toolbox.'

As a ball-player of slight build, Tobin had been warned what to expect and duly encountered it on his first-team debut. 'I knew that the first thing they were going to do was clatter me from behind and then give me a whack in the ribs,' he said. 'The older defenders at Everton had shown me how to go over the top in a tackle and break someone's leg. They were doing this to help me, so I could see it coming and learn how to protect myself. As a professional footballer, you have to have a bit of nasty in you or you don't survive. It was part of the game back then.'

Tobin had grown up on a council estate where he'd learned the art of survival; this was further honed when he joined Everton. 'Where I was brought up, things went on that meant you sometimes had to fight your way out of situations,' he said. 'At Everton, we had this punishment called "the yellow bib". At the end of five-a-side, players and coaches used to vote for whoever they thought had been the worst player and he had to wear the bib the next day. It was a matter of pride to make sure you avoided it. You weren't allowed to wash it, so it stunk of sweat, shit and just about everything else. I tried to bring this in later when I was coaching in America but I got crucified for it. The parents wouldn't have it. That shows how much things have changed.'

The 3-3 draw at Cambridge United was noteworthy because it was the first time all season that a Rochdale player had scored more than one goal in a match – Dave Carrick, two. They drew 0-0 at Spotland against Wrexham and a late equaliser by Keith Bebbington secured a 2-2 home draw against Aldershot. The three consecutive draws hadn't reflected a significant tactical change. 'We were never told to "park the bus" or drop off to make sure we didn't concede,' said Tobin. 'Walter always told us to go out there and play our own game. I thought we had some good players. Some of them were coming to the end of their careers and had lost a yard of pace but it always seemed to be little moments that cost us. I know it's impossible but I'd love to view videos of those games, to see where we were going wrong. We didn't deserve what happened. The training was good, everything was good. We never gave up. It was unbelievable really and after losing or drawing, we'd ask: how the hell has that just happened?'

Dave Seddon felt the dynamic among the squad was awry. He was one of only a handful of players either from Rochdale or living in the town. 'There were little groups within the squad and they all tended to stick together. Their only real connection with the club and Rochdale itself was to come in for training or on a matchday, and then drive off again,' he said. Seddon had been brought up in Bamford and attended Rochdale Grammar School, where he'd represented Lancashire at five different sports – basketball, athletics, rugby union, cricket and football. As a boy, on alternate Saturdays, he watched Rochdale with his father, Jack, a plumber, and Bury with his grandad, Vernon Greaves. 'If players were needed to do anything locally for the club, it was always me and Paul [Fielding],' said Seddon. 'We'd be invited to push piles of pennies over in pubs or pick up cheques for charities. The rest of the lads all lived so far away.'

He was offered a professional contract on a wage of £35 per week with an appearance bonus of £5 per match. He was also granted a signing-on fee of £250, to be paid over three years. He left his job as a schoolteacher, although it meant him taking a pay cut. A year later he was released by Walter Joyce. 'He called me into his office and said, "I'm letting you go." I wasn't given any reasons why and we didn't even have a conversation. I took it as "well, this is what happens". I was upset and disappointed, mainly because I don't feel I'd shown the best of my ability, being constantly played out of position.'

He returned to teaching and played for Stafford Rangers on a part-time basis for several seasons. In his first season, they reached the FA Challenge Trophy at Wembley, losing 3-2 to Scarborough. 'We had so much camaraderie at Stafford and it made me realise it was missing at Rochdale. Football isn't only about ability – most players at a certain level are much the same – it's about the dynamic of the team. If you mix and all get on and encourage one another it breeds confidence and the whole team plays better. I'm still in touch with five or six lads from the Stafford squad but I've not seen my Rochdale team-mates since the last game I played with them,' he said.

Fred Ratcliffe had done his best to encourage greater fraternity between the players. In the face of criticism that money was better spent on new signings, he'd refurbished the players' lounge during the season, even inviting Alan Hardaker, secretary of the Football League, to conduct the official opening. Ratcliffe told the press at the opening, 'When things are going badly for the team, this is one way of restoring their morale. Instead of drifting off home, without a word of consolation, they will be able to come into the new lounge with their wives and girlfriends and mingle with the directors and our guests.' The players 'mingled' for the first two or three matches after the lounge was opened but soon began to race to their cars once more, kitbag in hand. None recall Walter Joyce being particularly concerned about team bonding; there were no social events organised.

Stan Townsend had travelled up and down the country covering matches and knew all the players and staff at the club. 'The players lost confidence in themselves, basically, and didn't know how to remedy the situation,' he said. 'I could see they were becoming very nervous about every game. They kept waiting to turn the corner or have a change of luck but it never occurred. I know they say teams make their own luck, but it just never came. All the confidence had gone and their body language showed that they were beaten before they went out to play. It's a shame because a lot of the teams they played weren't all that good.'

Rochdale lost 3-1 against Blackburn Rovers at Ewood Park and, two days later, lost 1-0 at Halifax Town, despite playing well.

* * *

Mr Grubberman said locals had thrown bricks through his windows and tipped rubbish over his car. He was also barred from nearby pubs. 'The pictures in my windows are not provocative. I don't like the curtains of some of my neighbours but I don't break *their* windows. There are no other men in my cult at the moment but I am looking for the right ones. It could sweep the country. I intend opening another temple in Oldham and possibly in Whitefield,' he said. He'd recently 'married' 'Tara', who had lived with him for three weeks. 'Tara is not like other women,' he said. 'She is not jealous and possessive. I have explained to her that I am doing this work for women who need help with their problems.'

Rochdale Rates Dept sent a form to Mr Grubberman seeking extra information about his ecclesiastical status but didn't receive a response. An amount of £116.27 was outstanding.

* * *

The final fixture of the season was at Spotland against Halifax Town on Saturday, 27 April 1974. Rochdale's run without a win had lasted 21 matches. 'We are determined to go out on a good note,' said Walter Joyce. 'The younger lads are beginning to enjoy their football and now want more games. Our recent performances have augured well for next season.' He reported that the players were still 'smarting' after outplaying Halifax five days earlier but still losing.

Only four of the players picked to play in the final match had started the season in the first team – Keith Hanvey, Alan Taylor, Bobby Downes and Leo Skeete. Rochdale scored after six minutes but conceded a minute before half-time. The match ended 1-1. Five years earlier, in August 1969, when Rochdale had played their first match in the Third Division, the attendance against Leyton Orient had been 7,114. In April 1974, 1,320 watched against Halifax Town and a few hundred of them were Halifax supporters.

The final piece of business was the announcement of the retained list – the players Joyce wished to remain in the squad for at least another season; 31 different players had been used throughout the campaign. Joyce finished as he'd started back in August, emphasising that he wanted to invest in youth. Eleven players were released, including Graham Smith, the club's then record appearance holder with 317 matches. Walter Joyce repeated his mantra one more time: 'It is felt with the players we have kept, that all of them have more potential and are younger.'

Graham Smith was 27 when he was released. He moved to Stockport County, where he spent five seasons, making more than 150 appearances. 'At 27 you've still got plenty of football left in you,' he said. 'In fact, I'd say you are just coming to your peak. He wanted all these young ones in his squad but you need experience as well.' Smith remains diplomatic about Walter Joyce. 'He was a nice enough fella. Before he came to Rochdale, everything he'd done had been in youth football. Perhaps he could have done with an older chap by his side, someone with more managerial experience. He probably tried to bring through the youngsters too quickly,' he said.

Andrew Hilton, son of former director Leonard Hilton and a lifelong Rochdale supporter, summed up the feelings held by many in Rochdale, then and now: pragmatism at its most pure. 'Walter Joyce, the same as all Rochdale managers, had a difficult job on,' he said. 'Not many players wanted to come to Spotland and he had little money, if any, to spend. He did his best and seemed to get on with most people. They weren't good days, let's put it like that. While my dad was worrying about the team and how they were doing, he also had to think about the ground, which was in a very bad state. He used to fret about the wall at the corner of the Sandy Lane End and Willbutts Lane – it was about to fall down at any time.'

Trevor Butterworth was a regular visitor to Spotland, either to watch the team or drop off supplies of kit and equipment. The same as Stan Townsend, he knew everyone, from the tea ladies to Fred Ratcliffe, and all in between. He was savvy, a working-class lad made good; he'd later join the board and serve the club for many years. Before then, he'd observed shrewdly, seeing how the club was run and how this manifested itself in the team's performances. 'I'm of the belief that if a football club is run properly, results naturally follow on the pitch,' he said. 'The board had let things go. They were each getting older and all it had come to for them was putting in money every week. Everything felt to be sliding away. When we [a new board] took over a few years later, we divided up the various jobs and roles between us and tried to keep on top of everything. I think the previous board had become disillusioned.'

The board overseen by Fred Ratcliffe had, in fact, originally allocated each other specific roles but these had become indistinct over the years. Subsequent board members felt a club within a club had formed, and this small group of men enjoyed the fraternity offered by one another and within the wider football world. They had, in effect, become an itinerant social alliance – a 1970s version of the Pickwick Club where, instead of stopping off at the George and Vulture or Spaniards Inn, they sipped sherry with similar self-made, middle-aged men at Portsmouth and Carlisle, and many locales in between. 'Fred was the figurehead and more or less said what went on and what didn't,' said Butterworth. 'He was very much tied up with his business, though, so couldn't always give the club his time. I think they were all happy enough to be going to the matches together but they weren't doing the organising that they should have done.'

Butterworth recalled one of the older directors often falling asleep at board meetings, although he claimed to be 'resting his eyes'. On one occasion, the other directors each left the boardroom, treading quietly. He continued snoozing and woke up to find himself alone in the room. 'Football is always a results business, everyone agrees this, and when you think back to the 1973/74 season, to win two league games out of 46 is completely unacceptable,' said Butterworth.

The Rochdale players dispersed at the end of the season, shaking hands in the club car park, wishing each other all the best for the summer. A few were particularly excited because they had secured deals to play in the United States. They were part of a wider group of British lower-league footballers whose lives were about to change drastically by virtue of a memo drafted in Manhattan, New York.

In early 1974, the NASL had been expanded to 15 clubs, organised for the first time on a nationwide basis. An internal memo, circulated among staff at the NASL headquarters in Manhattan titled 'Procurement Programme: Coaches, Players, Referees', had advised owners of football club franchises – which each lodged $75,000 to take part in the NASL – to 'consciously target lower-level players at clubs in financial trouble in England'.

The NASL had determined that most positions in a football team comprised journeymen, runners and tacklers, and these could be sourced at low cost. The recommended maximum payment over the course of a four-month summer season was $7,000 – substantial by English standards but a pittance compared to the earnings of American sportsmen playing basketball, American football, baseball, etc. English clubs in 'financial trouble' were earmarked because NASL officials knew they would be appreciative of having their players' wages covered by a third party during the close season.

These players were required because they couldn't call upon 'home-grown' talent to fill their squads; there was little football infrastructure in the United States. Also, the nation's fascination with celebrity meant they preferred to focus resources on a smattering of star names or 'fantasisti' (famous players with technical and superlative ability) at each club, which, within a few years, would see the likes of Pelé, George Best, Franz Beckenbauer and Eusébio sharing pitch space with hobnail, tin-bath grafters from clubs such as Southport and, indeed, Rochdale.

Ken Bracewell, Walter Joyce's old pal, was typical of the men entrusted to build football clubs from ground level in the United States. He'd found himself at Denver Dynamos, aged 38, after a nomadic life typical of many footballers. Unlike most, his had an international dimension. He'd played for Toronto Italia in the 1960s, a team formed by Italian immigrants in Canada. He'd also spent three seasons with Atlanta Chiefs (later known as Atlanta Apollos) in the NASL. In contrast, while playing for

Margate in the Southern League, he'd set up a window-cleaning business with another player, Tommy Marshall.

At a time before agents, Bracewell was briefed by Calvin Kunz Jr, the Harvard-educated 'corporate farmer' whose family owned the Dynamos, to find players and backroom staff. Bracewell plundered his contacts book and signed 15 British players, mostly from Lancashire and Yorkshire clubs, while his 'flair' players included strikers Kaizer 'Boy-Boy' Motaung (he'd founded South Africa's most famous football club, Kaizer Chiefs, in 1970) and Iris DeBrito from Brazil. The Dynamos' home ground was the Mile High Stadium, a former landfill site on the outskirts of Denver city centre, which had been converted into a magnificent amphitheatre with a 43,000 capacity. They shared it with American football's Denver Broncos and baseball's Denver Bears.

On Sunday, 5 May 1974, a week after the football season had ended in England, Denver Dynamos played their first-ever competitive match, a 3-2 defeat against Toronto Metros. Lining up for the team photo on that humid night, resplendent in white shirts, arms tucked behind their backs, were four Rochdale players – Jim Grummett, Lee Brogden, Mike Poole and Stan Horne. They lived close to one another in apartments supplied by the club in Littleton, a small city of 27,000 people, a 20-minute drive from the stadium. On their journey to training each day, they passed through the districts of Castle Pines, Lone Tree and Aspen Park; memories of Rochdale and the rain soon began to fade. 'They treated us like superstars,' said Stan Horne. 'I was given a Ford Mustang by the club. It was as if we were royalty.'

Rodney Marsh, the foremost ambassador of football in the United States, famously summed up its appeal: 'English football is a grey game played on a grey day before grey people. American soccer is a colourful game played on a sunny day before colourful people.' The NASL introduced new features that were later adopted across the globe. Players had their names printed on the back of their shirts and were given specific squad numbers that didn't necessarily correspond to their positions. As well as keeping a tally of goalscorers, they also counted a player's 'assists' – passes that led directly to a goal. Draws were outlawed because Americans felt it was unacceptable that they should invest time and money in a match where neither team was deemed a winner. If the scores were level at full time, a 'shoot out' was held, where players, 35 yards out from the goal line, had five seconds to either shoot or dribble past a goalkeeper. 'We were introduced individually to the crowd over the speakers and everything was geared towards making you feel special,' said Horne. 'The atmosphere around the game was completely different than in England. People were much more open and friendly. Mike Poole was the only single lad among us – I think he fell in love about four times in the few months we were out there!'

Before he left England, Poole had been presented with Rochdale's player-of-the-year award, which was both a reflection of his talent and his team-mates' ineffectuality – they had conceded more goals than any other team in the Football League. 'I'll be back next year, fitter and raring to go. Believe me, we have lads here with a lot of ability and with a good start next season, we will do well,' Poole told the press.

Don Tobin, among other Rochdale players, later made the same journey across the Atlantic. He played initially for California Lightnin', a team founded by Warren Hoffnung, a nuclear physicist, aerospace executive and entrepreneur. Tobin's hair was long and flowing and his cheeky charm quickly made him a popular figure. 'I was on the plane flying into LAX Airport and I am looking at all these houses with swimming pools and thinking, "What's this all about?" It was unbelievable, it really was,' he said. 'I was met at the airport, taken to the training ground and shown all the facilities. A few days later, I was at Newport Beach, this beautiful place that was a movie-star land, and given the keys to an apartment right on the beach. The football out there suited me. There was none of that "hoof it and run" stuff. The ball was played more to feet. We were playing in beautiful grounds in beautiful weather. I think all us British lads really appreciated it after some of the pitches we'd played on in England.'

Throughout the short season in the United States, both Horne and Grummett played in all 20 matches for Denver Dynamos, while Brogden appeared in 18, and Poole 17. There were parallels with Rochdale's season, although not as extreme. The team finished bottom of the Central Division, winning five and losing 15 matches. Their average home attendance had been 4,840. Bracewell left at the end of the season and was replaced by John Young, a former semi-professional player from the United States. None of the Rochdale players were re-signed. The average attendances later fell to just over 3,500 and the franchise was sold to Minnesota, nearly 1,000 miles north of Denver; they became the Minnesota Kicks.

Back in Rochdale, Walter Joyce drove to Spotland to collect the couple of suits and the training gear he kept in his room. While he was there, Beryl made him a cup of tea and passed him a few letters. They were the usual mix of lads asking for trials, circulars from the Football League and bank statements, which he put to one side for Fred Ratcliffe. He couldn't help himself – he began writing down the names of players still at the club. In the margins, he made a list of possible additions. Port Vale had released two or three players he rated and he'd been tipped off about a lad from Manchester who had been banging in the goals at youth level. Before he knew it, he'd mapped out a football pitch on the pad and was filling in names to particular positions. The new season was still three months away but he already had that familiar tingle of anticipation and excitement.

Epilogue

WHEN I was young, I assumed that footballers who played for the same team were best friends and stayed that way for life. They also remained permanently at their playing age, lived near to one another and thought and talked about their days together, again and again. In the case of my team, Rochdale, whatever these players did next, wherever they went, they were always and forever *Rochdale*. When they did finally grow old, I imagined them in a retirement home, still wearing their Rochdale tracksuit tops, watching reruns of old matches: the fluky win at Port Vale, that 1-1 draw at Wrexham on a drizzly, foggy night.

It is not like this, of course. Football squads are fluid. Players pull on the shirt, give it their best, but nearly all have been at another club before and will later move to another. At the start of a new season, they sit and stand together for the team photograph; however, this is but a moment in time. The week afterwards, the tall player (back row, second left) has moved to Walsall or Halifax Town. By Christmas, three more have been transferred and two new players have arrived. On an icy pitch in January another tears a cruciate ligament. The papers say he'll be out for six months; he doesn't play for the club again.

Footballers are each passing through; playing for themselves before they play for the club whose badge is on the shirt. Of these players, one or two may have been injured or lost form and dropped down a division, maybe two, believing they'll re-establish themselves at a new club. Others have joined from non-league and view it as an interim move before they sign for a bigger club. Another is nearing 30 and wants to carry on playing and earning before retiring or moving into coaching or management. In contrast, a player still in his teens has worked his way up through the youth and reserve teams and is desperate to pull on a first-team shirt. Each player is on his own mission.

In writing this book, I tracked down as many former players as possible. Although I've long moved on from my reverie of the Retirement Home for Aged Spotland Heroes, I was surprised at the level of disengagement among ex-players. None had kept in touch with one another and they were even unaware of who was living or had died; it seems the profile of perpetual flux was especially true of the Rochdale squad of 1973/74. I was also amazed that *none* of the players or coaching staff remembered the depth of awfulness of the season. They had to be reminded that the team had won only twice in 46 league matches. As if learning this for the first time, they shook their head or sighed. Several were unable to conceive that the season had been *that bad*.

Until I began my forensic examination, I'd received and believed a narrative of the season handed down on the terraces, fan to fan, generation to generation. In short, we were an impoverished club forced to call upon raw novices who had given their all but were ground down into the Spotland mud. This 'so it goes' viewpoint served to exonerate everyone connected to the club, from the boardroom to the dressing room. No money, no fans, no players, no hope. Poor souls, what chance did they have? Well, they had as much chance as a handful of other clubs and *they* didn't fail so monumentally. Southport, the next worst team in the Third Division, did three times as well – they won six league matches during the season. It was also a misnomer that Rochdale had been short of players; 31 represented the club during the season.

Clearly there were reasons particular to Rochdale AFC that caused the team to be magnetised to the bottom of the division and fixed there so rigidly. Self-belief and single-mindedness are attributes that can make one manager successful and another a failure. Results are the only true unit of measurement. By this reckoning, Walter Joyce and his management team failed by an unprecedented degree. Joyce held dear a strategy that had worked at Burnley and Oldham, two clubs with whom he had long-term associations. Both had nurtured young players and integrated them into the first team with remarkable success, especially at Burnley. Until arriving at Spotland, Joyce had worked solely with youth and apprentice professionals. Understandably, he considered this his area of expertise. He believed passionately that a team comprised of fit, impetuous, hard-working, well-coached young players was superior to one peopled by senior, seasoned pros.

Such a belief was dependent, surely, on the quality of the young players around whom a team was built. Burnley had, by popular consensus, one of the best scouting systems in the Football League, while Oldham had assembled a crop of players who would serve the club with distinction for more than a decade. Rochdale, in comparison, had an ad hoc, haphazard youth system that brought forth one or two gifted players (David Cross, for example) but not in sufficient numbers to form the bedrock of a team. Most of the young professionals at Rochdale were also of small stature at a time when pitches were heavy, and brawn was a necessary constituent of the game. In such circumstances, Joyce's commitment to youth bordered on belligerence: what did he see in those frail, raw players?

Fred Ratcliffe wasn't without a ruthless streak. He'd fired managers before but, surprisingly, there was barely a hint through the season that Joyce might be summoned before the man in a fur coat to receive a warm handshake and a letter of dismissal. Joyce was shown the forbearance reserved ordinarily for a manager who had previously brought sustained accomplishment to a club. In some quarters, the board's loyalty might be viewed as commendable and a rare example of sporting decency – a contract rightfully honoured. Alternatively, others might see it as a dereliction of duty – allowing a manager to remain in situ despite the worst run of form ever known in English football and the coincident haemorrhaging of support.

If the team was defeated on the pitch, it was perhaps a reflection of the defeatism emanating from the boardroom. In fact, many hold that the Rochdale directors of the early 1970s, drained of resources and energy, had covertly accepted that the club was on a gradual wind-down to extinction. Fatalism had set in and this was probably why Joyce and his backroom team remained – the rigmarole of sacking him and finding a new manager was simply too much of a chore. Who would come to Rochdale anyway? That a board would ask such a question – often echoed by fans – revealed the level of disillusionment and dearth of ambition.

All the while, during the winter of 1973/74, the basic fundamentals of living – keeping warm, getting about, buying food – had become a slog. The political system was on the brink of collapse. The streets were dangerous places. Teenagers were restless, fighting with each other or rival supporters or those of a different ethnicity. Football might have offered hope, a respite from the misery, and it did in many towns and cities as their clubs scored goals and won matches. Rochdale, the town and the team, were in perfect disharmony, the life draining from both.

In better, brighter days, those responsible for the club (directors, management, players and fans) might have done more, given more, but it felt to be a winter without end, where apathy had become a natural state. Whether they stayed at home and watched the news – this loop of despondency – or put on their overcoats and trudged up to Spotland, it had the same sense of futility.

Interestingly, and happily, the players appear to have passed through the season without suffering trauma. Their careers continued, either in lower or higher divisions, or the same one. They remember 1973/74 as 'poor' or 'disappointing' but the fact that none recall the damning statistics shows that they haven't dwelled on or *become* the season, wearing it as a branding. Many later enjoyed relative success at other clubs and this enabled them to reflect on this season at Rochdale as merely part of their progression as sportsmen. They claimed a 'soft spot' for Rochdale and said they 'still looked out for their results' but their interest was superficial; it had to be, for their next club demanded a singularity of focus.

It was different for those left behind with this mess of a club – fans, directors and staff (especially fans). Here, there *was* trauma. They didn't move on elsewhere and slip free of the curse. The club's heart was broken and the ignominy was worn as chain mail for many years. The recovery was long and slow, shadowed by the fear that the club – perpetually near or at the bottom of the Fourth Division – might lose its place in the Football League. In such circumstances, it was inevitable that the club's survival and continual membership of the Football League would become badges of pride: we're still here.

Being 'here' is wonderful, of course, and many clubs (old foes such as Southend United, Torquay United, Notts County, Chesterfield, Halifax Town, Wrexham et al.) covet our league status and stability but, from there (1974) to here (2022), has been a long recovery.

Eventually, the 1973/74 season will become coated by the dust of time, a footnote that falls from the pages of the club's history. But, let this book stand as a reminder of how desolate it had become and also how splendid it was that a dedicated, loyal set of people – Rochdalians – hung on with brilliant resolve to their beloved football club. Up the Dale.

Afterwards

ROCHDALE AFC remained in the bottom division for 36 consecutive seasons. They twice finished at the foot of the Football League in this period, in 1977/78 and 1979/80. They were promoted in 2009/10, relegated two seasons later, promoted again in 2013/14 and relegated once more after seven seasons. They are currently back in the fourth tier. Support for the club has grown substantially since 1973/74, with an average home league attendance of approximately 3,500. Spotland – now called the Crown Oil Arena – has been shared with rugby league club Rochdale Hornets since 1988. The ground has been extensively rebuilt, with only the Sandy Lane terrace remaining from the early 1970s.

Players

Steve Arnold, age 71, played for Weymouth in the Southern League and spent a period on loan to Dorchester Town. He retired through injury but two years later turned out for Connah's Quay Nomads and, later, West Kirby.

Bill Atkins, age 83, spent two seasons with Darlington before retiring from football in 1975. He ran his bakers and confectionery shop in Keighley for 30 years. In 2002, he was made an entrant into Stockport County's Hall of Fame to mark his scoring record of 37 goals in 92 matches for the club from 1967 to 1969.

Keith Bebbington, age 79, joined Winsford United after being released by Rochdale. In February 2013, the tankard he received for being a member of the Stoke City team that were runners-up in the 1963/64 League Cup Final was sold at auction for £212.

Colin Blant, age 75, had two seasons with Darlington before a short period at Grimsby Town. He joined Workington in November 1976 when they went on to finish bottom of the Fourth Division and weren't re-elected back to the Football League. He ran a newsagents shop in Heywood and was caretaker at St Joseph's RC School in the town for several years. He later coached at Rochdale AFC's School of Excellence. He lives in Newcastle with his wife, Pauline. They have a grown-up daughter, Ashleigh. Colin is suffering from dementia.

Barry Bradbury was released and joined local side, Castleton Gabriels. He died in September 2021, aged 69.

Paul Brears, age 67, recovered from injury and played for another two seasons with Rochdale before joining New Mills in the Cheshire County League. He was reunited with former Rochdale coach, Harold Holburt, in the early 1980s when Holburt was manager of Mount Pleasant of Oldham in the Manchester League.

Mike Brennan, age 70, joined Macclesfield Town where he played part-time, while also working for one of the club's directors in his clothing manufacturing business. He was a postman in the Wilmslow area for 18 months, playing for various non-league clubs, until he was invited by former Rochdale coach, Frank Campbell, to join West Adelaide Hellas in Australia. He emigrated to Adelaide with his wife, Glynis, and two children, Lee and Angela. They moved to Perth in 1984, where Brennan played and coached several high-level clubs. He finished his playing career at 39 in the Perth State League. He currently works for a construction company charged with building new headquarters for Chevron, the American energy company. He lives with Glynis in an apartment in the suburb of Osborne Park, ten minutes away from dozens of beaches on the Indian Ocean. He still attends the gym regularly and remains fit.

Lee Brogden, age 72, spent a season with the Denver Dynamos before retiring from football at the age of 25.

Ian Buckley, age 68, returned to Oldham Athletic after his loan spell at Rochdale and went on to play for Stockport County and Cambridge United. He also played for Durban City in South Africa and Newcastle KD in Australia.

Jimmy Burt, age 71, played four matches for Rochdale before moving into non-league football, where he played for Enderby Town and Corby Town.

David Carrick played for several non-league teams, including Altrincham, Macclesfield Town, Droylsden, Oswestry Town and New Mills. He suffered from motor neurone disease and died in 1989, aged 42.

Gary Cooper, age 72, joined Southport and scored the club's last-ever goal in the Football League in a 3-2 defeat at Watford in April 1978. He was an inductee in Southport's Hall of Fame in 2019, marking his 155 appearances for the club and 57 goals. He later worked for British Aerospace.

Malcolm Darling, age 75, joined Bolton Wanderers but made only eight appearances. He signed for Chesterfield in a £10,000 transfer and scored 33 times in 100 appearances. He went on loan to Stockport County before signing short-term contracts and playing a handful of times for Sheffield Wednesday, Hartlepool, Bury and Morecambe. He spent a summer with California Sunshine in the American Soccer League, where he scored four goals in four appearances. He finished his playing career at Darwen in the Lancashire Combination. He also managed Darwen before becoming manager of Great Harwood Town of division one of the North West Counties League in June 1985.

Roger Denton, age 69, returned to Bradford City after his loan spell at Rochdale but didn't play any more league matches. He now lives in Amphoe Cha-Am, Phetchaburi, Thailand and is a keen cyclist and golfer.

Bobby Downes, age 73, joined Watford in 1974 and was part of a squad that won two consecutive promotions from the Fourth and Third Division in 1977/78 and 1978/79 and also reached the semi-final of the League Cup. He played for Barnsley and Blackpool, where he was a player-coach. He was a youth coach at Watford and Port Vale, assistant manager at Wolverhampton Wanderers (caretaker-manager for six matches) and returned to Watford to become director of youth in 1996. He held the same position at Blackburn Rovers before becoming a scout for Preston North End and then head of recruitment at Nottingham Forest. He still works in the game as a scout for Sheffield Wednesday. He has two sons, David aged 38 and Michael aged 34.

Paul Fielding, age 67, left Rochdale in the summer of 1976 and joined Sligo Rovers in the League of Ireland. In his first season they were champions and qualified for the European Cup. They drew Red Star Belgrade in the first round and lost 3-0 in Belgrade and 3-0 at home; Fielding played in both matches. He became their player-manager in 1982, aged 27, and won the FAI Cup, beating Bohemians 2-1 in the final. Again, they qualified for Europe but were knocked out in the first round of the European Cup Winners' Cup by Valkeakosken of Finland. He had three separate spells at Sligo and also played for Finn Harps, Newcastlewest and Glenavon.

Peter Gowans made three full appearances for Southport before playing for and managing Nantwich Town. He later worked for British Rail as a clerical officer at Crewe Locomotive Works. He died in November 2009. He was 65.

Jimmy Grummett, age 77, spent the summer of 1974 playing for Denver Dynamos and the 1974/75 season with Boston

United in the Northern Premier League, before retiring at the age of 29.

Keith Hanvey, age 69, played for Grimsby Town and Huddersfield Town, where he made more than 200 appearances before settling in the area. He returned to Rochdale in 1984 and played 15 times. He was a rep for a window company before working as a commercial manager at Huddersfield Town, Halifax Town, Bradford City and Leeds United. He runs Hanvey Corporate Ltd, supplying hospitality packages for pop concerts, theatre shows and sporting events.

Stan Horne, age 77, became a builder after retiring from football, working with former Fulham team-mate, Wilf Tranter. In October 2021 he was retrospectively awarded a league championship winners medal for being part of Manchester City's squad of 1967/68. He made five appearances that season, which the Football League originally deemed insufficient to qualify for a medal. He still lives in the Manchester area and is an avid golfer.

Rod Jones, age 76, joined Barrow in the Northern Premier League before finishing his career at Mossley in 1977, where he teamed up with several ex-Rochdale players, including Dave Ainsworth, Andy Sweeney and Leo Skeete.

Eamonn Kavanagh, age 68, joined Workington Town, who, while he was with them, finished second from bottom of the Fourth Division in 1973/74 and 1974/75, and bottom in 1975/76 and 1976/77, when they weren't re-elected to the Football League. He played in central midfield for Scunthorpe United from 1977–80 and was briefly a team-mate of Ian Botham.

Len Kinsella, age 76, retired from football after being released by Rochdale at the age of 28.

Arthur Marsh spent a season at Darlington after leaving Rochdale. He worked as a police officer in Bedfordshire until his retirement. He suffered from Alzheimer's disease. He was married to Judith, who he'd met while playing for Bolton Wanderers, and they had two daughters, Joanne and Liza. He died in March 2020. He was 72.

Mike Poole, age 67, spent a season with Denver Dynamos and three spells with Portland Timbers. He also played indoor football for Houston Summit and Baltimore Blast before re-joining Rochdale for the 1981/82 season, playing another 27 matches for the club. During most of his time in the United States, Poole's shirt number was '00' – the number 1 shirt had already been allocated when he arrived at Portland.

Dick Renwick, age 79, reunited with former Rochdale manager Dick Conner at Darlington. He played 19 times for them before retiring from football in May 1975, aged 31. He lives in Burnley.

Dave Seddon, age 71, joined Stafford Rangers and played more than 1,000 matches in non-League football for various clubs. He became a head teacher and received an OBE for services to education when he turned around two schools in special measures – Baxter College in Kidderminster and Wodensborough High, Wednesbury. He plays as goalkeeper for the walking football team, the Hartshill Strollers.

Leo Skeete, age 72, signed for Mossley in August 1975. He moved from Liverpool to work at the engineering company, Weldem Ltd in Mossley, owned by the club's president, Ronnie Ward. In the 1976/77 season he scored 45 goals. During his time at Mossley he scored 174 goals in 350 appearances and is regarded as a club legend. He later played for Runcorn Town and Altrincham.

Graham Smith, age 76, spent five seasons with Stockport County before joining Buxton and becoming player-coach at Ashton United and assistant manager at Thackley in Bradford. While a player, he passed his City and Guilds examination in plumbing and, after quitting football, joined the family firm, TA Smith & Sons, with his father, Tom, and younger brother,

Peter. He has been married to Jean for 54 years and they have three daughters – Nicola, Alison and Rachel.

Alan Taylor, age 68, joined West Ham United on his 21st birthday in November 1974. Ron Greenwood, West Ham's manager, was alerted to Taylor by a piece in a newspaper about lower-league footballers titled: '12 To Follow'. Taylor played in the 1975 FA Cup Final when West Ham beat Fulham 2-0 and scored both goals. He'd previously scored two goals in both the quarter-final (versus Arsenal) and semi-final (Ipswich Town). He came on as a substitute in the 1976 European Cup Winners' Cup Final, which West Ham lost 4-2 against Anderlecht. He joined Norwich City in August 1979 and had two spells with Vancouver Whitecaps in Canada before returning to England to play for Cambridge United, Hull City, Burnley and Bury. He finished his playing career at non-league Bury Town, Thetford Town and Dereham Town. He became a milkman before opening a newsagents in Norwich, which he ran with his wife, Jeanette, for 16 years. He also worked as a pallbearer for a funeral director.

Don Tobin, age 66, joined Witton Albion before signing for Sligo Rovers in Ireland. In 1978 he relocated with his wife, Joan, to the United States, where he played for a wealth of clubs in the indoor and outdoor leagues, among them California Sunshine, Tampa Bay Rowdies and Carolina Lightnin'. He has coached at the top level in the United States and now runs his own 'soccer' academy. He lives with Joan in St Petersburg, Florida on the Gulf of Mexico, a city that has an average of 361 days of sunshine each year. They have two grown-up children, Lee and Megan.

Staff/Directors

Rod Brierley, age 86, resigned as a director of Rochdale AFC in October 2008. He suffered a stroke in August 2021.

Dennis Butler, age 78, left the club in November 1975 to coach at Bury. He joined Port Vale as assistant manager two years later and was manager for the 1978/79 season. He coached at Swindon Town before retiring from football in 1980. He ran the post office at Bamford, Rochdale for eight years and worked for Rochdale Council in the education and council tax departments.

Frank Campbell relocated to Australia, where he coached Newcastle KB United before moving to Perth with his wife, Hazel. He died in 2008. He was 71.

Leonard Hilton retired from his bakery business at the age of 54. He resigned as a director of Rochdale AFC in August 1992. He had two sons, Andrew and Peter. Andrew runs A and J Hilton, a bakery that has been based in Norden, Rochdale for 33 years; it no longer supplies pies to Rochdale AFC. Leonard died in July 2016. He was 92.

Harold Holburt, age 85, left Rochdale for New Mills, returning to Spotland in 1977 to coach under manager Mike Ferguson. He later coached at Bolton Wanderers before scouting for Bury, Preston North End, Burnley, Leeds United and, finally, Sheffield United, a position he held until he was 85. 'I've worked with more than 35 managers – lots of great, well-respected people along the way and inevitably the odd prat. That's life and I have enjoyed it,' he said. He lives in Bolton with his wife, Dorothy.

Walter Joyce remained as manager for two more seasons. Rochdale finished 19th in the Fourth Division in 1974/75, avoiding having to apply for re-election by three points. In 1975/76 they finished 15th. He left the club 'by mutual agreement' in June 1976. He was coach and assistant manager at Bolton Wanderers from 1977 to 1985. He spent four years as youth development officer at Bury and also worked at Preston

North End before joining the youth set-up at Manchester United. In September 1999, while still at Manchester United, he returned to Burnley, where he'd spent most of his playing career, to make the half-time draw in a 3-0 win against Colchester United. After the match he complained of feeling unwell and died less than two weeks later. He was 62. His son, Warren Joyce, aged 57, played for Bolton Wanderers, Preston North End, Plymouth Argyle and Hull City. He was manager of Royal Antwerp, Wigan Athletic, Melbourne City, Manchester United reserves and Salford City Under-18 development squad; player/manager at Hull City; co-manager of Manchester United reserves and is currently manager of Nottingham Forest's Under-18 squad.

Angus McLean was briefly a coach at Southport before working at Hawker Siddeley (later British Aerospace) in Manchester. He died in July 1979 while on holiday in Guernsey, weeks after passing a works physical for insurance purposes, when he was deemed to be 'A1 fit'. He was 53.

Tom Nichol received an Order of Merit award from the Lancashire Football Association in 1983 and a medal from the FA in 2004 to mark his long service to football. He'd first joined Rochdale in 1953 and, in that time, worked alongside 21 different managers. He died in April 2005. He was 84.

Fred O'Donoghue scouted for Blackburn Rovers and Blackpool. He died at his home in Lostock Hall, near Preston, in September 2002. He was scouting for Bolton Wanderers at the time. He was 74.

Fred Ratcliffe resigned as chairman in 1980 after holding the position for 33 years. He was made club president. He died on Saturday, 31 August 1985 in Highfield Hospital, Rochdale; the club was joint top of the Fourth Division at the time. He was 71.

Joe Stoney became vice-president. He died at his home in Bamford in 1980. He'd been a director for 25 years.

* * *

Turner Brothers Asbestos – the European Union banned the import and production of asbestos in 1999. In the UK, neither TBA nor its insurers faced product liability claims or decontamination costs. This was because the company had been sold in 1998 to Federal-Mogul, a long-established US corporation specialising in motor parts (brake pads, gaskets, bearings and other vehicle parts had asbestos components). Faced with 350,000 individual claims, Federal-Mogul was forced to declare Chapter 11 bankruptcy, despite initially putting aside $2.1bn to cover settlements. These bankruptcy terms permitted troubled companies to reorganise over a set period of time without necessarily recompensing debtors. When it emerged from bankruptcy in 2007, Federal-Mogul set up a compensation scheme of £100m – a fraction of the original amount – to cover TBA claims emanating from the UK.

Third Division – Final Table 1973/74

		Pld	W	D	L	GF	GA	Pts
1	Oldham Athletic	46	25	12	9	83	47	62
2	Bristol Rovers	46	22	17	7	65	33	61
3	York City	46	21	19	6	67	38	61
4	Wrexham	46	22	12	12	63	43	56
5	Chesterfield	46	21	14	11	55	42	56
6	Grimsby Town	46	18	15	13	67	50	51
7	Watford	46	19	12	15	64	56	50
8	Aldershot	46	19	11	16	65	52	49
9	Halifax Town	46	14	21	11	48	51	49
10	Huddersfield Town	46	17	13	16	56	55	47
11	AFC Bournemouth	46	16	15	15	54	58	47
12	Southend United	46	16	14	16	62	62	46
13	Blackburn Rovers	46	18	10	18	62	64	46
14	Charlton Athletic	46	19	8	19	66	73	46
15	Walsall	46	16	13	17	57	48	45
16	Tranmere Rovers	46	15	15	16	50	44	45
17	Plymouth Argyle	46	17	10	19	59	54	44
18	Hereford United	46	14	15	17	53	57	43
19	Brighton & Hove Albion	46	16	11	19	52	58	43
20	Port Vale	46	14	14	18	52	58	42
21	Cambridge United	46	13	9	24	48	81	35
22	Shrewsbury Town	46	10	11	25	41	62	31
23	Southport	46	6	16	24	35	82	28
24	Rochdale	46	2	17	27	38	94	21

Appearances (league and cups)/goals

Steve Arnold	43	1
Bill Atkins	5	1
Keith Bebbington	28	3
Colin Blant	10	0
Barry Bradbury	13	0
Paul Brears	1	0
Mike Brennan	30	3
Lee Brogden	17	5
Ian Buckley	6	0
Jimmy Burt	4	0
David Carrick	10	3
Gary Cooper	6	0
Malcolm Darling	8	3
Roger Denton	2	0
Bobby Downes	48	5
Paul Fielding	14	0
Peter Gowans	32	1
Jimmy Grummett	20	2
Keith Hanvey	43	3
Stan Horne	27	3
Rod Jones	9	0
Eamonn Kavanagh	4	0
Len Kinsella	9	1
Arthur Marsh	30	1
Mike Poole	43	0
Dick Renwick	10	0
David Seddon	8	0
Leo Skeete	32	10
Graham Smith	36	0
Alan Taylor	42	3
Don Tobin	10	0

Bibliography

The Survivors, the Story of Rochdale Association Football Club by Steven Phillipps (Sporting and Leisure Press)

Rochdale AFC, the Official History, 1907-2001 by Steven Phillipps (Tore Publications)

Let's Do It, the Authorised Biography of Victoria Wood by Jasper Rees (Trapeze)

Smile for the Camera, the Double Life of Cyril Smith by Simon Danczuk and Matthew Baker (Biteback)

Scouting for Glory by Fred O'Donoghue (Firebird)

Pink Floyd are Fogbound in Paris: the Story of the 1970 Krumlin Festival by Ben Graham (Bleeding Cheek Press)

Imprinting the Sticks, the Alternative Press Beyond London by Robert Dickinson (Arena)

Tales of Deeply Vale Festival by Chris Hewitt (Ozit Morpheous)

Fast Forward, Music and Politics in 1974 by Steve Millward (Matador)

Rock 'N' Roll Soccer, the Short Life and Fast Times of the North American Soccer League by Ian Plenderleith (Icon)

Triumph and Disaster, 150 Years of Rochdale Hornets by Jim Stringer & Mark Wynn (London League Publications)

Magic Mineral to Killer Dust, Turner & Newall and the Asbestos Hazard by Geoffrey Tweedale (Oxford University Press)